Between Self and Community

Rutgers Series in Childhood Studies

The Rutgers Series in Childhood Studies is dedicated to increasing our understanding of children and childhoods throughout the world, reflecting a perspective that highlights cultural dimensions of the human experience. The books in this series are intended for students, scholars, practitioners, and those who formulate policies that affect children's everyday lives and futures.

Series Board

Stuart Aitken, geography, San Diego State University

Jill Duerr Berrick, social welfare, University of California, Berkeley

Caitlin Cahill, social science and cultural studies, Pratt Institute

Susan Danby, education, Queensland University of Technology

Julian Gill-Peterson, transgender and queer studies, University of Pittsburgh

Afua Twum-Danso Imoh, sociology, University of Sheffield

Stacey Lee, educational policy studies, University of Wisconsin-Madison

Sunaina Maria, Asian American studies, University of California, Davis

David M. Rosen, anthropology and sociology, Fairleigh Dickinson University

Rachael Stryker, human development and women's studies, Cal State East Bay

Tom Weisner, anthropology, University of California, Los Angeles

For a list of all the titles in the series, please see the last page of the book.

Between Self and Community

Children's Personhood in a Globalized South Korea

JUNEHUI AHN

RUTGERS UNIVERSITY PRESS

NEW BRUNSWICK, CAMDEN, AND NEWARK, NEW JERSEY

LONDON AND OXFORD

Rutgers University Press is a department of Rutgers, The State University of New Jersey, one of the leading public research universities in the nation. By publishing worldwide, it furthers the University's mission of dedication to excellence in teaching, scholarship, research, and clinical care.

LIBRARY OF CONGRESS CATALOGING-IN-PUBLICATION DATA

Names: Ahn, Junehui, author.
Title: Between self and community : children's personhood in a globalized south korea / Junehui Ahn.
Description: 1 Edition. | Newark, New Jersey : Rutgers University Press, [2023] | Series: Rutgers series in childhood studies | Includes bibliographical references and index.
Identifiers: LCCN 2022048906 | ISBN 9781978831384 (paperback) | ISBN 9781978831391 (hardcover) | ISBN 9781978831407 (epub) | ISBN 9781978831414 (pdf)
Subjects: LCSH: Socialization—Korea (South) | Child development—Korea (South)
Classification: LCC HQ783 .A385 2023 | DDC 303.3/2095195—dc23/eng/20230111
LC record available at https://lccn.loc.gov/2022048906

A British Cataloging-in-Publication record for this book is available from the British Library.

Copyright © 2023 by Junehui Ahn

All rights reserved

No part of this book may be reproduced or utilized in any form or by any means, electronic or mechanical, or by any information storage and retrieval system, without written permission from the publisher. Please contact Rutgers University Press, 106 Somerset Street, New Brunswick, NJ 08901. The only exception to this prohibition is "fair use" as defined by U.S. copyright law.

All photographs by the author

References to internet websites (URLs) were accurate at the time of writing. Neither the author nor Rutgers University Press is responsible for URLs that may have expired or changed since the manuscript was prepared.

♾ The paper used in this publication meets the requirements of the American National Standard for Information Sciences—Permanence of Paper for Printed Library Materials, ANSI Z39.48-1992.

rutgersuniversitypress.org

For my parents whose faith in and love
for me have made anything I do possible

CONTENTS

Note on Transcription and Romanization   ix

1   Introduction: A Journey into the Shifting South Korean
Socialization Landscape   1

2   New Personhood and Transformation of South Korean
Early Childhood Socialization   26

3   "Why Don't We Find a Unique Self Concept Developing
in Our Children?": The Heterogeneous and Conflicting
Socialization Landscape   36

4   "I Want to Copy My Best Friend's Artwork": Expressions
and Social Relationships in Children's Peer World   74

5   "Maybe We're Not Wrong": Communal Creativity
and Multidirectionality of Learning   135

6   Conclusion: A Journey and Beyond   173

Acknowledgments   183
Notes   185
References   189
Index   201

NOTE ON TRANSCRIPTION AND ROMANIZATION

This study draws on a collection of transcripts of children's and teachers' conversations. Data are presented by adapting the system developed by Jefferson and described in Sacks et al. (1974, 731–733). The following illustrates the transcription conventions used in this study.

SCENE 3.4: EXAMPLE NUMBER

(()) Materials in double parentheses indicate (a) nonverbal activities or (b) features of audio phenomena other than actual verbalization.

() Materials in single parentheses indicate specific features of the speakers such as the child's age or the speaker's job (e.g., teacher).

In rendering Korean terms, I have followed the Yale romanization system except for personal names.

Between Self and Community

1

Introduction

A Journey into the Shifting South Korean Socialization Landscape

When I first entered the Rainbow Room in Somang preschool, a preschool located in Seoul, South Korea, the classroom looked similar to the one I daily encountered in my previous fieldwork at a midwestern preschool in the United States. Classroom walls were decorated with children's artwork, poems, and pictures, along with posters made by teachers, which were full of words such as *I, myself, feelings, expression, self-confidence, creativity, diversity*, and so forth. Teachers at Somang constantly encouraged children to express and verbalize their own thoughts, ideas, and feelings in a variety of classroom activities and praised children's expressions using utterances not included in the typical Korean communicative repertoire, such as "Wow, that's great!" or "Wow, that's super. How did you make it?" Children were also eager to express themselves; for instance, when Ms. Choo asked who would like to present their weekend story during a Monday morning class, almost all the children in the Rainbow Room raised their hands. When only three children were chosen to present their stories, others sighed in disappointment. After and between presentations, the teacher encouraged children to ask questions and comment on presenters' stories, and children actively participated by making statements such as, "I also went to the supermarket with my mom yesterday," "My brother is nine years old. How old is your brother? He's only seven, right?" The overall structure of this weekend story time reminded me of show-and-tell time[1] in U.S. preschools. Even the way Somang children transformed the story time into a place where they jockeyed for power and authority was almost identical to the way children I observed in a U.S. preschool engaged with show-and-tell time.

Based on these observations, I tentatively but almost with confidence concluded that contemporary Korean socialization practices and ideology are geared toward cultivating children's self-expression, creativity, and individuality, the values believed by many contemporary Koreans to be prerequisite for success in the emerging globalized South Korea. This overall picture and interpretation, however, completely changed when Ms. Choo approached me one day and expressed her difficulties and frustrations. It was about mid-May, three months since I had started visiting the Rainbow Room. She began, "You've been with us for three months. What do you think of our children?" I answered, "It looks like they're getting more and more energetic," indirectly implying that the children's peer relationships were becoming more dynamic and complicated, which most captured my research interest at that time. She looked at me oddly and said, "We've had a really hard time for the last three months. We couldn't find what we initially expected from our children. There are noticeable achievements in other classrooms, but we don't have any. . . . Kids are just copying each other's work and are only interested in what others are doing. No diversity and no creativity. . . . And I don't understand why play activities are continuously interrupted. We can't find anything from their play. Why can't we find any diversity or creativity [sighed]?" Then, she started talking about one particular girl named Nuri: "She's too cocky. Kids think her drawings are the best in the class and envy her. But she doesn't care for others' feelings. She's problematic."

This conversation with Ms. Choo surprised me in many ways. To my eyes, Somang children's expressions displayed in their play and other everyday interactions were diverse and creative enough, even when compared to the ones I previously observed in the U.S. preschool. Moreover, Nuri had caught my eye as a student who was good at articulating her own unique ideas, thoughts, and preferences. If diversity, creativity, and self-expression were the goals of Somang socialization, as reflected in Ms. Choo's narrative above, Nuri seemed to be an exemplary student. On the contrary, Ms. Choo identified Nuri as a problematic student and criticized her as "cocky" and "not caring for others' feelings." She was also dissatisfied with her students' overall performances, especially their lack of creativity and diversity.

Ms. Choo's statements prompted many questions for me: Why does she problematize children's performances and behaviors while I never heard U.S. teachers complaining about their students' lack of creativity or diversity? Why is it problematic to be interested in other kids' work? What does Ms. Choo have in mind when she mentions the values of creativity and diversity? Why does she criticize Nuri's behavior and attitude even though Nuri seems to meet teachers' educational goals well? What were the teacher's initial socialization goals and expected outcomes? What kind of cultural assumptions, imaginaries, and aspirations reside behind this teacher's laments and frustrations?

This book is a journey to understand this puzzling observation and the questions entailed by it. Teachers' eager pursuit of individuality, creativity, and diversity, their ambivalent stance toward children's performance and behaviors, as exemplified in Nuri's case, and the overall curriculum designed to promote children's self-expression all pertain to the issue of a new type of personhood emerging in South Korea. Against the backdrop of South Korea's ever-intensifying drive for globalization, a new type of person, one who is individually motivated, self-confident, and creative, is called for as a prerequisite to leading a successful life in a rapidly transforming global world. This new personhood is considered

INTRODUCTION

highly desirable and is eagerly sought in almost every sector of South Korean society, including everyday personal relationships, the corporate sector, and social organizations. However, its pursuit is especially acute in socialization contexts, wherein children develop culturally distinctive understandings of the world and themselves. Recent South Korean early childhood socialization discourses are filled with discussions of raising a child equipped with so-called new or global values such as self-confidence, individuality, creativity, and diversity. Even though this new emerging personhood is considered indispensable to the demands of globalization, as the puzzlements and questions I described above allude to, the process of shaping a new personhood was not a straightforward replacement; instead, it entailed tension, conflict, and contradiction. By immersing myself into the views and lives of children and teachers of a preschool in Seoul, South Korea, I have been able to explore this uneven, complicated, and conflicting process of shaping and reshaping an ideal personhood manifested in the transformation of Korean early childhood socialization. Based on fifteen months of ethnographic fieldwork, I examine how both children and teachers interactively navigate, construct, and reconstruct their own multifaceted, conflicting, and contradictory models of "a good child" amid Korea's shifting educational and social grounds.

As an ethnography of socialization and globalization, this book has two major goals. First, it aims to show how globally dominant socialization ideologies and practices meet with local ones in a Korean preschool classroom, focusing on moments of tension, conflict, and transformation involved in indigenizing processes. It particularly illustrates how implicit local socialization values and practices, undermined as "old" and obsolete in current South Korean socialization discourses, lurk and greatly shape the contours of new personhood that local actors endeavor to construct and reconstruct. Second, by describing everyday local experiences of children and teachers in a Korean preschool, this book aims to show the role various agents of socialization play in the globalizing socialization sphere. It especially attends to the way children, as active agents of socialization, create, construe, and sustain their own meanings for global imports, thereby highlighting the dynamism children and their culture-laden peer world bring to Korea's shifting socialization terrain.

Globalization, Childhood, and Socialization

The anxiety and conflicts teachers and children experience as related in this book emerge largely from South Korea's rapidly changing socialization landscape, especially the dominance of globally circulating socialization ideologies and practices in the lives of local agents. Many anthropological studies of globalization and education as well as recent research into early childhood education have noted the imposition of particular Western socialization ideals in diverse cultural locations, and authors critically discuss the problems presented by discontinuities between globally dominating educational practices and culturally and historically situated local values and ideas (Anderson-Levitt 2003; Cannella and Viruru 2004). Early childhood education studies influenced by postcolonial theories, in particular, discuss how dominant Western discourses about young children have "colonized" the world of early childhood education through concepts such as "developmentally appropriate practice" or "preschool quality," ideas fundamentally rooted in Western child development philosophies and theories (Burman 1994; Dahlberg, Moss, and Pence 1999; Pence and Marfo 2008; Rao 2010; Viruru 2005; Walkerdine 1984).

The postcolonial scholarship of early childhood education has enhanced our understanding of the global circulation of early childhood educational ideas, especially the way perspectives of Western child development can serve as instruments of oppression. It has also provided practical insights into practices by urging early childhood educators to view dominant Western thinking about children not as "quality" standards but as "non-necessary" (Ailwood 2003) and proposing the importance of context-sensitive policy formulation and implementation. Missing from our understanding, however, is a detailed investigation of how the tensions between the global and the local are actualized in everyday classroom experiences, a focus that would help explain the nature of conflicts, confusions, and worries local agents, like caregivers and children in this book, experience in rapidly globalizing and transforming socialization spheres. Furthermore, the focus has been mainly on juxtaposing and stressing discontinuities between global imports and local contexts to the exclusion of indigenizing processes wherein local educational cultures collide with, survive, or adapt to the global exogenous influences. Given that every import gets "creolized" or "indigenized" to reflect local realities as much of social science on globalization has shown (Appadurai 1996; Hannerrz 1996; Kearney 1995; Lewellen 2002), due attention to the moments and spheres of indigenization is essential to the investigation of the meeting of globally circulating socialization ideas and local child-rearing cultures, especially in exploring the role local agents and their mundane enactments play in these processes, a main concern of this book.

To investigate how global socialization ideologies and practices impact and shape local preschool classroom experiences, especially the dilemmas, confusions, and agonies local actors face, this book builds on anthropological research on globalization, education, and socialization that addresses issues of transformation, indigenization, and resistance involved in the global circulation of educational ideas and systems (Anderson-Levitt 2003; Erickson and Mohatt 1982; Flinn 1992; Fuller 1991; Holloway 2000; Schriewer and Martinez 2004; Steiner-Khamsi 2004; Tobin, Hsueh, and Karasawa 2009; Watson-Gegeo and Gegeo 1992; Weisner and Lowe 2005; Woronov 2008). Challenging world culture theory that insists on the convergence of school cultures around the world (Boli and Ramirez 1986; Chabbott and Ramirez 2000; Fiala and Lanford 1987; Meyer and Ramirez 2000), these studies argue for culturally specific appropriations and diversification of imported educational ideas, variations in lived experiences, and tensions between local models and imported systems. This literature, in particular, articulates the significance of investigating everyday local experiences arguing that global imports get "indigenized" through workings of local actors who make decisions regarding how to enact or resist imported educational policies, practices, or ideas (Flinn 1992; Levin 1992; Philips 1992). While acknowledging a common set of educational discourses and taken-for-granted features of modern schooling that tend to set limits on our ordinary thinking about "good" education and child development, these studies nonetheless demonstrate the importance of exploring globalizing forces as experienced by local actors who actively transform and sometimes resist imported models, thereby creating within a roughly common structure distinctive lived experiences (Anderson-Levitt 2003, 18).

Attention to everyday local experiences and indigenizing processes is particularly important to the case this book deals with as the dilemmas, confusions, and anxieties Korean teachers and children confront today can be adequately understood and explained when mundane and everyday local practices and experiences are fully examined in detail. As illustrated in Ms. Choo's narratives opening this introduction, the current South Korean socialization landscape is characterized by local actors' active consumption of Western educational ideologies and unintended consequences that local actors often regard as failure to achieving new educational goals. Given that local actors eagerly pursue globally dominant socialization ideologies, the perceived failing outcomes they lament are less likely to emerge from educational policies or programs themselves but involve microlevel practices such as the inevitable gap between imported models and actual practices (Anderson-Levitt 2003, 18) or local actors' transformations of imported models to reflect local realities (Flinn 1992; Philips 1992).

Of particular interest to the current study are the findings from educational anthropological research that highlight the power of implicit socialization practices in the indigenization of global imports. In Tobin, Hsueh, and Karasawa's (2009) study on changes and continuities of preschool cultures in China, Japan, and the United States, for instance, the authors show that local educational beliefs and practices, such as Chinese beliefs in the power of exemplars and the utility of critique, or Japanese practices of resisting interventions in children's fights and maintaining a high student-teacher ratio, have been preserved through implicit ideologies and practices despite dramatic and sometimes wrenching processes of reform. Moreover, recent educational ethnographies argue that the failure of reform efforts often emerges from highly contentious and conflicting educational landscapes wherein local actors are asked to abide simultaneously by distinct and often mutually contradictory values (Fong 2007; Woronov 2008). Woronov's (2008) study of Chinese reform efforts to increase students' creativity, for instance, shows that Chinese creative education is constrained by state-mandated standardized curricula and testing systems accompanying the newly introduced aims of producing creative citizens. Fong (2007) examines Chinese discourses about the unsatisfactory personalities and behaviors of children born under China's one-child policy and argues that children's unsatisfactory behaviors result mainly from the difficulty of following mutually contradictory values that parents promote rather than from the children's singleton status per se.

These findings inform us that the forces of globally dominating socialization ideologies are not located solely in public discourses or policies, nor are they confined to explicit aspects of school curricula. Rather, it is through everyday enactments and implicit embodied practices that global imports shape local experiences and exert influences on the contours of socialization. The heterogeneous and conflicting socialization landscape presented before, such as Ms. Choo's keen pursuit of new values while at the same time displaying strong reservation toward Nuri who is equipped with these values, or her evaluation of children's performances as lacking new values, are related to traditionally implicit socialization goals and practices teachers still have in mind and to the ongoing transformations of the indigenous model for socialization that reflects these implicit local values. Attention to various moments of everyday inconsistencies and disruptions, then, is needed to fully account for the meeting of the global and the local in socialization spheres.

This book describes a variety of ways and processes in which these disjunctures appear in a South Korean preschool, especially focusing on the gaps between imported models and actual practice on the ground, different and sometimes conflicting enactments among local actors, or uneven implementation across cultural contexts. By examining the complex and uneven ways that globally dominating socialization ideologies are implemented and practiced in local everyday socialization contexts, I am to contribute to the scant ethnographic studies that deal with the impact globalization has on early childhood education and child-rearing practices of preschool-aged children. The detailed ethnographic account of the meeting of the global and the local in a South Korean preschool, in particular, provides empirical materials to discuss the underlying multiplicities and complexities that serve to produce converging similarities as well as dynamic particularities resulting from the global circulation of particular socialization ideologies across different regions of early childhood socialization.

Children's Agency in Globalizing Socialization Landscapes

Although an increasing number of studies on globalization and childhood articulate the significance of examining everyday experiences of local actors, little of this research pays attention to how children actively participate in indigenizing processes. Mostly adults such as teachers (Anderson-Levitt and Diallo 2003; Falgout 1992; Flinn 1992), parents (Levin 1992; Rosen 2003), or administrators (Napier 2003; Silova 2004) appear as principal local actors, and children and their engagements in and contributions to globalizing socialization are rarely addressed. Most globalization research implicitly assumes that children passively adopt cultural inputs already indigenized by adults without any resistance or transformation. As Wyness (1999) articulates in his commentary on the relationship between childhood and educational reform in globalized contexts, the absence of children and their perspectives has been pervasive in discourses and practices of educational reform themselves as well as scholarly research on them.

The marginalization of children's experiences and perspectives is not simply a matter of globalization research but prevalent in most traditional studies of children and socialization. Based on functionalistic and deterministic theoretical formulations, these studies typically view children as passive objects and helpless spectators continually assimilating and responding to influences external to them, having little autonomy and contributing nothing crucial to their own socialization or to cultural reproduction (Hardman 2001). However, contemporary studies from a variety of disciplines such as anthropology and sociology of childhood (Bluebond-Langner and Korbin 2007; Briggs 1998; Corsaro 1997; Carsoro and Miller 1992; Hirschfeld 2002), childhood studies (Clark 2003; Dyson 2016; James 2007; James and Prout 1997), developmental psychology (Rogoff 1990, 2003), and language socialization (Goodwin and Kyratzis 2007; Miller et al. 2012; Ochs and Schieffelin 2012; Pontecorvo, Fasulo, and Sterponi 2001) challenge the traditional adult-centric view of socialization that directs attention to the deterministic power of adults and instead reconceptualize socialization as a process of negotiation, reinvention, and reproduction to which children contribute as skillful social actors. Recent scholarship on children and childhood, in particular, demonstrates that even very young children constitute and reconfigure important sociocultural and political issues such as racism, gender, labor, and migration (Castañeda 2002; Christou and Spyrou 2012; Connolly 2004; Hirschfeld 2002; Thorne 1993; Rosen 2007; Van Ausdale and Feagin 2001). Given that children are crucial local agents as empirical findings from the "competence paradigm" (Hutchby and Moran-Ellis 1998) suggest, due attention to children's experiences, especially their contributions to the construction of globalized education and socialization is essential for adequately accounting for the indigenization of globally circulating socialization ideologies and practices.

A few insightful studies on globalization and childhood recently address how children as social actors actively participate in and influence indigenizing processes. Ouyang's (2003) research on Chinese English-teaching reforms, for instance, illustrates that Chinese students evaluate imported English-teaching methods based on local models of learning and he demonstrates that students' agency determines the extent to which global imports are accepted, rejected, or creolized. Similarly, Fong (2007) explores how Chinese children, exposed to conflicting and contradictory mixes of traditional and new neoliberal socialization values, construct their own models of personhood by inference from their diverse and often contradictory experiences, not by simple replication of adult didactic instructions. Xu (2014), through a combination of detailed ethnographic research and experimental method, shows that Chinese young children often labeled as self-centered "little emperors" construct their own moral universe that differs markedly from adult norms amid China's rapid social transformations and a looming moral crisis. These studies all suggest that children are not passive witnesses to or passive recipients of global imports but rather social actors who actively navigate and react to globalizing socialization inputs and further construct their own indigenized models.

This book elaborates on this recent scholarship that highlights children's subjectivities and agency in globalization of socialization landscapes by exploring how South Korean young children strategically transform, reinterpret, and reconstruct globally circulating socialization ideas and practices to address goals of their own culture-laden peer world. Although Ms. Choo in the narrative presented earlier portrays her students' performances and behaviors as deficient with respect to the "new" and thereby "good" socialization values such as creativity and diversity, when children's perspectives are considered, their pursuit of uniformity and comparison can be seen to be, perhaps unexpectedly but nonetheless, as an outcome of their strategic use and appropriation of the new Western curriculum.

Furthermore, unlike previous works that tend to focus on children's reactions to or experiences of global imports, this book extends previous research by examining the ways that children's agentive participation shapes teachers' enactment, reinterpretation, and reconceptualization of global imports. The studies highlighting the bidirectionality of the socialization process have shown that children not only react to adult initiatives or directives but also significantly constrain, encourage, or facilitate adults' socialization activities, thereby themselves structuring their own learning experiences (Pontecorvo, Fasulo, and Sterponi 2001; Rogoff 1990). In the bidirectionality paradigm, therefore, parental action and children's participation are no longer conceived as separable elements but as mutually interacting and often affecting the process of socialization.

Although a growing body of research has focused on the bidirectional and collaborative nature of learning, none of these works so far has addressed children's direct influence on adults' indigenization of globally circulating socialization ideologies. My study aims to fill this gap by describing how South Korean young children's strategic and selective appropriation and reinterpretation of global imports facilitates and mediates teachers' reform of their curricula and pedagogical practices. The book shows that children's own transformed practices and meanings do not remain as discrete elements of peer culture but provide an impetus for teachers to reflect on their own highly inconsistent and conflicting socialization practices and ideologies and thereafter actively modify them and construct new models of personhood based on these reflections. It details how anxieties and agonies like those of Ms. Choo's presented in the beginning of this chapter are caused mainly by children's refusal to passively internalize global imports teachers explicitly try to infuse. In Ms. Choo's case, she was later inspired to modify and transform her pedagogical goals and styles as a result of her pupils' performances. The detailed analyses of the processes of this transformation articulate the dynamism children's agency brings to the indigenization of global imports and more broadly to the globalized and globalizing South Korean socialization landscape.

Psychological Globalization and Transformation of Personhood

Among various domains of socialization and globalization, this book particularly focuses on the ways that configurations and experiences of self and personhood shape and are shaped by global forces imposing on socialization spheres. As Mauss (1985) states in his classic paper on the category of the person, the idea of person or self is a human universal constituting an essential part of human life. The notion of person or self is held to be fundamental in that it is basic to the rest of human thinking and dominates our intellectual life. Given that the category of person or self as a human universal governs other social realities as Mauss (1985) and others (Hallowell 1955; Kirkpatrick and White 1985; Lutz 1985; Shweder 1990; Wellenkamp 1988; White 1992) have articulated, asking how people think and talk about persons, what this does for people, and how it shapes social realities are fundamental questions to be dealt with in the inquiry of the link between local subjectivities and sociopolitical structures. In particular, the fact that the main purpose of parenting and formal education is to cultivate beliefs, skills, and feelings supporting particular cultural ways of understanding the world (Bruner 1996), the self or personhood is a major domain of socialization that affects the lives of local actors in shifting milieus.

Although scholars from various disciplines discuss the social impact of globalization, few offer insights into the resonance of this global time-space compression with psychocultural processes such as constructing one's self, personhood, identity, consciousness, and emotion (Casey and Edgerton 2005). A scant but insightful set of studies from psychological anthropology, however, has shown how psychocultural processes mediate and become mediated by globalization (Fong 2007; Hinton 2005; Linger 2005; McHugh 2004; Strauss 1997; Weisner and Lowe 2005; Xu 2014). Strauss's (1997) work on postmodern subjectivities, for instance, critically reexamines a dominant account of postmodern selves as "schizofragmentation," characterized by floating emotions and inability to organize coherent experience. She argues that the widely shared rhetoric about postmodern selves does not adequately describe psychological experiences of political economic changes. Based on extensive interviews with urbanites and suburbanites in the United States, she shows that postmodern selves are not entirely fragmented or "random pastiches" as presented in the abstract rhetoric but rather are integrated through emotionally salient experiences that mediate internalization of social discourses. In her earlier work, Strauss (1990) also analyzes detailed psychocultural processes of social actors' internalization of heterogeneous and inconsistent social information and substantiates three different types of cognitive mechanisms for internalizing "heteroglossia" based on the analysis of the discourse of U.S. workingmen. In a similar vein, McHugh (2004) closely traces a Nepalese woman's experiences of global forces and shows how this privileged middle-class woman integrates the values of her community and those of "the West" and forges a self that is locally grounded yet effective in a cosmopolitan context. Studies by Xu (2014) and Fong (2007) presented above also detail psychocultural processes involved in Chinese caregivers' and children's remapping of themselves in relation to others under the rapid transformation of Chinese society which demands a conflicting and confusing set of imperatives. Anderson-Fye's (2003) work on Belizean adolescents' adoption of transnational ideas, in particular, illustrates the power of ethnopsychology as mediator of psychological globalization. Scrutinizing the ways that Belizean schoolgirls selectively incorporate transnational concepts, she shows that the Belizean ethnopsychology of self-protection plays a key role in the degree to which transnational ideas and images become salient among schoolgirls. Even though gender-based maltreatment and thin body image are both transcultural materials new to Belizean girls, the former becomes psychologically salient and gets integrated into girls' lives as it fits better with the local ethnopsychology while the latter is ignored due to its lack of fit with local ethnopsychology.

These findings from psychological anthropology's studies of globalization and psychocultural change inform us that self and personhood are not only major domains profoundly reshaped and reworked by sociopolitical changes but are significant mediators of these transformational processes. This book examines the interactive processes of psychological globalization—that is, the ways that globalization remaps local contours of self and personhood and the indigenization of global force as mediated by psychological processes including self and personhood. The architecture of Somang classrooms full of verbal glosses such as I, myself, feelings, and self-expressions, or Ms. Choo's eager pursuit of creativity and diversity presented in the beginning all attest to the impact globalization has had on the reconfiguration of "proper" notions of self and personhood. At the same time, conflicts and contradictions caused by the introduction of global materials, as reflected in Ms. Choo's agony over the unattainability of newly forming ideals of selfhood, her ambivalent attitude toward children's personalities, or different configurations of selfhood between teachers and children, raise the question of why certain ideas get easily incorporated into local experiences while others are ignored, resisted, or transformed. Strauss's (1990, 1997) discussion of the role emotionally salient experiences play in the internalization of heteroglossia and three different cognitive mechanisms of internalization and Anderson-Fye's (2003) theory of "goodness of fit" presented above provide theoretical materials to examine the mediating forces of psychological processes in the indigenization of globally circulating socialization ideas. The following chapters present ways that implicit local forms of selfhood and associated feelings and sentiments toward them work as powerful mediating factors in the transformation of local socialization amid its globalization.

To investigate the resonance of globalization with shifting contours of self and personhood, I employ discourse-centered approaches that treat language not as merely referential but as social action that creates and transforms social reality in interaction (Ahearn 2001; Hanks 1996; Miller, Fung, and Mintz 1996).

Discourse-oriented approaches provide theoretical and methodological means to discuss the mutual constitution of subjective experiences and sociocultural structures without dichotomizing or essentializing them. Several theoretical currents, such as ethnopsychological studies (Kirkpatrick and White 1985; Lutz 1985; Shweder 1990), language socialization research (Miller et al. 1992; Ochs and Capps 2001), and developmental psychological work (Bruner 1986, 1990; Nelson 1989; Snow 1990) concerning self and personhood have stressed the need to move from viewing self as a discrete concept or symbol coded in terminologies or metaphors and instead to attend to "self in discourse" where processes exert forces in defining social relations, directing practical actions, and shaping sociopolitical realities. Following this view of "self in discourse" and other socialization research that regards discourse-level language as an important locus of inquiry for understanding childhood socialization (Briggs 1998; Fivush and Haden 2003; Fung 1999; Fung and Chen 2001; Miller et al. 2012; Quinn 2005a), I employ a particular version of ethnography that combines participant observations and interviews with "micro level analysis of talk" (Miller et al. 2012, 6), an approach that has characterized language socialization research from its inception (Ochs and Schieffelin 1984). I closely analyze everyday classroom talk to examine the creation and transformation of self through discursive practices. Here, everyday discourses of teachers and children and peer talk, a focus of close analysis in this book, are not merely a site of internalization wherein participants internalize the outside public signs and ideas of selfhood but a place where newly forming intersubjective assemblages of selfhood emerge and experiences of self arise amid both personal and collective realities and are potentially transformed.

Beyond Binaries: Self, Cultural Values, and Socialization

In line with most contemporary ethnographic writings after the interpretive turn in anthropology,[2] this book aims to represent intricacies, contradictions, and uncertainties of social realities and human actions observed in the field without imposing generic or supposedly objective units of analysis. In particular, the global phenomena observed in this book entails fragmentations, conflicts, and contradictions at its core. Therefore, it is essential to treat major themes of the inquiry such as self, cultural values, and socialization not as fixed and bounded entities but as emergent, situated, and contested so as to adequately account for the multidimensionality of global experiences. Even though the ethnography itself should display this perspective, I nonetheless briefly mention how I view and treat these major themes in the book.

As already alluded to above in the explanation of the discourse-centered approach I employ in this book, I treat the self and selfhood as culturally and historically constructed ideological practices affecting a social field. This is a view of the self as pragmatic acts and communicative performances and it departs from mid-twentieth-century anthropological studies of self which tend to posit a bipolarized model wherein the Western self is characterized as predominantly autonomous, acontexual, and independent in contrast to a relational, collective, and context-dependent non-Western self (Dumont 1982; Geertz 1984; Keeler 1983; Levy 1984; Myers 1979; Rosaldo 1984; Shweder and Bourne 1984). This bipolar model of the self is the product of a move to de-essentialize previous Western psychological and philosophical thinking of the self as a fixed and bounded entity filled with inner reflective psychological essence. However, these mid-twentieth-century anthropological studies of self and personhood, nonetheless, in their efforts to fix the subject/object, reason/feeling, self/society distinction operative in the Western notions of self, created another version of a binary that essentializes and dichotomizes the Western and the non-Western selves as respectively egocentric and sociocentric[3] (for critiques, see Ewing 1990; Harter 1999; Holland and Kipnis 1994; Killen and Wainryb 2000; Kusserow 2004; Lindholm 1997; Murray 1993; Raeff 2006; Spiro 1993). To adequately describe the shifting contours of selfhood as experienced and embodied by Korean participants, I view the self as informed by cultural meanings and themes and, at the same time, multiplex, emergent, flexible, and contradictory serving as an operation in a contentious field of social activity as stressed by many contemporary discussions on self and personhood (Abu-Lughod and Lutz 1990; Ewing 1990; Kondo 1990).

Although I emphasize the nonessentialist emergent dimensions of the self in my analyses, ethnographic descriptions in this book reveal a bipolarized model of selfhood due to the very characteristics of the way that the self is conceived by and practiced in the contemporary South Korean socialization scene. As is closely discussed in chapter 2, the South Korean socialization terrain, in their adoption of globally dominant socialization ideologies, tend to posit an "imagined dichotomy" wherein "the Western" is imagined as exclusively loaded with "new" and "better" values of creativity, diversity, or self-expression while "the traditional" or "the Korean" is characterized by the "old" and "backward" values of hierarchy, uniformity, or obedience. Similarly, although all cultural values have complex and nuanced meanings, the current South Korean socialization discourses articulate those cultural values categorized as "the Western" (e.g., creativity or diversity) are only "good" and "desirable," whereas those conceived as "the Korean" (e.g., uniformity or hierarchy) have "bad" and "backward" sides. This imagined dichotomy and simple treatment of cultural values as ethnographic realities are likely to be misconstrued as a scholarly analysis or interpretation. Despite this risk, I nonetheless describe the imagined dichotomy as used by my informants and refer to cultural values with simple terms such as creativity, self-expression, uniformity, or hierarchy because these are the ways that participants of the contemporary South Korean socialization scene conceive of and talk about the self and personhood. Moreover, as I demonstrate in the book, this simple and dichotomous treatment of selfhood and cultural values are the very place from which many of the complexities, disruptions, and contradictions of the contemporary globalized South Korean socialization terrain, the main inquiry of this book, emerge.

INTRODUCTION

As with conceptualization of the self and personhood, I conceive of socialization as taking place in sites of struggle, negotiation, and conflict wherein diverse actors jointly and mutually reconstruct and reinterpret cultural and semiotic resources and thereby not only produce and reproduce cultural knowledge but play a dynamic role in the processes of social change. This proposed view of socialization is an attempt to challenge the assumption of determinism, functionality, linearity, and outcome-centeredness prevalent in much of earlier theorization of socialization (for reviews, see Alanen 1988; Levine 2007; Schwartzman 2001) and pays more attention to the dynamic, multidirectional, emergent, and processual qualities of socialization, which I view as crucial especially in investigating socialization in the contexts of social transformation and change like the South Korean case in this book. In examining the heterogeneities and dynamisms of socialization, I particularly focus on two important aspects of socialization. First, while I look at both explicit and implicit mechanisms of socialization, I pay particular attention to the power of implicit, unmarked, and embodied aspects of socialization in cultural learning and reproduction. As Quinn (2005b) points out in her discussion of the universal features of child-rearing, although children receive a plentitude of explicit injunctions, admonitions, lessons, and corrections to their behavior, important cultural lessons are much more frequently and continuously conveyed in implicit messages. Following theorizations of socialization that stress these implicit aspects of socialization (Bruner 1996; Chapin 2010; Rogoff and Lave 1984),[4] I show how these habitual, unconscious, and embodied practices, conveyed repeatedly, redundantly, and unmistakably, make so-called characteristically Korean socialization values and ideologies, survive and endure despite explicit inculcation of global ideals. Second, in exploring dynamisms of socialization, I focus on the role children and their peer culture play in the production of meanings crucial to cultural reproduction as well as in the acquisition of cultural sensibilities. Challenging an earlier theorization of socialization that solely directs attention to the deterministic power of adults and conceives of children as passive objects being acted on, I follow more contemporary scholarship of socialization and childhood that highlights children's agency and perspective (Bluebond-Langner and Korbin 2007; Caputo 1995; Corsaro 1997, 2017; Corsaro and Miller 1992; Hirschfeld 2002; James 2007; James and Prout 1997; Pontecorvo, Fasulo, and Sterponi 2001). Again, I conceptualize socialization as taking place in sites of negotiation, reinvention, and reproduction to which children actively contribute as builders and transformers of culture as well as initiators of their own cultural learning. From this point of view, the tensions, dynamisms, and conflicts embedded in socialization emerge largely from children's active participation in their own socialization processes where they not only embody culturally valued conduct, sentiments, and virtues but also appropriate and transform various cultural and semiotic resources to construct their own culture-laden social world and sometimes even bidirectionally influence and constrain adults' practices through everyday interactions and negotiations.

Fieldwork

To investigate the meeting of the global and the local in a South Korean early childhood educational sphere, I conducted ethnographic fieldwork in a Korean middleclass preschool that I call by the pseudonym Somang. I got to know Somang preschool through the introduction of my colleague who is a professor of early childhood education at a university in the metropolitan area. After finishing my PhD in the United States, I came back to my home country and was looking for a place to do my second research in Korea. Based on my previous research on classspecific socialization practices and peer culture in the United States at a preschool in Michigan, I was planning to do my second research in a similar setting with some cross-cultural continuities. Somang preschool seemed to fit into this category in terms of its socioeconomic background and organizational features such as class sizes, student-teacher ratio, and classroom routines. The fieldwork for this book began in December 2010 and lasted until February 2012. During fifteen months of this fieldwork, I tried to immerse myself in the lives of Somang children and teachers and understand their perspectives, experiences, sentiments, and aspirations. I regularly visited classrooms three or four times a week, followed everyday classroom routines, and closely observed teachers' interactions with children as well as children's peer interactions. The observations took place in a variety of school settings, from structured settings such as teacher-led activities or group times to relatively unstructured settings such as free play or lunchtime. As will be detailed in the following, I also conducted both formal and informal interviews with teachers. Teacher-children interactions in structured settings and interviews with teachers were all video or audio recorded. Video recordings of interactions in unstructured settings took place when interactions were relevant to the topic of study and when the researcher, through recordings, could capture details more fully than through observation alone. I collected other materials such as children's artwork, poems, and writings, artifacts of the classrooms, and other documents in which teachers recorded assessments or observations regarding children's activities, play, and behaviors in educational settings.

Like any ethnographic research, this book is the product of the interaction of the ethnographer and hosts as well as the nature of, and shifts in, the power relations between the two parties. The interpersonal relationships that are established between the anthropologist and those she visits are, then, central to the process of cultural understanding. My relationships with my host had its own unique features which are not the exclusive outcome of the individual characteristics of me as a fieldworker but the encounters of my multiple identities such as adult, professor, and woman one the one hand, and research questions I brought to the field on the other hand, with cultural features of the host community. Although the intricacies of these relationships might be beyond my awareness and interpretation, I nevertheless present my sense of my positioning in the field below. I introduce sociocultural dimensions of the Somang preschool, my research processes

INTRODUCTION

and specific methodologies employed, and the kinds of relationships I had with the host community that affected my data collection.

Somang Preschool

Somang preschool forms the basis of this book. It is located inside the well-known apartment complex of the Kangnam area in Seoul, South Korea. Kangnam, which literally means the southern part of the Han River, is a largely affluent neighborhood known for its "education fever" (*kyoyukyeol*)—that is, a preoccupation with the pursuit of formal schooling (Seth 2002, 9). Reflecting characteristics of this area, children in Somang preschool are mostly from middle- and upper-middle-class families. Parents are highly educated, most of them holding at least a bachelor's degree and tend to have professional and managerial jobs. Having pursued higher education, a marker of high prestige and social rank among middle-class Koreans (Lett 1998; Sorensen 1994), Somang parents have demanding educational goals for their children. In the apartment complex where Somang preschool resides, one can easily encounter shuttle buses from a variety of private after-school educational institutions lining up to pick up students. The ages of these students range from two-year-old children who have just started speaking to eighteen-year-old high school students who are taking the national college entrance exam. Somang parents consider that preschoolers are initiating their educational path to the university. This view leads parents to closely compare preschool curricula in the area in order to choose one they think will give their children a competitive edge and guarantee success in their long educational journey.

The major motivation for parents to choose Somang preschool is its emphasis on newly imported Western educational ideas such as self-expression, creativity, autonomy, and individuality. Somang preschool advertises itself as pursuing the "new" and "advanced" education that produces today's successful child who could compete in the global economy as self-sufficient and creative. Targeting parents' aspirations to raise their children as fitting into the creative elite class, this preschool positions itself as a corrective to the problems of traditional Korean education and attracts educational consumers for being equipped with educational means to find and develop the full potentials of their children.

As a means to raise the creative, independent, and self-sufficient elite, Somang preschool implements an Italian curriculum called the Reggio Emilia approach which originated in a small town, Reggio Emilia, in Italy and then spread to the United States in the 1980s and recently to East Asian countries such as South Korea, Japan, and China (New 2007; Tobin, Hsueh, and Karasawa 2009). The Reggio Emilia approach was introduced to South Korean early childhood education around the late 1990s and started to be implemented by some preschools in the early 2000s. South Korean early childhood education's adoption of the Reggio Emilia curriculum is related largely to the emerging significance of Western values as important organizing factors for South Korean society and more specifically to South Korea's educational reform in the late 1990s which "dramatically changed the rhetoric of educational values from 'uniformity and equality' to 'creativity, excellence, and diversification'" (Park 2007, 191). Against a backdrop of educational reform and the shift of focus in socialization values, a group of early childhood scholars and educators who were critical of the South Korean early childhood educational system for being teacher-centered, uniform, and repetitive conceived of the Reggio approach as an alternative and actively participated in disseminating its philosophy and practice to South Korean early childhood education. The Somang preschool was founded in 2009 by one of those educators who believed the Reggio approach to be an effective pedagogical means to inculcate so-called new socialization values such as individuality, creativity, or self-expression which are thought to be required for success in a changing globalized South Korea. Most of the Somang teachers did not have much experience with practicing the Reggio Emilia curriculum but were exposed to its philosophy through previous education in a university and other teacher training programs. In particular, they firmly believed that the Reggio approach, especially its child- and play-centered pedagogy, was an effective way to raise a new type of person. They were very active in implementing the Reggio approach to their curriculum.

Somang provides day care and preschool programs for children aged one to five years old. During my stay in Somang preschool, there were eight age-based and one mixed-age classroom. Among these, I observed two three-year-old and one four-year-old classroom from December 2010 to February 2011, and one classroom of three-year-olds and one of mixed-aged children (four- and five-year-olds) from March 2011 to February 2012. The class sizes ranged from fifteen to twenty-two children with two or three teachers. Teachers are all female except for an English teacher who regularly visited each classroom three times a week. Teachers tend to have a bachelor's degree from major South Korean universities and some have earned a master's degree or finished the coursework in early childhood education MA programs. Many teachers, therefore, are academically oriented and reflectively approach their pedagogical practices. All the names in this book are pseudonyms.

Getting to Trust Each Other: Teachers and Me

I first visited Somang preschool on one very cloudy and cold day in December 2010. From the gate of the apartment complex where Somang preschool is located, I could feel the "education fever" of this community by signs of after-school institutions in annexed buildings. I barely encountered residents on the street and could see only some residents entering apartment buildings using security cards, which gave me the impression of a gated community. I later got to know that this somewhat desolate landscape was due to the time and the weather of that day. The street and playgrounds tend to get crowded and lively in the afternoons with children and parents, especially during sunny and warm days. Somang building lies in one corner of the apartment complex and has a typically clean and tidy exterior. Inside the building is a refined interior with huge classrooms and nice facilities.

When I first met the director, she identified Somang preschool as an institution pursuing "good education." Differentiating Somang education from the ones practiced in other institutions and calling it "new," she also emphasized that their "good education" appreciates, develops, and maximizes the full potential of every individual child. I did not fully understand the meanings and contexts of her introduction at that time and simply assumed that their educational goals pertained to social demands of raising a new type of person. As mentioned in the opening of the book, this hasty conjecture took on a different shape and more nuanced meanings as I came to know and observe more detailed and diverse contexts of Somang everyday socialization practices.

After sharing my research interests with the director, I was allowed to visit the classrooms I preferred. I chose three classrooms that fit into the age range of three to five and began by visiting the Rainbow Room, the four-year-olds' classroom. On my first visit to the Rainbow Room, Ms. Shim, the teacher, welcomed me and included me in the class by introducing me to students, alluding to my presence in her conversation with children, and constantly offering eye contact with me. At the end of the day, she even handed me the packed cookies children made as part of classroom activities of that day. Receiving the cookies, I expressed my gratitude for allowing me to be part of their class and said, "See you tomorrow." At my goodbye phrase, she paused for a moment and asked, "Are you coming again?" From her puzzled face, I had a hunch that something went wrong. She seemed to understand my visit as one-time class observation which teachers had some experiences of before. I replied, "I'd like to come again if you would allow."

I was able to visit the Rainbow Room the day after but not as welcomed or included as before. The teachers were kind and polite to me, but at the same time I could feel their uneasiness toward my presence. I was placed in similar situations in other classrooms. This was a somewhat unexpected circumstance for me as I tended to envision my relationships with informants based on my previous fieldwork in the U.S. preschool. Even though my relationship with the U.S. teachers had deepened as we became accustomed to each other, my presence did not seem to put much burden on them from the beginning. My identity as a doctoral student, foreigner, Asian, and young woman made the U.S. teachers regard me as a researcher learning their educational practices and therefore someone who needed help and guidance from them. As I reflect on the opposite responses from the two field sites, I realize how contextual, relational, and politicized the conduct of fieldwork is as many anthropologists have argued since the so-called reflexive turn of the 1980s.

I was perplexed by unacceptance at first but soon noticed that teachers' discomfort and uneasiness emerged mainly from my identity as a university professor. Teachers placed me in the category of "professors" with whom their typical relationships had been hierarchical. I realized that teachers positioned me as an authoritative figure who came to observe, evaluate, and correct their pedagogical practices and skills. For instance, on our way to the picnic in the beginning of the school term, Ms. Park approached me on the bus and asked about the theme of my research. I answered that I'm broadly interested in children's peer relationships and Korean socialization practices. She then suddenly said, "Our class and kids might look chaotic to you." In this statement, she assumed that I expected some particular order in their classroom interactions and would rashly judge their children as well as pedagogical practices as not reaching certain criteria. This anxious and defensive attitude seem to be related to teachers' previous experiences with professors of early childhood education and more broadly with their training in early childhood education wherein evaluation of pedagogical practices is considered to be essential for feasible educational outcomes.

Knowing that I was being placed in a particular position vis-à-vis the teachers (teachers are projecting the professorial category onto me), I employed several research strategies to subvert power relations and hierarchy inherent in teachers' perception of me. First, I made considerable efforts to position myself as a researcher who is interested in insiders' views, experiences, and perspectives rather than imposing certain criteria on them. The effort included signaling to teachers that I barely have any knowledge of early childhood education, nor am I an expert in that field, all of which were in fact true. In my interactions with teachers, I also continuously acknowledged their expertise in the field. Knowing that I not only did not intend to evaluate their pedagogical practices or possess the abilities or knowledge to evaluate them, teachers began to conceive of me as a researcher to whom they could show their everyday natural classroom interactions and as someone who might need help from them. They sometimes taught me by explaining various methods, approaches, or trends of Korean early childhood education or introducing textbooks and research papers that could enhance my knowledge, especially regarding the Reggio approach that Somang preschool adopts. Afterward, teachers actively shared their views, thoughts, and feelings toward a variety of issues including their own socialization practices, pedagogy, children's interactions, and parents' attitudes.

Second, overturning perceived power relations involved not only persuading teachers of my intent but personally constructing an egalitarian and faithful relationship with them. I negotiated my positionality through everyday acts such as how I talked, where I sat, or how I arranged to help them with chores. Such little actions enabled me to blend into their lives as someone at least not authoritative, if not fully equal. Teachers started talking to me about their difficulties, complaints, despair, and agonies as well as joys, hopes, and imaginaries. They also included me in their more personal spheres by inviting me to talks, coffee times, or dinners after school.

Third, to construct and maintain an egalitarian relationship with teachers, I allotted the first half of fieldwork mainly to participant observation of everyday classroom interactions and to unstructured, informal interviews with teachers. By allowing teachers to express themselves in their own ways and paces and observing naturally occurring interactions, I could have teachers initiate our relationships and refrain from imposing my research questions on them. The semistructured and in-depth interviews pose lists of preplanned open-ended questions and were conducted at the end of fieldwork when we had established a close rapport and could openly discuss my research. During these more structured interviews, I asked teachers about their educational goals, their experiences with imported curricula, views on children's senses of self, their perspectives on children's behaviors and social interactions, and their conceptualizations of a "good" child. Scheduling fieldwork in this way also enabled me to reserve my tentative and preconceived research questions and have research questions emerge from and be shaped by the field.

Even though I do not believe that my relationship with the teachers was fully equal or that I became an "insider," arranging the fieldwork and relationships in this particular way permitted me to form relations of trust that are important in fieldwork. Teachers who were defensive and tended to show idealized views and behaviors at first began to express difficulties, dilemmas, complaints, or critiques regarding their pedagogical and socialization practices and openly show their diverse, contradictory, and conflicting attitudes and behaviors to me, all of which became ethnographically vast, rich, detailed materials with which to discuss main findings, themes, and arguments of this book. On my final visit to Somang preschool, Ms. Choo told me that they first thought of me as a *fraktsiya* who spied on them for the director. We laughed heartily at her remark.

Entering into Children's Peer World

Another important feature of my fieldwork emerges from the conflicts between the perspective this book takes and power relations and hierarchy existing between adults and children in the real world. Although this research deals with teachers' socialization practices, much is devoted to understanding children's perspectives and social worlds. As mentioned before, the book aims to bring voices of the children to the current thinking of socialization and globalization. This aim involves challenges not only at the level of theoretical debate but also in the process of actual fieldwork. "The adult ideological viewpoint," which stresses the exclusive power of adults in defining children, is not only embedded in socialization theory but the reflection of the everyday folk notion of adult-child relationships as shared by many modern societies including South Korea. Especially in institutional settings like preschool, teachers as adults clearly have much power and authority over children. As Thorne (1993, 20) notes, "Children have little choice about being present, and members of a smaller, more powerful group [teachers] regulate their use of time, space, and resources." Therefore, my sheer status as an adult in an institution that draws sharp generational divisions and marks them with differences in power and authority posed complicated obstacles to my research objective of discovering children's perspectives. I knew that children's identification of me as a typical adult would make it difficult for me to gain access to their secret world. At the same time, teachers would also have some expectations for me as an adult such as keeping order and imposing an agenda. My fieldwork required challenging these views that both children and teachers held and positioning myself as an atypical adult. Several research strategies were employed for this purpose.

First, although my physicality made it impossible to be a true member of the children's world, I tried my best to identify myself as the children's equal rather than a typical teacher or a parent. At the beginning of the fieldwork, this was mainly done by employing Corsaro's (1997) "reactive method of field entry," which he used for his study of children's cultures in three different communities. That is, I entered into play areas, sat down, and waited for kids to react to me. This is the opposite of what most teachers do in the classroom as they usually do not sit down in play areas, and when they enter, it is usually to settle disputes, lead play, or ask questions. After a while, the children began to ask me questions and draw me into their activities and gradually defined me as an atypical adult. I did not attempt to initiate play, settle disputes, or direct activity. As time went by, children who first identified me as one of the teachers came to recognize me as part of their play—for instance, frequently asking me to put on costumes and play roles that often involved ones children usually do not prefer but that may be necessary for play activities such as the customer of a hair salon who has to sit still while a hairdresser cuts and perms hair, which is not an easy job for preschoolers. They also enjoyed sitting with me at the lunch table, which is an emblem of "best friends" in Somang children's peer world. I also tried to dissociate myself from authority and power typically attributed to adults in the classrooms. I usually did this by not participating in activities that signify adult authority or skills such as sitting on adult chairs, distributing lunch, helping with bathroom issues, or leading groups. I tried to help teachers in other ways—for example, cleaning up tables and floors while children were out playing or after school. I went through the days with or near the children rather than along the paths of teachers. With these relationships, children did not modify their behaviors and talk when I approached them, which they often do when teachers are present. This methodology permitted me to observe and become a part of their activities without affecting the nature or flow of their peer interactions.

Second, my efforts to discover children's perspectives involved not only constructing certain types of relationships but also constant reflections of my own observations as an adult. As any ethnographic representation, my observation of children's interactions is always filtered through my own interpretation of cultural events, and this interpretation could unwittingly entail common adult assumptions of children's daily activities as mostly trivial in comparison to adult ones. I tried to overcome this barrier by arranging fieldwork schedules in a specific way. That is, during the first three months of my fieldwork, I mainly focused on how children interact with each other and how they engage in various activities. I focused on areas where teachers' influences were minimal such as outside playgrounds, gym, and pretend play areas in the classroom. Even in the activities where teachers' roles were influential such as group time or storybook reading time,

INTRODUCTION

I tried to focus on how children engage with and react to teachers' inputs. It was after three months that I started paying attention to how teachers interact with children. Even though children's and teachers' models cannot be treated as separate entities and in fact are always deployed in shared contexts, this process enabled me to discover children's views and experiences without imposing adult models' models.

Third, as I reflect on my understanding of children's worlds, I realize the force of empathy and emotion in the process of knowing as Rosaldo (1993) argued in his now well-known analysis of Illongot headhunting. Even though being attentive to power relations inherent in my relationship with children and the politics of knowledge production was useful as a research strategy as mentioned above, empathetic observation was most crucial in my understanding of children's perspectives and experiences. It was often through my own feelings akin to those of the children that I was able to gain a level of intellectual depth and understanding of the children's world. Aligning myself with children often drew me into perplexing situations in which I found myself in between children and teachers. Children, for instance, offered to play with small prohibited objects such as personal toys or goodies they brought from home or hid those items in their pockets at the very moment they might be caught by teachers. Seeking closer ties, I always accepted children's requests and offers of prohibited items, but this often made me feel like going back and being a child by breaking rules and being afraid to be caught by teachers. The anxiety, fear, and uneasiness I felt at those moments became sources of insight into what it is like to be a student, to make friends, and to follow peer rules and expectations in an institutional setting like preschool. I still remember the school excursion day to the aquarium when I was assigned by the teacher to be a partner with Minjun. Before the departure to the aquarium, the teacher of the Tree Room paired up the children and asked them to hold each other's hands and take care of their partner all day. As pairing aimed at preventing possible risks and accidents such as getting lost, the teacher tended to pair a mischievous child with an amenable one. When an energetic, mischievous child such as Minjun was left out as the odd child, the teacher paired Minjun with me. It was obvious that I was expected to perform the role of an amenable and good child who leads Minjun to follow teachers' directions and thereby safely finish the school excursion. Soon after I was paired up with Minjun, I realized how difficult it is to accommodate to the needs of one's partner and achieve the communal goal of enacting socialities expected and emphasized by teachers. Minjun kept dragging me to the gift shop to look at shark toys and Nemo balloons. I had to pull on his hands not to be separated from the group and to look at real fish in the aquarium. Spending the day with Minjun, I felt the imponderabilia of adjusting to a peer's desires and interests as well as the difficulties of negotiating incompatible goals and behaviors. The feelings I experienced at those moments broadened my insight into children's peer world, especially the prevalence of conflicts, the pursuit of power and authority, and the shifts of alliance formation and exclusion, all of which I discuss in detail in the following chapters. Through what Behar (2012) calls emotional intelligence, I was able to understand that arguing over whose painting is best or yielding one's belongings to others is not a trivial matter as often considered by teachers and more broadly adults. It is a serious business requiring highly sophisticated political and social skills, and I, as an adult, obviously did not possess those skills.

The Plan of the Journey: Chapters

By being gradually immersed into the lives of Somang teachers and children, I was able to better understand the seemingly puzzling views, attitudes, and behaviors teachers and children display in their classroom interactions and the feelings and sentiments embedded in these everyday moments of rapidly transforming socialization spheres. The initially incomprehensible observations such as Ms. Choo's complaints, her inconsistent views of ideal personhood, or children's fondness for uniformity introduced in the beginning became more intelligible and explicable as diverse moments of local actors' everyday lives were witnessed and then contextualized within the micro- and macro-sociocultural universes surrounding them. This book emerges from this journey to understand the motivations, imaginaries, and perspectives of teachers and children who are experiencing the drastic change of their mundane environments and to interpret the contradictions, heterogeneities, and dilemmas involved in the experiences of these local actors, building on findings from earlier scholarly works and theorization of globalization and childhood as well as historical and cultural contingencies.

The journey starts from introducing the social, cultural, and historical contexts this research is situated in. In the next chapter, I introduce the recent transformations of the South Korean socialization landscape, locating it in the history of educational reforms, the emergence of new types of personhood, and the structural transformations of Korean society amid its democratization, globalization, and neoliberal turn. The chapter especially discusses the active and reckless consumption of globally dominating socialization ideologies as the main feature of current South Korean early childhood socialization and details the ways "the Western" and "the traditional" are imagined and redefined in this process of adoption. It shows that as globally dominating so-called Western socialization ideologies are consumed in the contexts of nurturing creative new citizens with a broad array of skills and develop as a correction to unsatisfactory qualities of current Korean children, the Western socialization practices are overidealized as if they have only positive sides while the so-called traditional Korean ones are reified as backward and evaluated in contrast to the imagined Western-ness.

Against these backgrounds, the next chapters present the lived experiences of local actors beginning with those of teachers. Chapter 3 revisits Ms. Choo's laments and agony and her ambivalent and contradictory attitudes toward children's behaviors and sets up widely shared and frequently expressed views, feelings, and attitudes of teachers as the central theme to be explained. Toward this end, the chapter first explores the way Somang preschool adopts the Reggio approach, the globally circulating curriculum, focusing on its selective indigenizing processes. Then, closely describing everyday local practices and interactions in the classrooms, it examines the discontinuities between the idealized model teachers explicitly articulate and real practices enacted in everyday contexts. I show that even though the explicit curriculum prioritizes newly introduced Western socialization values and deprecates the perceived older values, the enacted practices entail traditional values and ideas in conflict with the explicitly stated new positions. Teachers, while making concerted efforts to promote new values that they believe offer a competitive edge to children in a globalized world, still expect their children to be equipped with traditional virtues such as modesty, considerateness, or reservations and even heavily emphasize hierarchy, collectivity, competition, or comparison, the values criticized for hindering the development of children's true selves, through embodied and implicit practices and also through explicit instructions in less formal areas. These findings reveal that teachers' complaints and agony over the unattainability of new ideals and their inconsistent attitudes toward children are closely related to the conflicting and contradictory desires and expectations they have for their children, complex models of personhood they have in mind, and more broadly the fragmented and heterogeneous socialization landscape these local actors are exposed to. The chapter especially pays attention to the power of what Tobin, Hsueh, and Karasawa (2009) and Bruner (1996) refer to as "implicit cultural practices" and "folk pedagogy" in the reproduction of core socialization values and argues that explicit reform efforts promoting a new type of personhood backfire because they are in conflict with traditional embodied beliefs and practices that linger as implicit, unmarked, situated, and taken-for granted features of socialization not readily subject to scrutiny, criticism, or reform.

Chapter 4 moves on to the experiences of children, describing what it is like to live as a child in this rapidly changing fragmented and chaotic socialization environment. Placing children's voices and perspectives at the center of analysis, I examine the ways that children view, experience, and respond to global forces. The detailed description of children's peer interactions shows that children, rather than passively assimilating global imports as provided and interpreted by teachers, do creatively and strategically reconstruct and reinterpret them and construct their own meanings, practices, and understandings of them to address themes of their culture-laden peer world. The findings, in particular, defy the adult-centric views upheld by teachers and previous studies on children and childhood that regard children's interactive styles and behaviors as symptoms of underdevelopment and instead demonstrate that children possess highly sophisticated understandings of heterogenous and conflicting socialization ideologies and even sometimes provide critical insights into the inconsistent and contradictory indigenized socialization milieu surrounding them. For instance, when unsatisfactory behaviors and attitudes of children, such as their eager pursuit of uniformity or copying are viewed from children's perspectives, they are no more the failures of pedagogical goals as Ms. Choo believed in the narrative presented earlier but are acts of belonging and inclusion, which indicates children's deep understanding of the very nature of self and expression—that is, their inevitable sociality. Children's understanding here contrasts sharply with that of teachers who treat self and expression as if they unfold in social vacuum, an untenable view as many anthropological studies on selfhood have demonstrated (Geertz 1984; Shweder and Bourne 1984; White and Kirkpatrick 1985). The chapter argues that children's own coconstructed interactive practices, models, and meanings as shown in this case of fondness for copying and sameness, are not only distinct from but even in some respect more refined and penetrating than those of teachers. Detailing rich interactive and communicative peer practices and rituals, this chapter discusses the depth of knowledge children possess regarding their complex and conflicting socialization environment and the active role they play in their own socialization processes as well as in the indigenization of globally circulating socialization ideologies and practices.

Chapter 5 carries along children's contributions to the rapidly changing socialization landscape but further extends their agency by focusing on how children's own created and transformed cultural practices and meanings bidirectionally shape teachers' indigenization of global forces. To this end, it traces the microhistory of classroom activities and curriculum and details the ways that children's transformation of global imports influence teachers' reform of the curriculum and pertaining pedagogical practices. The microhistories illustrate that characteristically traditional socialization values rarely articulated and even dismissed for inhibiting the cultivation of new global ideals in teachers' initial adoption of the Western curriculum later come to constitute a significant component of the revised curriculum. Children, through active transformation of global imports, incite teachers to reflect on their eager and somewhat reckless pursuit of globally dominating socialization ideologies and then spur them to actively practice local socialization values and to create the indigenized model of ideal personhood which intuitively combines local values with global imports. Based on these findings, the chapter argues that children, by mediating, constraining, or facilitating teachers' enactment of everyday practices, wield great influence on indigenizing processes and even, in collaboration with teachers, implicitly resist the hegemonic force of Western early childhood ideologies in their lives.

The final chapter sums up overall findings and links them to broader theoretical and applied concerns. The South Korean early childhood socialization landscape described in this book is full of fragmented, conflicting, and contradictory desires, imaginaries, and motivations. This heterogeneity emerges not only from the conflict between global desires and local virtues but also from different positions local actors occupy in social spheres. The book reveals that local actors, both teachers and children, endeavor to solve the dilemmas presented by this chaotic landscape in a variety of ways such as developing their own strategies, constructing new hybrid indigenized models of personhood, implicitly resisting global imports, or sometimes eagerly pursuing global ideals. The chapter discusses how these findings speak to and critically broaden previous scholarly works of globalization and childhood and the practical implication these ethnographically grounded descriptions, explanations, and interpretations have for the globally shaping and rapidly changing early childhood socialization and education.

2

New Personhood and Transformation of South Korean Early Childhood Socialization

> Kids are so different depending on where they came from. . . . The kids from private school studied too much, so they don't know how to play. The worst case is kids from kindergartens attached to elementary schools. They're all same, I mean uniform. It's like North Korea. Everyone claps together, sings together. You should go there sometime and see what's happening in there. They ask children to simply follow directions and do the same things and say it's exemplary good practice. (Looking at children playing restaurant) They didn't know how to play when they first came here, but now they play much better.[1]

This narrative by Ms. Shim, a teacher at Somang preschool, illustrates Korea's shifting socialization landscape and the dominance of new socialization ideologies on the lives of Korean caregivers and children. Ms. Shim, here, employs an analogy to North Korea in explaining the excellence of their curriculum and pedagogical practices. She disparages the pursuit of uniformity, conformity, and the collective orientation practiced in other institutions as "backward," and places a high value on "playing well," which reflects the Westernized play-oriented and child-initiated curriculum adopted in this preschool. The way Ms. Shim uses the comparison to North Korea, which typically represents premodern and underdeveloped stages in South Korea in explaining uniform and teacher-centered instructions, demonstrates that she conceives of the newly adopted curriculum and the accompanying socialization values as more modern and advanced in contrast to other teacher-centered programs.

This dichotomous, hierarchical, and teleological view of socialization values and pedagogical practices saturates not only Somang everyday discourses but more broadly recent Korean socialization discourses and ideologies in general. Both everyday and official discourses circulated by educators, medical authorities, child psychologists, policymakers, and parents are full of discussions about the importance of moving away from traditional practices of raising a hardworking social conformist toward new practices aiming to produce a creative and self-confident global citizen. Ms. Shim's narrative raises several questions: Why does she evaluate children from kindergartens attached to elementary schools as "worst" while valorizing her students as "playing well"? Why is the pursuit of uniformity and sameness considered "worst" by this teacher? Why does she highly regard "playing well" and what does she specifically mean by "playing well"?

To understand narratives like that above now prevalent in South Korean socialization terrains and the impact they have on practices and experiences of contemporary Korean caregivers and children, it is necessary to examine the recent transformation of Korean socialization landscapes and their historical, cultural, and social contexts. Toward this end, this chapter first introduces the nature of recent shifts in Korean socialization ideologies and practices and then contextualizes the changes in larger social backgrounds such as educational reforms, the emergence of new types of personhood and subjectivities, and the broader structural transformations of Korean society such as democratization, globalization, and a neoliberal turn. After this, I discuss globally dominating socialization values and practices in the sphere of Korean early childhood education and situate the Somang preschool in this context. The chapter concludes with a discussion of the characteristics of the transformation, especially the way the "Western" and the "traditional" are imagined and redefined in the process of transformation.

From Uniformity to Self: The Self in Korean Socialization Practices

Within Korea, discourses on children's self concepts are at the center of new calls to reform early childhood socialization practices and ideologies. Influenced by Western early childhood education and socialization, and more broadly by the Westernization and globalization of Korean society, recent early childhood socialization discourses are filled with discussions of how to cultivate and foster children's selves. Under new discourses of self, characteristically traditional Korean socialization practices based on hierarchy, uniformity, and collectivism are evaluated as "old" and "backward" and contrasted with "new" and "better" socialization values such as individuality, creativity, and diversity.

Notably, these so-called new socialization values and practices are advocated as scientific and proper in mass media and popular parenting advice literature. Experts appearing in newspapers, magazines, and television talk shows frequently address promoting children's selves as a principal way to raise a successful child in the emerging Westernized and globalized Korea. These experts, in particular, criticize traditional Korean socialization practices for being didactic, uniform, and hierarchical, thereby obstructing the development of an individual child's uniqueness and potential. Instead, they suggest Western socialization practices as healthier and more advanced approaches that can move children away from traditional values of uniformity, hierarchy, and standardization toward new values of individuality, diversity, and creativity.

Experts' stratified views of socialization ideologies and practices have strongly affected the way Korean parents raise their children. Unlike previous generations who tended to obtain childcare information from their parents or grandparents, contemporary Korea parents, especially middle- and upper-middle-class parents, depend heavily on so-called expert resources in seeking out "good" and "right" child-rearing practices. As mentioned above, these "expert resources" are full of Western middle-class child-rearing ideologies and practices. Medical and scientific authorities introduce Western child-rearing practices and ideologies, themselves products of certain cultural and historical conditions (Apple 2006; Barlow 2004; Ochs and Kremer-Sadlik 2007; Sirota 2010; Seymour 2004; Wolfenstein 1951), as "proper" and "scientific" through various avenues such as children-rearing literatures, parenting classes, and television talk shows. Informed by advice from these authorities, contemporary South Korean parents orient their socialization goals toward producing an autonomous, self-confident, and creative child and follow authorities' prescriptions for cultivating these somewhat unfamiliar qualities. Parents, in particular, deal with authorities' critiques of traditional socialization practices and actively reflect on the parenting practices by which they themselves were raised. In this reflection, their own socialization experiences such as emphasis on conformity, hard work, and obedience are evaluated as hindering the development of an authentic self that the parents themselves lack. For instance, in conversations with me, parents often spoke of their parents' strict disciplinary style that coerced them to live "as they were directed" and blame this regimentation for their current state—that is, not being able to "live as they want" or to "know what makes them happy." These same parents, therefore, make concerted efforts to prohibit themselves from enacting embodied socialization practices such as asking children to follow their directions or forcing them to be devoted to assigned roles and instead practice "proper" and "scientific" modes of raising their children such as providing diverse choices, attending to children's authentic needs, preferences, and feelings, or encouraging children's self-expressions.

Early childhood educational practices configure similar trends. In preschool classrooms, teachers strive to make their educational practices less didactic and controlling and more individualized and child-centered. Traditional educational practices such as large-group activities and teacher-driven instructions, once regarded as necessary for producing compliant, responsible, and group-oriented citizens, are now criticized for prohibiting the development of children's true selves. Rather, teachers prefer small-group activities, individualized and child-centered instructions, free-choice time, and learning through play, all of which are typical quality standards of early childhood education in the United States (Tobin 2005). They also try to make their everyday interactions with children less hierarchical and controlling, thereby giving children more opportunities to express and cultivate their inner selves rather than adjusting themselves to group rules or others' expectations. Ms. Shim's narrative in the beginning of this chapter reflects this stratified view of pedagogical styles. She disregards practices such as clapping together or following teachers' directions as historical burdens to be discarded and instead advocates play-centered pedagogy for allowing ample opportunities for creative expression and cultivation of individuality.

Educational Reforms and Transformation of Korean Society

Behind the recent shift of the focus in socialization values and practices reside social transformations of the last few decades and more specifically recent educational reforms considered the most radical and comprehensive in the history of South Korean education (Mok, Yoon, and Welch 2003; Seth 2002). South Korea is well known for its educational exceptionalism and the enormous social demand for education. The nation's rapid economic growth in the second half of the twentieth century is typically accounted for by the educational system that has successfully provided the quality workforce required for economic success (Lim 2013). Many scholars of Korean education note South Korea's remarkable educational development, especially the rapidity of its growth and the intensity with which prestigious degrees are pursued (Seth 2013, 25). The strong zeal for education among Koreans, referred to literally as "education fever" (kyoyukyeol), has been consistently reported by various international agencies and foreign observers. The survey by the Organisation for Economic Co-operation and Development (OECD) in 1998, for instance, reports that 98 percent of parents responded that university education of their children is their primary goal, and about a half century earlier, the UNESCO report found similar results then stating that "the strong zeal for education among Koreans cannot be matched anywhere in the world" (OECD 1998, 7). The expenditure for education also attests to South Korea's popular zeal for educational advancement. Family expenditures for private after-school education almost equaled the country's education budget by the late 1990s, and Koreans were found to be spending the highest percentage of their personal income on education among citizens of OECD member nations (J. H. Lee 2004).

The origins of the popular zeal for educational advancement are explained in various ways. Many Koreans attribute it to the nation's "Confucian" cultural heritage. Literatures on Korean education, on the other hand, point out the significance of credentials, especially diplomas, as the most important criteria of evaluation in a wide range of social spheres such as employment, marriage, and interpersonal relationships in Korean society (OECD 1998). Numerous factors shape the zeal for education, but it is undeniable that enthusiasm for education is driven largely by the desire of Koreans for the high status that degrees confer.

Interestingly, the persistent desire of Korean families to enhance their social position through education is always accompanied by strong egalitarian ideals. That is, as much as Koreans pursue upward social mobility through education and construct a highly stratified educational system in which universities are hierarchically ranked, they also eagerly seek and embrace egalitarian philosophy. In his review of the history of Korean education, Seth (2013) pinpoints the long-standing tension between egalitarian educational philosophies and the reality of rank and status consciousness as a major characteristic of Korean education. This tension is reflected in the series of educational reforms, and the egalitarian ideals, in particular, strongly shaped educational policies, goals, and practices introduced before the mid-1990s.

In public policy, the egalitarian educational philosophy is enacted in two ways. First, the government carried out policies that assure equal educational opportunities to all citizens. Under the firm belief that educational opportunity should be open to all, the government made strenuous efforts to minimize the effects of familial disparities on student achievement (Abelmann, Choi, and Park 2013a, 2013b). President Park Chung Hee's high school equalization policy in 1974 and the subsequent Chun Doo Hwan's banning of all kinds of private after-school education in 1980 are exemplary instances that prohibit any structures militating against equal access to schooling. Second, ideologically committed to egalitarian ideals, the government established policies that assure uniformity of education, especially uniform in content and standards in schools. The Central Educational Research Institution was established to devise a national curriculum, and a rigidly uniform curriculum was introduced in the mid-1950s. Similarly, clinging to the idea that the college entrance system ought to be fair, the government supervised a nationwide uniform college entrance exam and forced universities to use it as the only criterion for admitting their students. This pursuit of educational uniformity focused school practices on rote memorization, repetition, conformity to rules, and teaching to the test. Ironically, policies aiming to equalize educational opportunity and ensure uniform contents and standards reinforced stratification of higher education in which many people were quick to assign every university within one hierarchical structure. Firmly believing in the fairness of the educational system and upward mobility afforded by college credentials, everyone strived to get into high-ranked colleges through hard work and strenuous effort. The economic and symbolic return conferred by college rank spurred every Korean to pursue uniform educational goals and paths.

The commitment to educational equality and the pursuit of educational uniformity is closely related to the type of personhood required during Korea's government-driven economic development in the second half of the twentieth century. Authoritarian governments' modernization projects demanded a hardworking, uniform, collective workforce, the members of which easily conform to collective pressures and devote themselves to the economic development of the nation. The educational system that promotes uniformity, homogeneity, and control supported and suited well the authoritarian development of intensive industrialization and rapid economic growth. With globalization and neoliberalization of Korean society, however, this hardworking conformist no longer fit economic and social demands, and a new type of personhood was needed to cope with social transformation. The newly emerging personhood had to be creative, autonomous, and self-reliant to cope with economic restructuring and globalization in which labor had to become increasingly flexible (Shin 2000). As the so-called International Monetary Fund (IMF) crisis accelerated a critique of Korean crony capitalism and the call for venture capitalism strengthened, social demands for a creative, global elite class heightened, and autonomy, creativity, and diversity were celebrated in the name of global advanced values.

Educational reform was critical to this project of nurturing a creative and competitive citizen. In 1998, for instance, the first minister of education Lee Hae Chan stated in a public letter to parents that "20th-century society demanded uniformity and homogeneity, but the society of the 21st century is different because it needs people who can think more creatively and more flexibly." In the mid-1990s, the Korean government enacted a series of educational reforms evaluated as the most radical in the history of South Korean education (Mok, Yoon, and Welch 2003; Seth 2002). The reforms aiming to transform the citizenry to become creative citizens "dramatically changed the rhetoric of educational values from 'uniformity and equality' to 'creativity, excellence, and diversification'" (Park 2007, 191). Largely dismissed were particular features of the authoritarian developmentalist educational system, especially its egalitarian ideology and standardization, as backward historical burdens (Park 2007) while decentralization, student-centered instruction, and diversification believed to promote students' excellence and creativity were pursued. The Korean educational system began to seek, at least ideologically, new modes of being in a rapidly globalizing and transforming world.

South Koreans' active embrace of new types of personhood and accompanying values are related not only to globalization and neoliberalization of Korean society but also to the postauthoritarian context of Korea and experience of the IMF crisis as Song (2003) articulated in her analysis of South Korea's neoliberal turn. That is, a liberal ethos that emphasizes democratic individual freedom and rights at the postauthoritarian historical moment coincided well with the global and neoliberal subjectivities, values, and policies being promoted (Abelmann, Park, and Kim 2009), thereby encouraging Koreans to celebrate creative, independent, and self-sufficient personhood in the name of liberal values while dismissing conformity, uniformity, and collectivity as authoritarian burdens (Park 2007). The long-standing westernization of Korean society, especially the influence of the teleological, dichotomous, unilineal view of the world in which the "Western" developed and the "non-Western" developing or underdeveloped countries are hierarchically positioned, also accelerated Korean society's vigorous espousal of new subjectivities and educational values.

Emerging Personhood and Shifting Socialization Practices

The significance of new modes of being extended well beyond school-aged children and had considerable impact on Korean parents' upbringing of their preschool children. As reflected in the term "educational fever" (kyoyukyeol), Korean parents tend to view their children even as young as one-year-olds as being in a pathway to the university and afterward the job markets and make strenuous efforts to prepare them in the changing globalizing world. Aiming to raise their children as members of a creative, global elite class, parents actively espouse the rhetoric of stratified socialization values and seek to implement practices that could cultivate new emerging qualities. Responding to parents' demands and more broadly to educational reforms and transformation of Korean society discussed above, Korean early childhood education and the private educational market actively adopted a variety of so-called Western curriculums and pedagogies (S. Lee 1987).

Even though early childhood education itself is a Western convention, Korean early childhood education, in their adoption of this foreign institution, has a history of embracing specific strands of Western pedagogies and considering them as advanced and scientific (Kwon 2004; S. Lee 1987; Park, Lee, and Jun 2013). The Montessori program, for instance, was introduced to Korean early childhood education in the 1970s and actively implemented by many Korean preschools and kindergartens. Even though parents were unaware of specific features and contents of this particular pedagogy, its "Western" atmosphere, combined with the teleological view of "the Western" as developed and refined, encouraged them to perceive it as advanced and proper pedagogy. In line with this long-standing trend, Korean early childhood education started to actively implement a variety of Western curriculums such as Waldorf, Reggio Emilia, Project Approach, and Play-Based Learning to meet the new call for raising a creative and self-reliant child in the 2000s.

If previous curriculums, especially characteristically traditional Korean ones, were burdened by fixedness and homogeneity, the Western curriculums were valorized for allowing ample opportunities for children to express and cultivate themselves. Preschools and kindergartens, in particular, highlighted child-centeredness and play-oriented features of these curriculums and claimed that these pedagogical features promote children's creativity, individuality, and autonomy, the values required in the transforming globalized world. Along with the adoption of specific curriculums, Korean early childhood education also used Western quality standards such as U.S. National Association for the Education of Young Children (NAEYC) standards of quality or Developmentally Appropriate Practices (DAP) in evaluating their local preschool programs as well as guidelines for building the National Kindergarten Curriculum (Kwon 2004; Shim and Herwig 1997). Under these standards, child-centered pedagogy, active and hands-on learning, learning through play, or small group activities were evaluated as "good" practices while teacher-centered instruction, mandated curriculum, or content-focused learning were assessed as lacking quality.

The parents, especially middle- and upper-middle-class parents who hope to raise their children as members of a global elite, scrutinize a variety of preschool curriculums available and choose the one that they consider fits best to their socialization goals. Parents' knowledge about different strands of Western curriculums varies. Some parents simply advocate Western curriculums as providing refined and advanced education, and others are aware of specific pedagogical philosophies of each curriculum and able to distinguish them.[2] Regardless of the level of their knowledge, however, parents all espouse the stratified socialization rhetoric that previous traditional socialization practices only produce narrow achievers suited to older economies while the new Western ones raise a global creative elite fitted to the new global cultural economy. Parents especially view preschool years as a time when children can fully navigate their preferences, authentic selves, and dreams before getting into the mainstream public educational system that is still burdened by uniformity, outcome-focused instruction, and too much emphasis on studying. In addition, the persistent structural limits such as a class system that preclude any real second chance for children drive parents to perceive children's searches for their true selves as a mission to be preferably completed as early as possible. Parents, therefore, use this relatively safe period of preschool years as a chance to allow their children to find their true selves and plan their future pathways.

The Reggio Emilia approach is one of those Western curriculums claimed to be effective in helping children find their true selves. Introduced to Korean early childhood education in the 1990s, the Reggio curriculum began to be adopted by a few preschools located in affluent residential areas in Seoul. Reggio preschools advertised their curriculum as "new" and "advanced" in that their pedagogical practices provide abundant ways and opportunities for children to express themselves. Naming its program as "emergent," the Reggio approach does not practice a preplanned curriculum but instead has children learn by exploring, observing, hypothesizing, and questioning their own thoughts and ideas in play or other unstructured activities. Teachers closely listen to and observe children in classroom activities and provide the environment and tools to further children's interests. Reggio preschools highlight this particular feature of the Reggio approach and assert that children are able to cultivate their true selves because the self-guided and child-initiated program pays attention to each individual child's preferences, interests, and potentials. This is a point where many parents, including parents of Somang preschool discussed in this book, get attracted to and decide to send their children to Reggio preschools.

Imagined "Western" and Redefined "Traditional"

As with the borrowing of any foreign ideas and practices, globally dominating so-called Western socialization ideologies get transformed and indigenized in the process of adoption to reflect local realities. The most salient feature of localization involved in the influx of globally dominant socialization values and practices within the Korean socialization sphere lies not only in that the "Western" and the "Korean" or "traditional" are hierarchized as discussed before, but the meanings of "Western" and "Korean" themselves are reinterpreted and redefined to meet local demands. Similar to Chinese parents in Xu's (2017) study who always evaluated the current environment of child-rearing in China in reference to or comparison with the "imagined West," Korean socialization discourses create an "imagined dichotomy" wherein Western socialization practices are heralded as exclusively loaded with "new" and "better" values of creativity, autonomy, or self-expression while traditional Korean practices are characterized by "old" and "backward" values of hierarchy, uniformity, or obedience.

The tendency to overidealize "the Western" is evident in the way the term "self" (*ca-a*), which is a relatively new and unfamiliar concept in Korean society, is used in recent socialization discourses. In spite of the ideological importance placed on the idea of fostering children's selves, there is no consensus among practitioners, educators, and parents on how to define the term "self." Rather, the term "self" acts as floating signifier, changing meanings in different social settings and is treated as a panacea for the perceived problems of Korean children such as a lack of creativity and autonomy. Moreover, even though the concept of selfhood has many different strands, meanings, definitions, and forms within the West and "the Western self" concept does not necessarily preclude a sociocentric orientation (Bellah et al. 2007; Kusserow 2004; Raeff 2006), Korean socialization discourses on self often posit an idealized, autonomous, abstract individual existing free of society. This strawman or idealized self only resides in popular imaginations and is configured as an omnipotent being to be emulated.

As much as "the Western" is imagined and overidealized, the so-called the "Korean" or the "traditional" is also redefined and reified in the process of borrowing global imports. Recent socialization discourses point out only certain strands of Korean socialization practices and contrast them with overidealized Western practices. For instance, they typically list uniformity, hierarchy, and collectivity as traditional Korean socialization traits and blame them for the current undesirable and unsatisfactory states of Korean children, stereotypically characterized as lacking creativity, diversity, and autonomy. Other aspects of Korean socialization practices such as the pursuit of equality addressed by many scholars as one of the main features of the Korean educational system (Beach 2011; Park 2007; Seth 2013) are rarely mentioned as the liberal nuance of this value does not create a sharp contrast with the imagined Western parenting styles. In a similar vein, even though competition is typically classified as Western in the Western and non-Western selfhood dichotomy (Hofstede 1980; Markus and Kitayama 1991; Shweder and Bourne 1982) and is perceived as rising in prominence only in Korea's recent rapid industrialization and economic development, socialization discourses categorize competition as characteristically Korean. As Korean socialization practices are always evaluated in reference to the imagined Western ideals, excessive competition, one of the main perceived problems of the Korean educational system, has not been categorized as "Western" but is perceived instead to be something "Korean" or "traditional."

Moreover, the so-called Western and Korean values are heuristically treated as if each value has only discrete meaning, similar to Chinese discourses about unsatisfactory singletons in Fong's (2007) study. That is, South Korean media, educators, and psychologists, in stressing the superiority of new values and the drawbacks of traditional ones, treat socialization values as if they have only one side, thereby dismissing the intricacies and complexities embedded in each value. Even though all of society's values have both "good" and "bad" sides, only emphasized are the desirable aspects of so-called newly imported Western values while typically Korean values are treated as undesirable. Therefore, traditional Korean values, despite their "good" sides, are often undermined and flattened as "bad" and "backward." For instance, even though uniformity has been a major means to guarantee educational equality in the history of Korean education, recent early childhood socialization discourses rarely acknowledge this "good" side of uniformity. Rather, uniformity with other values such as hierarchy and collectivity is typically defined as oppressive and authoritarian and apt to hinder the development of true selves. The liberal ethos in postauthoritarian Korean society has reinforced this perception of Korean traditional values as too strict and oppressive.

The heuristic use of values as well as the posited imagined dichotomy are related to the sociocultural backgrounds out of which Western socialization ideologies and practices developed in South Korea. As Western socialization practices are understood as means to cultivate desirable personhood and alternatives to unsatisfactory qualities of current Korean children, they are overidealized and treated as having only positive sides that meet these local demands. Similarly, so-called Korean traditional socialization practices are always evaluated negatively in contrast to or in reference to an imagined Western-ness. This is the context in which the ethnographic stories this book presents are situated and unfold.

3

"Why Don't We Find a Unique Self Concept Developing in Our Children?"

The Heterogeneous and Conflicting Socialization Landscape

> At the beginning of the semester, we hoped to raise a child who has a self. But we couldn't find it. . . . Kids are all into making the same things and interested in what others are doing. They just compare each other's work and copy the one they think is the best. So we can't see any creativity or diversity. . . . Same for the play. They argue over what role they would get and who controls the play for a while, but then they don't proceed to play. It just ends there [sighs].

In this narrative, Ms. Choo, a teacher from the Rainbow Room in Somang preschool, criticizes the pursuit of uniformity and hierarchy she witnesses among her students. She negatively views children's tendencies to compare and copy each other's artwork and their obsession with roles, status, and power in play. She particularly agonizes over the difficulty she experiences in addressing the initial socialization goal of promoting children's independent senses of self. When Ms. Choo was assigned as the main teacher of the Rainbow Room with Ms. Park, they set up "raising a child who has a self" as a major socialization goal and accordingly contrived various activities to cultivate children's self-expression, creativity, and individuality. However, as Ms. Choo's lament in the narrative above illustrates, what she found among her students was a longing for uniformity and hierarchy, lingering characteristics considered today to be negative aspects of Korean traditional socialization practices.

As introduced in the beginning of the book, I frequently encountered narratives like the above during my fieldwork in Somang preschool. As much as teachers eagerly pursued so-called new socialization values and practices, they also expressed the challenges of socializing a child to come to know and have confidence in his or her own unique preferences, feelings, and thoughts. Teachers, in particular, were perplexed by discrepancies between their socialization goals and outputs, as illustrated by Ms. Choo in the above narrative when she agonizes over a divergence of her socialization goal of cultivating children's selves and the lack of creativity and diversity she confronts.

Teachers typically reacted to this perceived problem in two ways. First, they attributed children's unsatisfactory qualities, such as a lack of creativity or diversity in the classroom, as symptomatic of the outside world wherein traditional values such as uniformity, hierarchy, and competition still prevail. In particular, teachers frequently criticized parents' socialization practices for being too "traditional" and not "new" enough. Looking at the children at the artwork table all drawing princesses, for instance, Ms. Park said to me that "it's because they think there's an answer to it [the drawing task]. Even though we work hard to convince them there's no answer and ask them to express whatever they feel or have in mind, it doesn't work because they hear other things from the outside world." She continues, "Jungwon's mom once complained to us that we don't give right answers and directions to children. She thinks that if we do activities about poems, we have to give definitions of 'poem' and provide examples of good poems to children. As you see, our program is different. We don't think there's any right or good answer. But parents still think in old ways." Such experiences with parents reinforce teachers' belief that failing socialization outcomes in the schools originate largely from the outside world. Moreover, as their newly adopted Western curriculum is geared toward the promotion of children's selves, teachers assume that there is no possibility that children's undesirable behaviors and attitudes stem from their school-based socialization practices.

Second, even though teachers' first and most typical reaction was to compare children's striving toward uniformity and hierarchy with the values explicit in the outside world such as children's homes or the larger Korean society, they nonetheless believed that they could identify and nurture children's selves if they could improve socialization practices. Teachers, therefore, critically scrutinized their curriculum and reformulated it in ways that they presumed would promote children's development of a unique self-concept. This involved reorganizing classroom activities and encouraging novel activities for themselves as instructors such as discussions with other teachers, conferences with outside experts, and participation in teacher training workshops. Somang teachers, for instance, regularly participated in teacher training workshops and conferences organized by the Korean Association for the Reggio Emilia Approach. In one conference I went to with teachers, teachers from Reggio preschools in Italy presented their philosophies and pedagogies in Italian and it was translated into Korean by the interpreter. As the interpreter was not a professional or had any knowledge on the Reggio approach, the translated contents were hardly understandable. However, teachers who must be tired after spending weekdays with their children devoted their whole weekend listening to what these authorities had to say, hoping to find any clue to improving their pedagogical practices. One could also easily hear teachers painstakingly ponder over and reflect on their curriculum with other teachers and with outside experts hoping to make adjustments in ways that would allow the children to attain desired socialization goals. Emergent aspects of the Reggio curriculum, especially Reggio's emphasis on constant modification of the curriculum according to observations of children's play and interactions, reinforced teachers' tendency to find answers through the improvement of their socialization and pedagogical practices.

In this chapter, I examine the paradoxical goals and outcomes Somang teachers lament, coupled with perspectives from teachers. Teachers' interpretations are understandable and may have some merit, but the close examination of implicit as well as explicit socialization practices enacted in everyday classroom interactions reveals that there is much to be taken into account. Toward this end, the chapter probes the competing ways that the term "self" (ca-a) and accompanying values such as creativity, independence, individuality, and diversity are deployed in contemporary Korean early childhood socialization discourses and practices. I argue that the problems teachers confront while trying to inculcate new socialization values result mainly from transformations and contradictions inherent in the indigenizing processes rather than directly from the influence of the outside world or the unfaithful enactment of imported curricula.

Specifically, in this chapter I first examine how Somang preschool implements the Reggio Emilia approach with particular focus on the indigenizing processes. I explore the way that certain aspects of this Western curriculum are selectively chosen and reinterpreted, and sometimes amplified, to meet local demands. I discuss the tendency to posit a dichotomous framework in embracing globally dominant so-called Western socialization ideologies, the issue discussed in chapter 2. Second, by closely examining everyday local practices and interactions in Somang preschool, I show that even though the explicit curriculum prioritizes newly introduced Western socialization ideas and devalues the perceived old values such as uniformity, obedience, and collectivity, everyday practices implicitly entail these traditional socialization values and ideas in conflict with the explicitly stated new positions. By exploring how traditional values are transmitted alongside newly imported ones and how new values are sometimes interpreted within traditional frameworks, I suggest that children's undesirable behaviors cannot be attributed solely to the outside world, as is often asserted by teachers, but are closely related to Somang everyday socialization and pedagogical practices. Third, furthering discussions of the gap between idealized models and real practice, I explore the ways that traditional Korean socialization values and practices are preserved and transmitted through the workings of informal and unmarked mechanisms of transmission rather than through explicit and conscious efforts. By examining how traditional socialization goals and values such as conformity, collectivity, and hierarchy are embedded in implicit beliefs and practices, I argue that explicit reform efforts backfire because they are in conflict with traditional beliefs and practices that linger as implicit, unmarked, situated, and taken-for granted features of education not readily subject to scrutiny, criticism, or reform.

"Self, Self, Self": Explicit Curriculum and Indigenization of Western Socialization Practices

Reflecting recent shifts in the South Korean socialization landscape, Somang preschool proclaims the cultivation of children's selves and other accompanying values such as creativity, diversity, and self-confidence as major educational and socialization goals. Naming their practices as "good education," the director and teachers share a firm belief that their curriculum is different from the ones enacted in other typical Korean early childhood institutions and special in that it promotes qualities assumed to be required for success in an increasingly globalized Korea. In particular, they consider the Reggio Emilia approach, the curriculum that Somang preschool has adopted, as being equipped with special pedagogical means to produce a creative, independent, and self-confident child.

Among various aspects of the Reggio approach, Somang preschool perceives child- and play-centeredness as major characteristics of Reggio philosophy. As Loris Malaguzzi (1993, 45), one of the founders of the Reggio approach states, Reggio philosophy conceptualizes children as "active constructors of knowledge, full of curiosity and creativity" and pursues a flexible curriculum that "emerges from children's ideas, thoughts, and observations." Naming it an "emergent curriculum," the Reggio approach takes place in a form wherein children are given opportunities to express, explore, question, and hypothesize their thoughts and ideas. Teachers, instead of pursuing preplanned goals and standards, are encouraged to facilitate children's learning by planning activities based on children's interests and asking questions to further children's understanding. Somang teachers view this emergent and child-centered aspect of the Reggio curriculum as characterizing the Reggio approach and effective in addressing their socialization goal of cultivating children's selves as the following narrative by Ms. Kim illustrates:

> We want to raise a child who has a self, I mean who is not swayed by others. Our classroom might look chaotic to outsiders, but I think that's how the children learn to find their selves. . . . You know what, honestly, as a teacher, it's much more convenient to just teach children in previous ways. Just teach what we planned and ask them to follow us. But that's not a good education. Reggio is difficult, but it's real education. We start from listening to children's thoughts and help them to flower. We never force them to do something, judge them, or compare them. So they can express themselves and find their own self and own dream without competition. And I guess it will look like a rainbow in the end.

In this narrative, Ms. Kim states "raising a child who has a self" as the major goal of her socialization and conceptualizes the self as an autonomous and independent state that exists free of others' influences as reflected in the statement "who is not swayed by others." Articulating that "good education" helps children to foster their inner selves, the teacher argues that child-centered and self-oriented components of the Reggio approach enable children to find their own unique selves by providing opportunities to explore and express themselves. Here, child-centeredness is contrasted with "previous ways" in which teachers simply provide preplanned contents to children and force them to follow teachers' directions. Unlike previous traditional practices based on standardization, teacher-centeredness, comparison, and competition that produce uniform personhood, she believes that their "real education" will allow children's true selves to "flower," resulting in unique, multiple, and diverse selves that taken together look like a "rainbow."

Similarly, Ms. Chung in the following interview excerpt valorizes the child-centered and emergent features of the Reggio curriculum and compares it with a preplanned curriculum in which teachers unidirectionally infuse planned contents and knowledge to children. She especially espouses Reggio's documenting practice as a powerful means to cultivate children's inner selves:

> Even though we have too many other things to do, I think documentation is really good. I just wish I didn't need to do other things. We see lots of things while doing documentations. In other institutions, there are planned schedules by semester, month, and week. But we plan moment by moment based on children's outcomes that we find through documentation. . . . It's not like teachers just infuse what they think. When I document children's interactions, I find children producing new ideas and thoughts. What we do is supporting them to do more of those new thinkings and documentation is very helpful for it. Learning the same things all together is easier for teachers. But it's not good for children.

Ms. Chung here claims that even though enacting a preplanned curriculum is more convenient and easier for teachers themselves, this didactic, teacher-centered, and uniform pedagogical practice is of no help to children. On the other hand, the cumbersome and difficult practice that requires teachers to incessantly observe, document, and reflect on children's play and interactions is beneficial to children as it provides means to find and further children's creativity and diversity. Ms. Chung articulates that documentation enables teachers to discover and cultivate children's new and creative ideas and thoughts which could hardly be found in the previous content-focused and preplanned curriculum.

In both interviews, the teachers express the difficulty of enacting the Reggio curriculum as reflected in the statements "Reggio is difficult" and "learning the same things all together is easier for teachers." Nonetheless, their firm belief in the superiority of the Reggio approach led Somang teachers to eagerly pursue and copy this foreign, unfamiliar, and difficult approach. Regarding Reggio's child-centeredness as an effective means to address their socialization goals, Somang teachers actively copy Reggio's child-centered and emergent features in their enactment of the curriculum and everyday pedagogical practices. As Ms. Kim states they "start from listening to children's thoughts," classroom topics of study derive from teachers' observations and documentations of children's play, talk, or interactions, and teachers provide various materials and projects that may provoke children to further explore a topic that has originally grown out of the children's own practices or comments.

For instance, Arum Room conducted the "block project" which has grown out of observations of children using blocks to build an apartment complex in which they live. Ms. Seo, the Arum Room teacher, observed Jiwon, Sungeun, Hyungjun, and Juwon making an apartment complex during playtime and found the children using chairs to reach the top of the building that exceeded their heights. She approached them to closely observe, record, and ask about the children's building processes. Then, later in the day, Ms. Seo asked Jiwon to present their work to the whole class during group time. Having Jiwon standing beside the apartment building she made with other children, the teacher asked questions such as the name, function, and construction process of the work. Ms. Seo especially found children's use of chairs interesting and therefore asked questions comparing heights of Jiwon and the building and had Jiwon articulate the process of using chairs to overcome the children's physical limitations. Through Ms. Seo's facilitation, children's use of chairs became an indication of children's creativity and self-confidence as reflected in the poster posted later in the Arum classroom with statements such as "Creative ways to solve problems," "Children's confidence through creativity," and "Success through creativity."

The observation and documentation of the block play, then, became the basis of the next curriculum. Instead of cleaning up blocks after playtime, Ms. Seo left the apartment complex in the block area. Children added additional blocks to the original one to make it taller and bigger. In the process of their construction, Jinseo and Jiwon brought paper from the artwork area and asked the teacher to write a sign saying, "Don't Destroy" and hung the sign in the building using tape. Observing children making the sign, the teacher provided additional paper, colored pens, and tape for the block area. Children then started to attach papers to blocks and the apartment complex gained a new look. Through children's play, the apartment complex later was transformed into dinosaurs. As before, Ms. Seo closely observed and documented the children's play and incessantly prompted children to verbally express their thoughts and feelings about the work by asking questions such as "Wow, that's super. What is it?" "How did you make it?" or "Why did you make in that way?"

Here, Ms. Seo not only faithfully copies Reggio's child-centered pedagogy but also makes a concerted effort to have children express their authentic ideas, preferences, and thoughts in every step of the project. At the same time, she pays close attention to any interaction and comment that seems to be unconventional or unique and interprets it as evidence of children's creativity, authenticity, or self-expression. The emphasis on self-expression is not confined to the way Somang teachers enact the emergent child-initiated pedagogy as shown in this case but prominent in broader contexts of Somang everyday educational practices. Much of the Somang official curriculum is allotted to activities believed to promote children's individuated self-expression. Children are, for instance, frequently asked to present in front of the whole class how they spent their weekend or how they made their artwork. In the presentations, they are expected to express their authentic preferences and feelings through artwork, music, or poems. Teachers also employ various pedagogical methodologies to provoke children's generation and expression of themselves such as praising children's performances by making statements such as "Wow, that's super," "Wow, that's great," or "What a great masterpiece," utterances not included in typical Korean communicative repertoires. Responding to teachers' practices, Somang children tend to show their works to teachers stating, "Look at this, Ms. Seo," "Ms. Chung, I made this. Mine is prettier than Jung's," or "Ms. Kim, this is my masterpiece." Through teachers' everyday pedagogical practices of encouraging self-expression and children's responses to their productions, children's play, interactions, comments, and artwork become the signs of their individuated senses of selves. The posters hung in the wall of Somang classrooms with titles such as "Not a failure but one more success," "The possibility of wire play expressed through self-confidence," and "Color and emotion" demonstrate the emphasis placed on the cultivation of inner selves and other so-called new values such as independence, self-confidence, and creativity.

The way Somang teachers implement the Reggio approach in their curriculum and everyday pedagogical practices so far indicates that they interpret the Reggio approach as a child-centered and self-oriented program, especially effective in promoting children's individuated senses of self. The Reggio approach originally conceptualizes a child as unique, creative, and full of potential as mentioned before (Malaguzzi 1993), but it does not necessarily posit an individuated child existing free of society. Rather, it places a strong emphasis on children's construction of knowledge through their relationships and collaborations with peers, teachers, and the community (Gandini 1993). Literature on the Reggio approach articulates that children should be treated as social beings existing as part of a group and learning through relationships with community and the surrounding environment (Cadwell 1997; Edwards, Gandini, and Forman 1998; Fraser and Wien 2001; Gandini 1993; New 1993). However, as recent Korean socialization discourses posit a hierarchical, dichotomous framework and conceive of fostering children's selves as an alternative to problems of the previous educational system, they typically postulate an imagined autonomous, acontextual, self-reliant individual as an ideal form of personhood to be pursued as reflected in Ms. Kim's narrative when she states they "want to raise a child who has a self, I mean who is not swayed by others." That is, even though the putative anomic Western self is a straw man invented by Western ideology (Hollos and Leis 2001; Lindholm 1997; Spiro 1993) and "the Western self" concept does not necessarily preclude sociocentric trends (Bellah et al. 2007; Kusserow 2004; Raeff 2006), Korean socialization discourses essentialize the Western self as a solely abstract, acontextual, bounded individual free of external societal influences.

Introduced in this context, the Reggio curriculum is viewed by Somang teachers as exclusively consisting of new socialization values and pedagogical practices considered good, important, and worthy of emulation. Other aspects of the Reggio approach, especially those aspects that appear to be similar to characteristically Korean socialization ideals such as relationality, collectivity, or hierarchy are eliminated and the elements even remotely related to new socialization values are amplified to meet the local demands for raising a creative, autonomous, and expressive child. Similar to the borrowing of the Reggio Emilia approach in the United States (Tobin, Hsueh, and Karasawa 2009), the Somang curriculum eschews the politics and socialism of the original system such as community support, children's relationships in learning, or parental involvement and emphasizes child-centeredness, children's exploration and expression of thoughts and feelings, and the arts and aesthetics. Furthermore, Somang teachers reinterpret Reggio's child-centeredness and promotion of self-expression as an individuated practice that occurs in an independent, autonomous, and acontexual being, not involving interactions with others. Through selective adoption and reinterpretation, the Reggio approach, then, becomes a child-centered and self-oriented curriculum that effectively aims to attain the newly established socialization goal of raising a creative, autonomous, self-confident citizen while other sociocentric trends existing in the original form of the Reggio approach are undermined.

"Don't Compare with Other Friends": Dissociating from "Old" Values in the Explicit Curriculum

South Korean preschools' adoption of a Western curriculum involves not merely the abatement of its socialism and politics but also active abandonment of any sociocentric trends seemingly close to what they consider characteristically "Korean" or "traditional." Along with strongly embracing child-centered and self-oriented aspects of the Reggio approach, Somang teachers work hard to dissociate themselves from any pedagogical practice they regard as hindering the development of children's individuated senses of self. In accordance with the imagined dichotomy teachers hold about socialization values and practices, teachers typically consider comparison, competition, uniformity, or standardization as "old" and "bad" values to set aside if they are to attain newly established socialization goals. Explaining how she taught her students to write a poem, Ms. Shim, in the following interview excerpt, dismisses comparison-based instruction as traditional pedagogical practice that obstructs the socialization goal of promoting children's authentic self-expressions: "The first few months were difficult. Children from other preschools just wanted to do many things. . . . Children were used to comparison. Teachers [in other preschools] always compare

44 BETWEEN SELF AND COMMUNITY

children's performances, so children tend to just do many things to win in a competition. . . . I never compared their performances. You saw children writing poems, right? They didn't even know how to write. But I taught without comparing them. I just encouraged them to express. Now they write a bunch of poems every day."

Here, Ms. Shim perceives comparison-based instruction as an obstacle to children's learning and stresses the effort she made to discard this "old-fashioned" and "backward" educational practice. She assumes children's tendencies to pursue quantities rather than qualities of activities stem from their exposure in other institutions to comparison-based pedagogy in which standardized evaluations prevail. She goes on to explain how the movement away from comparison magically improved children's performances. Ironically, as reflected in her statement "Now they write a bunch of poems every day," she evaluates educational outcomes based on quantities. This is contrary to her earlier critique above of children's pursuit of quantities ("children tend to just do many things to win") as "old" and problematic.

The negative attitude that teachers express toward comparison is not confined to pedagogical styles but extends to any practice related to comparison, competition, or uniformity. Teachers, in particular, problematize competitive and comparison-based peer interactions prevalent in children's peer world and actively constrain children who initiate comparative educational performances. In the following scene, Ms. Shim steps into children's interactions and discourages attempts to compare and evaluate each other's work.

SCENE 3.1: "CREATIVE READING TIME"

Participants: Ms. Shim (teacher), Jinhyuk (boy, 4 years), Jungyeon (girl, 4 years), Siwon (girl, 4 years), Minju (girl, 4 years)

1. ((Children are drawing pictures based on the book they read together))
2. Jungyeon: ((looks at Minju's picture)) Why is everything orange color?
3. Jinhyuk: It's not orange. It's all brown.
4. Jungyeon: And why, why . . .
5. Siwon: Where? ((Jinhyuk, Jungyeon, and Siwon turn their heads to look at Minju's picture))
6. Ms. Shim: Minju, draw as you think. You're doing very well.
7. ((Siwon looks at the picture of Jinhyuk who sits beside her))
8. Ms. Shim: Siwon, yours are interesting, too. You don't need to compare with others.
9. ((Siwon looks at Jinhyuk's again and looks at Jungyeon's picture for a while))
10. Ms. Shim: ((to Siwon)) Don't copy friends'. Do it as you want by yourself.

Beginning with Jungyeon's statement "Why is everything orange color?" the children at the table display interest in Minju's picture. Interpreting this movement as the indication of an evaluative attitude, Ms. Shim interrupts children's conversations and asks Minju to be confident in her authentic thoughts and feelings and not to be swayed by others' evaluations as reflected in the statement "Minju, draw as you think. You're doing very well" (line 6). In the scene that follows, Ms. Shim similarly perceives Siwon's observation of others' work as an intention of comparison and imitation and tries to encourage her to abstain from attempts to adjust her genuine preferences and ideas according to external standards and evaluations as shown in lines 8 and 10 ("Siwon, yours are interesting, too. You don't need to compare with others," "Don't copy friends'. Do it as you want by yourself").

Similarly, in the following example, as children produce competitive talk regarding the subject of their poems during poem writing time, Ms. Shim discourages children's attempts to compare their performances, the practice that she regards as often leading up to copying. In line 9, by explicitly stating "Yoobin, everyone has a different idea. So you should just write what you want," the teacher urges Yoobin to pay attention to her genuine inner needs and wants and express them as she wishes.

SCENE 3.2: "POEM WRITING"

Participants: Ms. Shim (teacher), Yoobin (girl, 4 years), Siwon (girl, 4 years), Jungwon (girl, 4 years), Junhyuk (boy, 4 years)

1. ((Children are writing poems in poem writing area))
2. Siwon: I'll write about the princess (*kongcwu*).
3. Yoobin: I want to write about the princess, too.
4. Siwon: You can write about the princess.
5. Jungwon: I'll write about the pepper (*kochwu*) (laughs).
6. Junhyuk: I'll write about the pepper, too.
7. Siwon: I'll write about the pepper, too.
8. Yoobin: I want to write about the pepper, too.
9. Ms. Shim: Yoobin, everyone has a different idea. So you should just write what you want.

Interestingly, the children in the above scene make puns while producing competitive talk. As Siwon declares to write about the princesses (kongcwu), Jungwon in line 5 takes a competitive stance by proclaiming the pepper (kochwu) as the subject of her poem. Here, the words *kongcwu* and *kochwu* have similar sounds and *kochwu* is a homonym that has meanings of pepper and genital of boys. As Jungwon's paralinguistic laughing behavior suggests, she humorously exploits similar-sounding words and dual meanings of the term to be in a better position in competitive talk. Her usage of puns might be a place wherein values of creativity, diversity, and self-confidence that Somang teachers avidly seek are apparent. Ms. Shim, however, hardly pays attention to the children's

46 BETWEEN SELF AND COMMUNITY

creative and unique uses of language and instead disrupts their talk which she interprets as involving comparison and competition and seeking uniformity. The excessive emphasis placed on new socialization goals and the tendency to discard any seemingly "traditional" or characteristically "Korean" values made teachers oblivious to children's linguistic competence and their emerging creativity and self-confidence.

Teachers were also burdened by estranging themselves from standardized and didactic pedagogical practices. As Reggio's child-centeredness is typically contrasted to teacher- and content-focused programs, teachers strive to abstain from enacting any educational practice that could possibly impose their own ideas and preferences on children and endeavor to make every interaction with children equal and unimposing. In the following scene, for instance, Ms. Chung deliberately refrains from providing answers to children's questions and instead prompts children to find their own answers.

SCENE 3.3: "ARTWORK TIME"

Participants: Ms. Chung (teacher), Sungeun (girl, 3 years), Seoyun (girl, 3 years), Minseo (girl, 3 years)

1. ((Children are making artwork weaving colored paper))
2. ((Sungeun is standing beside the artwork table and looks at colored slips of paper to weave into her square grid))
3. Sungeun: Ms. Chung, which color is pretty? Which color is pretty?
4. Ms. Chung: Which color? Do you mean the color I like? Or the color you like? I like light colors.
5. ((Sungeun looks vacantly at the colored slips of paper))
6. Sungeun: Dark color?
7. Ms. Chung: What kind of colors do you think are dark? ((points to purple paper)) This one?
8. ((Sungeun shakes her head))
9. Ms. Chung: Which one do you think is dark? Choose what you think is the dark color.
10. Sungeun: I want dark.
11. Ms. Chung: I don't know which color is dark.
12. Seoyun: I'll have light pink.
13. Minseo: I'll have light pink, too.
14. Ms. Chung: What do you think is the light pink? What kind of color do you think of as light pink?
15. Minseo: ((points to the pink paper)) Lighter than this one.
16. Ms. Chung: ((nods)) Oh.
17. Sungeun: ((to the researcher)) Which color is a pretty color? Which color is a pretty color?

. . .

18. ((Seoyun tries to put colored slips of paper into the square grid and fails))
19. Seoyun: ((to Ms. Chung)) How should I do it?
20. Ms. Chung: Well, I don't know. ((Ms. Chung keeps cutting colored paper to provide more pieces for the children))
21. Minseo: Not fat ones ((shows her grid to Seoyun and Ms. Chung))
22. Ms. Chung: Not fat ones, why?
23. Minseo: Because you can't put many if you use fat ones.

While Sungeun asks Ms. Chung for advice in choosing the color of the paper, Ms. Chung regards her question as pursuing a standardized answer and shifts the focus of the conversation to talking about individual preferences by asking her back "Which color? Do you mean the color I like? Or the color you like? I like light colors." The teacher's expression of her own taste that she likes light colors elicits Sungeun's utterance that she perhaps likes dark colors, but as the teacher further asks her to present specifics of dark colors, she hesitates to specify (lines 7–8), repeats the statement that she wants the dark color (line 10), and finally seeks help from me by asking again "Which color is the pretty color?" (line 17). The way Sungeun responds to the teacher's questions indicates that Sungeun is not used to exploring her own preferences or at least does not have particular tastes in regard to the colors of the slips of paper at this moment; therefore, she seeks guidance from adults. The teacher, however, refuses to give any opinion by explicitly stating that she does not possess any knowledge about dark colors ("I don't know which color is dark" [line 11]), fearing that her opinion might hinder opportunities for Sungeun to fully explore and develop her own preferences, wants, and tastes. The teacher's negative stance toward providing guidance to children is also reflected in the way Ms. Chung responds to Seoyun's ask for help. In line 20, Ms. Chung refuses to provide clues to figure out ways of putting paper slips into the square grid, the task Seoyun confronts in weaving. She explicitly states that she does not possess solutions and ignores Seoyun's struggles by not paying attention to Seoyun and continuing her own work.

The major motivation for teachers to refrain from providing guidance to children emerges from the fear that any movement or signal from teachers would impose their ideas and thoughts on children, therefore impeding an individual child's chances to fully explore and cultivate his or her own self. That is, as children typically regard teachers as authority figures and the children-teacher relationship tends to be hierarchical, teachers were anxious about the influence that they might have on the development of children's individuated senses of self. Even though Somang teachers perceive this unimposing and egalitarian pedagogical practice as a characteristic of the Reggio approach, Reggio's child-centeredness in its original form does not necessarily entail the withdrawal of adults' guidance and support. Rather, as mentioned before, the Reggio approach stresses the importance of learning through collaboration and relationships with peers, adults, and the community (Cadwell 1997; Edwards, Gandini, and Forman 1998; Gandini 1993; New 1993). Moreover, a deep connection between the school staff and the larger community, and parent and community involvement are the core ideas of Reggio Emilia preschools in Italy (Tobin 2005). In the process of vigorously pursuing the socialization goal of producing a creative and self-competent child, teachers tend to confuse imposing a standardized answer with providing guidance or scaffolding in learning and therefore pay little attention to Reggio's collaborative and relation-based learning. Under this indigenized curriculum, children, then, are deprived of opportunities to learn through interactions with others and instead are expected to learn individually, somehow not affected by others.

Self-Expression or Selfish Expression? The Self in Actual Educational Contexts

Although Somang's explicit curriculum is highly geared toward the promotion of children's selves as discussed so far, the ways the term *self* and accompanying values are enacted in actual educational settings are complex. Even though Somang teachers all agreed on the importance of fostering children's selves and rigorously pursued the goal through indigenization of an imported curriculum, the definitions of "self" and "self-expression" are not coherently understood nor is the socialization of self evenly practiced. Rather, teachers understand these terms differently in different socialization contexts and sometimes even implement practices in a way that works against their stated socialization goals.

"Nuri's Problem": Problematizing Excessive and Self-Absorbing Expressions

One particular example is clear from teachers' reactions to what were considered children's excessive use of self-expression. While teachers ideally valorize children's abilities to generate and express their own unique ideas and thoughts and strive to attain this socialization goal, they, at the same time, critically view children's self-expression in educational contexts. The ambivalent and contradictory attitude toward children's self-expression is apparent in the ways Somang teachers deal with what they called Nuri's problem. Nuri, a four-year-old girl in the Rainbow Room, was good at expressing and articulating her own creative ideas and thoughts. She was the first student in the Somang preschool who caught my eye as behaving very similarly to the children I observed in my previous fieldwork in the United States. She seemed to embody some behaviors and attitudes expected of American middle-class children. She always raised her hands to answer teachers' questions during group time, was active at articulating her ideas and thoughts, and took a lead in peer play. I got the impression from her that Korean children who are raised under the transforming new socialization landscape look quite akin to the U.S. middle-class children I had studied previously. The creativity, self-confidence, verbal skills, and leadership that Nuri presented in various educational contexts were clearly the qualities Somang teachers wanted their children to develop. To my surprise, however, this exemplary student was treated as somewhat problematic by Rainbow Room teachers mainly for two reasons.

First, teachers often criticized Nuri's performances for being excessively self-promoting and insufficiently modest. Looking at Nuri in front of the whole class presenting how she spent the weekend, for instance, Ms. Chung, a teacher in the Rainbow Room, whispered to another teacher sitting beside her, "Oh, too good," using a tone of voice that conveyed disapproval. The other teacher, Ms. Park, in a similar context, described Nuri as a student who is academically outstanding but lacks modesty and empathy. She says, "She'll be a good student when she goes to school. She speaks very well; her drawing is best among her peers. . . . But she's too cocky and overweening. She does not care about others' feelings." In response to Ms. Park's comments, Ms. Choo, another teacher from the Rainbow Room, said, "Right, she reminds me of the kids in my school days who were smart and got good grades but were kind of disagreeable; someone with whom I didn't wanna get along."

Nuri's performances were officially acknowledged and even praised, yet the very qualities that made her outstanding in terms of the explicit curriculum also caused her to be viewed as pretentious and inconsiderate. Although teachers never articulated it in their interviews, their discourses regarding Nuri's performances demonstrate that what they actually have in mind when they encourage children to express themselves is not just free expression of authentic feelings and thoughts but also modest, considerate, and thoughtful expression of oneself that considers the feelings and needs of others, not just one's own.

Second, along with issues of overconfidence and arrogance, teachers also problematized Nuri's performances for exerting too much influence over her peers. As Nuri had good drawing and crafting skills, was good at expressing her own ideas and thoughts, and had leadership skills, she frequently took a lead in children's free play and other school activities. Children often played contentedly under Nuri's direction and envied and copied her drawings and other artwork. The leadership and excellence Nuri showed in various school activities were clearly the qualities that teachers emphasized in their explicit curriculum. The same instructors who praised Nuri, however, also pointed out that her influence was excessive and thereby hindered other children's development. Many of the children aspired to reproduce Nuri's drawings, conform to her lead in activities, and even mimic her outfits, thereby evaluating and competing with one another based on Nuri's performances.

Teachers believed that Nuri's leadership and excellence obstructed other children's opportunities to cultivate their own preferences and tastes and caused uniformity and hierarchy in children's performances. Looking at the girls wearing pink princess outfits and playing in the pretend play area, Ms. Choo, for instance, told me, "I heard from other teachers of the last year that Nuri was the one who brought princess outfits into vogue. She has been problematic for us, too. Everyone wants to draw like her, act like her. Kids even do as she directs. We would like to see diversity, but it's not easy." From Ms. Choo's view, the educational goal of finding children's diversity and uniqueness is thwarted by Nuri's excellence and popularity.

Ironically, this interpretation widely shared by Rainbow teachers and even the whole preschool led teachers at times to reinforce uniformity and sameness. That is, in response to Nuri's dominance, teachers in the Rainbow Room began to discourage Nuri's expressions and participation and encourage others' by intentionally praising other children's performances. When Jiwon, Nuri's best friend, for instance, looks at Nuri's drawing and says, "It's so pretty," Ms. Choo praises Jiwon's drawing by saying, "Jiwon, yours are also very pretty and cute. I like yours." Ms. Choo even said to Jiwon later that day when no one was around, "Jiwon, your house in the drawing today was really good. Honestly, I think your [drawings] are better than Nuri's." At the same time, teachers sometimes intentionally discouraged Nuri's expressions, for instance, by not giving her a chance to present her ideas during group time even when no one but Nuri raised their hands.

Teachers believed that this strategy would provide a learning environment in which every child could develop their own preferences and ideas rather than simply following a popular peer's ideas and thoughts. Teachers, however, did not realize that the way they cope with Nuri's dominance ironically reinforces the idea of a uniform standard and sameness. Although the teacher forcefully emphasizes excellence in Jiwon's artwork, and by extension everyone's, she does so in a way that initiates a new comparison and competition. Teachers' reactions, in part, emerge from the tensions between their need to cultivate students' confidence in expressing themselves with the reality that there are too many children in a classroom. Given that teachers' intentions are not to mandate equivalent self-expression but to equalize the incentive to express one's self, the teacher's strategy clearly differs from the traditional South Korean educational curriculum. However, it also diverges from what teachers ideally postulate in their new and explicit curriculum in that it forcefully discourages some children's expressions and aims to equalize children's confidence to express themselves. At the same time, in an attempt to give Jiwon confidence, the teacher implicitly structures her comments as though self-expression is inherently a competition evaluated by a uniform standard. Unlike the explicit verbal commitment to "promote children's selves," teachers, in fact, unconsciously but actively practice the values of uniformity, competition, and comparison of which they strongly and consciously disapprove.

The complex and conflicting stance Somang teachers have toward children's self-expression was evident in other cases as well. The weekend storytelling time in the Rainbow Room was an activity in which children were asked to present how they spend their weekend in front of the whole class every Monday morning. Rainbow teachers designed this activity to promote children's zeal for self-expression, especially to cultivate children's verbal skills to present their ideas, thoughts, and feelings. Teachers often mentioned this activity as representing the child-centered and self-oriented aspect of their curriculum and were contented with children's performances as Ms. Shim, in the beginning of my visit to Somang preschool once told me, "Kids didn't know how to talk about their experiences and feelings at first. But now we do weekend storytelling time for one and a half hours. It's a journey to find oneself." In everyday actual enactment of the activity, however, teachers often took a negative stance toward children's self-expressions. One Monday morning, almost all the children in the Rainbow Room raised their hands to present their weekend story and Ms. Choo had to pick only ten of them due to time constraints. As Ms. Choo announced the last child to present, other children sighed in disappointment. Looking at this in the back of the classroom, Ms. Park frowned at students, and Ms. Choo later said to me, "You saw it today, right? I picked ten kids, but they still said, 'Why not me?' and sighed. Same thing happens when I pick only one or two. They just can't help expressing their desires. They can't suppress themselves. They think of only themselves." Although teachers expect and strive to have children express their own thoughts, feelings, and wants in this activity, they, at the same time, criticize children's desires for expressions as too self-centered and not being considerate to others. Similar to Nuri's case, what Rainbow teachers have in mind when they enact this activity is not free expression of one's authentic thoughts, ideas, and feelings but thoughtful and considerate expression that sometimes should be restrained to allow others a chance.

Even though teachers rarely articulate the subtle and complex models of self-expression they have in mind, which are a part of their taken-for-granted habitus (Bourdieu 1977), they sometimes openly criticize children's excessive and inappropriate self-expression. In the following conversation during storybook reading time, for instance, Ms. Choo explicitly challenges and dismisses what she perceives to be an inappropriate instance of self-expression.

SCENE 3.4: "STORYBOOK READING TIME"

Participants: Ms. Choo (teacher), Junghan (boy, 4 years), Hyungjun (boy, 5 years), Bora (girl, 4 years)

1. ((Ms. Choo picks up the storybook titled *Pig Mom* from the bookshelf and moves to the group area where children are gathered for storybook time))
2. Ms. Choo: ((shows the cover of the book to the class)) Today, we're gonna read this book called *Pig Mom*.
3. Junghan: I know that book.
4. Other children: I know, too.
5. Hyungjun: I read that book before.
6. Ms. Choo: What's the name of main character, then?
7. ((No one answers))
8. Ms. Choo: ((raises her voice)) What's the name of main character?
9. ((Children become silent))

10. Ms. Choo: See? You guys don't know everything. Could you please sit and listen quietly so that other friends who do not know the book can also listen?
11. Ms. Choo: ((shows the picture of the mom)) Why do you think she is so angry?
12. Bora: I already know.
13. Ms. Choo: Young friend who knows why, do you wanna go out?
14. ((Bora shakes her head))
15. Ms. Choo: No? Then please listen quietly.

Ms. Choo, in this example, reprimands children's self-expressions for being pretentious and inconsiderate. As children express their knowledge about the storybook Ms. Choo has chosen to read for the whole group, she challenges their knowledge by asking them specific questions about the book. By asking questions children cannot easily answer and then explicitly mentioning that the children's knowledge is incomplete and fragmentary, she alludes to the importance of being humble, modest, and unassuming in expressing one's thoughts and ideas. The children's boisterous contributions are seen as particularly problematic and unsatisfactory because they do not consider the needs of others. The teacher says that children should not express their knowledge about the book for the sake of other members who have not read the book before (line 10). She even scolds Bora for responding to her question and evokes the idea of the collectivity by commenting, "Young friend who knows why, do you wanna go out?" (line 13). Even though the teacher did not explicitly state so to the children, what was expected in this particular context was for the most knowledgeable to control and regulate their desires to show off their knowledge, thus yielding a chance for other children who had little knowledge about the book to gain familiarity with it. Building a learning community here is given priority over exploration and expression of one's own opinions, abilities, and characteristics. Individuals are expected to attune their needs, desires, and goals to those of others and to the group.

Not So Much an Individualistic Self

The complex and contradictory expectations teachers have toward their children's selves were also manifested in the ways they evaluated an individual child's character and performance. While Rainbow teachers were critical of children for being passive and seeking uniformity when they aspired to draw as Nuri did or played under her direction, they also negatively viewed some children who shied away from Nuri's influences. In my conversations with Ms. Chung and Ms. Park during outside playtime, Ms. Chung said, "Among four-year-olds, I'm concerned about Sowon and Ara. These two are sort of strong kids and I think they kind of wander and don't belong anywhere. They are not in particular places, nor are they with particular kids. And they tend to wander a lot. I'm concerned that they are not included anywhere, and this is not a comfortable place for them. Sowon doesn't like the princess thing, so she isn't there. She goes to the boys' block area but can't stay there long. Same for Ara."

As alluded to in Ms. Chung's narrative, Sowon and Ara were not the typical Rainbow Room girls who wear pink outfits and like princesses. Unlike Ms. Chung's view that Sowon and Ara did not play with Nuri and the girls under Nuri's influence, they, in fact, frequently did but were not as immersed in the popular themes of their peers as other girls. For instance, Sowon and Ara, while playing with Nuri and Nuri's group, tend not to be obsessed with producing artwork similar to Nuri's or popular among peers. They also enjoyed playing in diverse areas with different peers, unlike other children who stuck to playing with, sitting with, and even eating with a particular group of children. Given that they do not follow other peers' tastes and have their own and choose play based on their needs and preferences, Sowon and Ara are individualistic characters displaying their own uniqueness and self-confidence, the values Somang teachers explicitly pursue in their curriculum. However, teachers express reservations about these two children's characters, interpreting their uniqueness and self-confidence as "strong" and "not belonging." The person who self-confidently pursues his or her uniqueness and sometimes stands out among the group, then, is at least not an example of the ideal selfhood Somang teachers have in mind.

I was able to infer the type of personhood Rainbow Room teachers had in mind when they positively assessed Ayeon's behaviors and performances. About the time when Nuri's behavior and attitude became "Nuri's problem" in the Rainbow Room, teachers abruptly started complimenting a four-year-old girl named Ayeon for being thoughtful and considerate. In a conversation with Rainbow Room teachers, Ms. Park said that "as we closely look into children playing, we find Ayeon quite popular among kids." Ms. Chung then mentioned, "I understood today why she is popular among kids. She helps others very well without a fuss. Jungjin dropped something this morning, and she was the first one picking it up while others were sitting still." Even though teachers did not explicitly compare Ayeon with Nuri, they often spoke highly of Ayeon's popularity stating, "Kids like to play with Ayeon" and regarded Ayeon as a possible alternative to Nuri who was viewed as exerting "unhealthy" influences over other children.

It was not clear from my observations of the Rainbow Room children's peer world whether Ayeon was as popular as teachers assumed. Ayeon was among Nuri's group and did not particularly stand out among them. The only difference she had with others might be that she tended to play without much conflict with others while other children often complained and expressed discontent in their peer interactions. The main reason teachers point Ayeon out as an ideal person seems to lie in that she tends toward being harmonious, thoughtful, and reserved. Rainbow teachers evaluated both Ayeon and Nuri as popular figures among peers. They positively viewed only Ayeon's character as she was not pretentious or careless like Nuri but reserved and considerate as reflected in Ms. Chung's statement that "she helps others very well without a fuss." In addition, unlike Sowon and Ara whom teachers were concerned about for being wanderers and "strong," Ayeon was included in the group without being particularly distinctive. The type of personhood expected in real everyday socialization contexts, then, is not entirely the individualistic, creative, and self-confident child as often explicitly declared but a person with some harmonious, group-oriented, considerate, and modest characteristics, or at least one equipped with both sides.

Not All Expressions Get Valued: Implicit Hierarchy and Evaluation

The complicated and contradictory models of self and personhood not only reside in the minds of teachers and sometimes come out but are also structurally embedded in teachers' enactments of explicit curricula in educational settings. Even though the Somang curriculum ideologically and explicitly pursues children's individuated, unique, and diverse expressions, the enacted curriculum unwittingly delivers the idea that expressions could be evaluated and ranked. This was most apparent in the way children's expressions were treated and circulated in the official classroom curriculum. As shown before, the Somang explicit curriculum is typically composed of three steps. Teachers first closely observe and document children's expressions displayed in their artwork, play, and interactions, then choose one that they find unique, creative, or meaningful, and circulate that idea around the classroom. In the process of circulation, the selected expressions get to be presented in group time, sometimes shared by all classroom members as an exemplary expression, and are often hung on the wall as a sign of children's selfhood and creativity.

For instance, as part of gymnastics class, Arum Room teachers planned a curriculum titled "Diverse Ways of Playing with Hula-Hoops." Unlike conventional gymnastics class in which children are asked to follow teachers' directions or simply romp around the playground, teachers handed out Hula-Hoops to each child and asked children to show how they would like to play with them. The gym bustled with children giving demonstrations of their individual ideas and Ms. Kim looked around the gym and picked Jiwok as the one to present his idea to the whole class. Responding to Ms. Kim's statement "Jiwok, let's show your friends how to play," Jiwok laid several Hula-Hoops on the floor and jumped between them. Ms. Kim then urged Jiwok to verbally articulate his ideas by stating, "Oh, that's a great idea, Jiwok. How about explaining your idea to the other children?" Jiwok, however, instead of verbalizing his ideas, kept adding more Hula-Hoops to the previous ones. As Ms. Kim failed to have Jiwok articulate his ideas, she asked rhetorical questions that presented Jiwok's ideas on behalf of him such as "Oh, so are you connecting them?" "So is it like a jumping game?" Ms. Kim shortly afterward asked other Arum children to follow Jiwok's demonstration and play with Hula-Hoops as Jiwok suggested. Although some children did not pay attention to Jiwok's demonstration and Ms. Kim's explanation of Jiwok's ideas, most children started to connect Hula-Hoops and jumped between them. A few days later, Jiwok's ideas were posted on the Arum Room wall as part of the weekly journal titled "Creative Ways of Playing with Hula-Hoops" with paragraphs emphasizing children's potentials, creativity, self-expressions, self-confidence, and so forth.

The explicit curriculum here clearly aims toward promoting children's creative and diverse expressions as reflected in the title "Creative Ways of Playing with Hula-Hoops." By having each child explore his or her own ways of playing with Hula-Hoops, teachers apparently provide ample opportunity for children to cultivate individuality and diversity. The enacted curriculum at the same time, however, implies that expressions are never equally treated but continuously evaluated and ranked by certain external standards. Jiwok's idea gets attention as exemplary and is shared and followed by other classroom members while other children's ideas go unnoticed. His idea and play are even displayed on the wall as a sign of creativity and draw the attention of everyone who visits the Arum Room. Other children's ideas were also expressed when children individually showed their own ways of playing with Hula-Hoops, but these were treated as momentary diversions and soon faded away. Teachers' intentions were not so much to prioritize certain expressions over others as to share expressions that seemed to fit their educational goals and displayed children's accomplishments and progress. When some expressions get more public and authoritative attention than others, however, this implicitly entails the idea that there is a hierarchy and ranking for expressions. The ostensibly diversity-oriented sphere is, in fact, a site of ranking and ordering in which children competitively vie for teachers' attention. We'll see how children respond to this disparity of expressions in the next chapter.

Reform Ideals and Situated Practices: Enforcing "Traditional" Values in Everyday Socialization Contexts

The ambivalent, conflicting, and contradictory ideas of children's selves were much more heavily and unconsciously practiced in noneducational and unofficial contexts. Although the ideology of fostering children's selves exerts much influence within the realm of the official curriculum despite different and conflicting enactments of it in actual educational contexts, the call for the promotion of children's selves goes largely ignored in school contexts perceived to be more mundane and informal as distinct from the formal learning settings. The enacted everyday practices even contrast sharply with the ideology of self that teachers, parents, and administrators actively and explicitly support at the ideational level.

Competition, Comparison, and Uniformity in Noneducational and Mundane Practices

The gap between the idealized model and actual practice on the ground is apparent in the way Somang teachers practice competition and comparison in everyday socialization contexts. As discussed before, Somang teachers typically regard comparison and competition as the most problematic aspects of the traditional Korean educational system and strive to dissociate themselves from enacting any comparison- or competition-oriented pedagogical practices. Moreover, they are highly critical of children's tendency to compare and compete in peer interactions and actively restrain children from initiating those interactions. For the teachers, competitions and comparisons are qualities that hinder the cultivation of children's true selves and therefore need to be discarded. However, when the context moves from formal education to everyday socialization practices, a different picture appears.

Unlike their efforts to eliminate competition- and comparison-based practices in formal teaching, teachers strongly encourage competition among children and constantly compare children's behaviors during everyday activities of maintaining the classroom or attending to conventions for group activities, school rules, and personal care. For instance, teachers frequently make statements such as "Please pick up the trash on the floor. Let's see who picks up first," "Let me see who cleans up the blocks well. Ready? Start!" or "Let me see who eats first." The song teachers often sing while waiting for children to gather for group time has the lyrics "Beautiful birds are sitting on the trees. Who's the one sitting most beautifully? Jungyoul? Jihoon? . . ." Through these discourses and practices, children are asked to compete with one another to be the first and the best in the class.

The tendency to use competition as a socializing method in settings outside formal teaching was often accompanied by practices of comparison as illustrated in the following teacher-children interactions.

SCENE 3.5: "LUNCHTIME"

Participants: Naeun (girl, 4 years), Bora (girl, 4 years), Ms. Jung (teacher)

1. ((After finishing her lunch, Ms. Jung approaches the children's table and sits beside Bora))
2. ((Naeun, sitting in front of Bora, finishes her lunch and puts her spoon back into the bag))
3. Ms. Jung: Wow, Naeun, you're the first. You're the best. ((Ms. Jung high-fives Naeun))
4. Ms. Jung: ((Looking at Bora who is playing with her spoons)) Bora, how much is left? Naeun is already done.

SCENE 3.6: "LUNCHTIME"

Participants: Hajun (boy, 3 years), Minju (girl, 3 years), Ms. Jung (teacher), Ms. Kim (teacher)

1. ((Hajun and Minju are having lunch at the lunch table))
2. Ms. Jung: Minju, Hajun is done.

"WHY DON'T WE FIND A UNIQUE SELF CONCEPT" 57

3. Ms. Kim: ((cleans the part of the table where children have already left)) I think Minju can also finish. Minju won't like to be the last one either.

In the scenes above, teachers explicitly compare children's performances in their attempts to complete one of the most difficult tasks in school routines both for teachers and children—that is, finishing an assigned amount of meal in a limited time. In scene 3.5, Ms. Jung praises Naeun for finishing lunch and mentions that Naeun is the first and the best among the children around the table. On the surface, such statements may be simple compliments for a child's achievements. However, the purpose of the praise lies less in acclaiming Naeun's accomplishments than in prompting Bora to finish her lunch by comparing her performance with Naeun's as shown by the teacher's statement "Bora, how much is left? Naeun is already done." In scene 3.6, as Hajun and Minju are left at the lunch table as the last ones, Ms. Jung explicitly compares their performances by stating to Minju that Hajun finished his meal. Even though Hajun had not finished his meal and was only a bit faster than Minju, Ms. Jung adopts the comparative frame to encourage children to accomplish this everyday burdensome task. In line 3, Ms. Kim even reinforces the comparative and competitive framework by implying that one of them will be the last one.

Similarly, in the next example, the teacher attempts to facilitate the school routine by explicitly comparing and ranking children's performances.

SCENE 3.7: "PICKING UP TRASH"

Participants: Nuri (girl, 4 years), Jiwon (girl, 4 years), Jihyun (girl, 4 years), Ms. Shim (teacher)

1. ((Rainbow children are picking up trash around the preschool))
2. Ms. Shim: ((Picking up trash from the floor)) How many did you pick up?
3. Jiwon: Zero.
4. Nuri: Zero.
5. Ms. Shim: How many did you pick up?
6. Jihyun: I picked up five.
7. Ms. Shim: Wow, Jihyun. You're so great. You picked up five. You're such a proud Rainbow Room member. Trash-picking king Jihyun. You're so great. You're the best.

Accompanying the children picking up trash around the preschool during outside playtime, Ms. Shim constantly checks and compares each child's achievements. Ms. Shim is the instructor who proudly told me how her "new" Reggio-based pedagogical practice of encouraging children's expressions without comparing them magically improved children's performances in poem writing. She was also the teacher who actively restrained children from initiating and participating in competitive and comparative interactions (scenes 3.1 and 3.2). During weekend storytelling time done on the same day as the clearing up of trash occurred,

Ms. Shim, observing children competitively presenting weekend stories, told the whole class, "Rainbow Room friends, you don't need to follow what others are doing. You don't necessarily need to do many stories just because others do many. You just need to do as much as you want." However, in the scene above, the same instructor actively uses comparisons in encouraging children to participate in the less formal school activity. Also, unlike educational contexts in which teachers make a conscious effort to avoid standardized evaluation, in the everyday context of cleaning the room or playground of trash which is embedded within the school day, children's performances are ranked and assessed based on a uniform standard and the child who picks up the most trash becomes the "trash-picking king." The teachers who harshly criticize standardized evaluation as "old" and "backward" hindering the development of children's full and diverse potentials in formal educational settings do not hesitate to score and rank children's performances in more everyday "noneducational" contexts. Evaluative statements such as "Children who have finished your meal, if you read the storybook in here, you're a perfect score," "Let's get together. Wow, Sihyun is the first," or "Wow, Haeun is cleaning very well. Jungyoon also cleans well. Uh, Minjun, are you cleaning up? Juwon, what are you doing without cleaning up?" are prevalent in everyday classroom discourses. Contrary to teachers' overly negative stance toward the expression of their views and opinions to children in formal learning settings, fearing that this might deliver evaluative intents to children, teachers, here in everyday more informal contexts figure as authorities who actively and explicitly evaluate, rank, and score children's performances.

In addition, teachers also ask children to refer to others in adjusting their behaviors to classroom rules and group needs. To prompt children to gather for group time, for instance, teachers make statements such as "Jihyun, look at other friends. They are all sitting here" or "Sowon, let's sit still. Other friends are all sitting still." Similarly, teachers, in encouraging children to finish their meal, often say, "Look at others. They're all finished" or "Oh my, Seoyun and Minseo are the only ones left. Look at others all finished." Although children are discouraged from following peers' ideas and tastes, producing outcomes similar to those of their peers, and even looking at others' works in formal educational settings, they are explicitly asked to be attentive to others around them, follow others' behaviors, modify their own behaviors to fit into the group in everyday informal contexts. Uniformity is an "old" and "backward" value to be discarded in the explicit curriculum but is a virtue to be embodied in everyday mundane contexts.

"Hyengnim Can Sit Still, Right?": Socialization of Role and Social Hierarchy

Along with the values of comparison, competition, and uniformity, recent South Korean socialization discourses regard the emphasis on role, status, and hierarchy as characteristically Korean traditional socialization practices that obstruct the development of children's true selves. Mass media and popular parenting advice literature often warn against imposing certain roles on young children and forcing them to be devoted to assigned roles. The Somang teachers and parents who belong to a generation whose life pathways were largely driven by familial pressures were responsive to such advice from authorities. They, in particular, reflect on their own upbringings during which they were asked to fulfill ascribed roles as daughter, son, firstborn, or the youngest of the family and to live up to the expectations of their parents. Attributing the ordinary and somewhat banal aspects of their lives to an earlier generation's child-rearing practices, this new generation is striving to dissociate themselves from imposing "ascribed role categories" in raising their young children.

In my interview with parents, a mother of a five-year-old girl and a two-year-old boy, for instance, told me, "I make an effort not to raise her as the firstborn. I was the firstborn and my parents always expected me to behave as the firstborn, like yielding to my brothers, being exemplary. Looking back, I think I never told my parents what I wanted. I never expressed my needs, so now I don't know how to express them. The worst thing is that I don't know what I like or want. I don't want Juyon to be like me. I want her to stand up just as herself, not as a daughter of someone or a firstborn of our family." Similarly, Ms. Kim, a teacher of the Rainbow Room, told me, "We don't set up certain standards for our children. In other institutions, children are expected do something according to their ages. But it's natural that a four-year-old does something better than a five-year-old. That five-year-old will have something that he or she does better than the four-year-old." In both narratives, caregivers view role- and age-based socialization practices as undesirable and unhealthy.

Unlike their stated ideology, however, Somang teachers heavily relied on what Douglas (1970) calls positional socialization in instilling socially appropriate behaviors and sentiments, especially in more informal settings. Positional socialization is a strategy that "inculcates the rules of conduct vested in the position or role that the child is expected to hold in relation to others at present or in the future" (Lebra 1994, 265). This socialization strategy appears across cultures but is reported to be stressed and elaborated in societies like East Asia in which hierarchy and social rank have long worked as important organizing factors for interpersonal relationships (Azuma 1994; Takanishi 1994). In their enactment of positional socialization, Somang teachers particularly utilized aged-based role categories such as elder brothers, elder sisters, younger brothers, or babies. Among these roles and statuses, *hyengnim* was the most prevalently and prominently used in Somang everyday classroom discourses. Hyengnim, a kin term composed of a kinship morpheme *hyeng*, meaning an elder brother, and *nim*, an honorific suffix, is a term of address and reference used among male kin members and close acquaintances to address and refer to someone older than the speaker. It was used both as a kinship and a fictive kinship term, but its usage has decreased and now is replaced by the nonhonorific form hyeng. That is, even though male speakers once addressed and referred to a male superior using both the honorific form hyengnim and the nonhonorific one, hyeng, contemporary Korean male speakers rarely use hyengnim and instead address and refer to a male superior as hyeng.

In Somang everyday discourses, this disappearing kinship term hyengnim is used to address and refer to a group of children who behave in socially appropriate ways, thereby deserving honorable social positions. Even though hyengnim is used among female kin, as a fictive kinship term it is more typically used by male speakers to their superiors of the same gender and thus recognized by Korean speakers as male-marked address and referent term. In Somang preschool, however, hyengnim is used as a gender unmarked form including both boys and girls. Other kinship terms such as *khunhyeng* (eldest brother), *hyenga*[1] (elder brother), and *enni* (elder sister) are interchangeably used in similar contexts even though not as frequently as hyengnim. The following scenes illustrate how Somang teachers use hyengnim in socializing children into appropriate emotional behaviors.

SCENE 3.8: "GROUP TIME"

Participants: Ms. Kim (teacher), Ms. Jung (teacher), Jina (girl, 3 years), Minseo (girl, 3 years)

1. ((Jina is sitting on Ms. Kim's lap crying during group time))
2. Ms. Jung: ((sits in front of the group to lead group time)) Would Jina also join us? Like hyengnim. You can do well.
3. ((Jina does not respond and puts her head into Ms. Kim's lap))
4. Ms. Jung: ((looks at other children)) Wow, you guys look like hyengnim.
5. Minseo: We look like the Rainbow Room, right?

SCENE 3.9: "PLAYTIME"

Participants: Junha (boy, 3 years), Ms. Jung (teacher)

1. Junha: ((approaches Ms. Jung)) Teacher, I'd like to see Mom ((almost cries)).
2. Ms. Jung: You're controlling yourself even though you wanna see Mom, right? Because you're a brave hyengnim.

In the examples above, the teacher refers to children who are not used to the new classroom environments and are having a difficult time controlling their inner feelings as hyengnim. She prompts them to produce role-proper emotional behaviors. In scene 3.8, as Jina who came to the preschool after a long break expresses her anxiety by crying during group time, Ms. Jung confers the role hyengnim to both Jina and other children and urges her to display emotions in a proper way as befits hyengnim. As Ms. Jung's attempt does not elicit the desired response as

"WHY DON'T WE FIND A UNIQUE SELF CONCEPT" 61

Jina's paralinguistic behaviors in line 3 show, she adopts a comparative framework and grants the role of hyengnim to other children in line 4. Minseo's statement that "we look like the Rainbow Room, right?" suggests that children also embodied these role-based socialization ideologies. Here, she confers the status of the Rainbow Room—that is, the five-year-old classroom on her four-year-old classroom members. Similarly, in scene 3.9, to Junha who expresses feelings of missing his mom to the teacher, Ms. Jung suggests he control his inner needs by granting the role of hyengnim to him. As the modifier brave before hyengnim alludes, hyengnim here is the one who is being equipped with the abilities to control inner needs and display socially appropriate emotional behaviors. Discourses on hyengnim such as "We can do well as we become hyengnim, right?" "Only hyengnim friends, look at here," "Please read like hyengnim" are prevalent in Somang everyday socialization scenes.

Along with the status of hyengnim, Somang teachers also adopted discourses on *aka* (*ayki*) (baby) and *tongsayng* (younger brother or sister) in enacting positional socialization. While hyengnim performs socially appropriate and rule-conforming behaviors, aka and tongsayng are social categories of incompleteness and inappropriateness. Those in these categories not only occupy socially inferior positions to hyengnim but sharply contrast with them in terms of performances and behaviors. Although teachers prompt children to display normative behaviors through discourses on hyengnim, they use the role and status of aka or tongsayng in pointing out and criticizing inappropriate behaviors as the following examples illustrate.

SCENE 3.10: "LUNCHTIME"

Participants: Jimin (girl, 3 years), Sungeun (girl, 3 years), Ms. Jung (teacher)

1. ((Jimin and Sungeun are underneath the lunch table and playing together))
2. Ms. Jung: ((approaches Jimin and Sungeun)) *Ayki-dul* (baby-plural suffix)! Ayki-dul! Are you done eating? Ayki-dul! Ayki-dul! You guys didn't even touch tofu. Tofu is good for your health.

SCENE 3.11: "LUNCHTIME"

Participants: Hajun (boy, 3 years), Minjun (boy, 3 years), Minseo (girl, 3 years), Sungeun (girl, 3 years), Ms. Kim (teacher)

1. ((Hajun, Minjun, and Minseo are comparing their spoons))
2. Ms. Kim: ((beside Sungeun who is packing up her lunchbox after finishing her lunch)) ((with loud voices toward Hajun, Minjun, and Minseo)) Sungeun, let's pack up. We'd better let *tongsayng-dul* eat.

In scene 3.10, the teacher addresses Jimin and Sungeun who do not conform to the classroom rules and expectations as ayki in her attempt to point out the inappropriateness of their behaviors and urge them to follow group rules. In a similar

62 BETWEEN SELF AND COMMUNITY

context, Ms. Kim in scene 3.11 indirectly criticizes the children who do not concentrate on eating during lunchtime by referring to them as tongsayng-dul in her conversation with Sungeun. Even though the teacher speaks to Sungeun, the intended effect of her utterance lies less in suggesting that Sungeun clean up but rather more in comparing Sungeun's praiseworthy behavior with the other children who are labeled with a pejorative identity of tongsayng for failing to meet the teacher's expectation.

These two types of social positions and roles—that is, the praiseworthy hyengnim and the pejorative aka or tongsayng—are often drawn on together in socialization scenes to explicitly compare children's behaviors and prompt children to follow and conform to group rules as the following examples show.

SCENE 3.12: "GROUP TIME"
Participants: Jiwok (boy, 3 years), Minhyun (boy, 3 years), Ms. Jung (teacher)

1. ((Jiwok kicks Minhyun who sits in front of him))
2. Minhyun: ((turns around to Jiwok)) Hey.
3. ((Minhyun turns back and Jiwok kicks Minhyun's waist stretching his right leg))
4. Ms. Jung: Jiwok, if you do that, it discomforts Minhyun.
5. ((Jiwok pretends not to hear Ms. Jung and stretches his left leg to Minhyun))
6. Ms. Jung: I'm so sad. I'm very, very sad. Very sad. Would you like me to treat you like aka? I think you're completely hyengnim. Not tongsayng but hyengnim. . . . Would you like me to yell at you? You can be good if you think deeply.

SCENE 3.13: "CLEANUP TIME"
Participants: Sungeun (girl, 3 years), Minseo (girl, 3 years), Juwon (boy, 3 years), Ms. Jung (teacher)

1. Ms. Jung: ((to Minseo and Juwon playing together)) *Ayki-ya* (baby-vocative case marker)! Ayki-ya!
2. Sungeun: Minseo-aki-ya! Minseo-aki-ya!
3. Minseo: Hey, I'm not an aki.
4. Ms. Jung: ((helps children cleaning up blocks)) Hyengnim classroom friends, let's clean up. ((looks at Minseo and Juwon and in a loud voice)) Aka classroom friends don't need to clean up. Aka classroom friends, you guys don't clean up and just keep playing.

In scene 3.12, the teacher attempts to correct Jiwok's behavior of harassing his classmate Minhyun by representing the feelings of Minhyun to him (line 4). However, as Jiwok does not pay attention to her discipline, Ms. Jung harshly reprimands Jiwok by appealing to the negative feelings caused by his misbehaviors and alternatively assigning the prestigious role hyengnim and the pejorative ones aka and tongsayng to him (line 6). The teacher first intimidates Jiwok suggesting she will treat him like an aka if he keeps behaving improperly ("Would you like me to treat you like aka?") and then confers on him the roles of hyengnim and tongsayng in turn ("I think you're completely hyengnim. Not tongsayng but hyengnim") to urge him to display role-appropriate behaviors. The ensuing utterances "Would you like me to yell at you? You can be good if you think deeply" imply that aka is one whose behavior deserves to be yelled at whereas hyengnim thinks deeply and behaves well. Similarly, in scene 3.13, the teacher employs discourses on hyengnim and aka in prompting children to conform to the classroom rules and expectations. As Minseo and Juwon play together during cleanup time, Ms. Jung negatively assesses their behaviors by bestowing on them a pejorative identity, aka (line 1). Ms. Jung's strategy elicits Sungeun's teasing of Minseo as aka in line 2 and Minseo's denial of the identity conferred in line 3. As Minseo and Juwon do not promptly amend their behaviors, however, the teacher reinforces their pejorative identity as aka by employing the comparative framework in which the children who conform to the school rules are assigned the prestigious role of hyengnim while Minseo and Juwon are addressed and referred to as aka.

Whereas discourses on hyengnim, aka, and tongsayng are the most prominent ones, teachers also employ age-specific categories in similar contexts. For instance, helping a four-year-old (five years in Korean age) boy Junwoo eating lunch, Ms. Kim says to him, "How old are you if you do it this way? I'm sorry, but you're four years old today. Let's pack up like seven-year-olds." Here, Ms. Kim evaluates Junwoo's behavior as that of a four-year-old, unsuitable for his real age as a five-year-old, and bestows an age older than his—that is, a seven-year-old— in disciplining him. Ms. Kim negatively viewed setting up age-based standards toward the children in an interview before ("We don't set up certain standards for our children. In other institutions, children are expected do something according to their ages"), but here, she criticizes Junwoo's behavior for being age inappropriate and urges him to display age-proper behaviors. Children may not be asked to perform according to age or status but instead are expected to think and feel independently in formal educational settings such as in making artwork, writing stories, or presenting their weekend experiences. They are, however, also constantly reminded that they have certain roles, social positions, and statuses and are expected to adjust their behaviors accordingly in everyday informal contexts.

"How Shameful It Is!": Socialization of Shame and Collectivity
Somang everyday socialization practices that employ comparison, competition, role, and status as major strategies examined so far often involved shame and shame-related scenes. Even though the dualistic formulation of shame versus guilt cultures has been strongly criticized, cross-cultural studies on shame, nonetheless, attest shame as an important part of experiences in many Asian

cultures (Crystal et al. 2001; Hu 1944; Kitayama, Markus, and Matsumoto 1995; Li, Wang, and Fischer 2004; Menon and Shweder 1994). The research on socialization of shame, in particular, finds shame-related practices and discourses as salient in socialization scenes of Asian societies such as Japan, Korea, Taiwan, and China (Benedict 1946; Doi 1973; Clancy 1986; Fung 1999; Fung and Chen 2001; Lo and Fung 2012). Cross-cultural studies that explicitly compare socialization practices across cultures especially suggest that shaming is an essential way in which young children learn the social and moral norms of a community in Asian cultures. The studies, for instance, demonstrate that Taiwanese parents expect their preschool children to feel ashamed of their misbehaviors more often than their Euro-American counterparts (Wang 1992) and Chinese children acquire shame-related terms earlier than American children (Shaver, Wu, and Schwartz 1992). Despite the hazard of characterizing societies as shame versus guilt cultures as Lebra (1983) mentioned in his critique of Benedict's analysis of Japan as a shame culture (Benedict 1946) and the hazards of evaluating shame as a less advanced emotion than guilt, studies so far show that shaming is seen as a necessary and integral part of moral education in many Asian societies including Korea (Lo and Fung 2012; Miller et al. 2002). Han's (2004) examination of verbal routines of shaming at a preschool program for Korean American children in the United States and Lo and Fung's (2012) investigation of shaming among Koreans support the pervasiveness of shaming in Korean socialization contexts.

The scenes illustrated before to discuss the prevalence of comparative and role-based socialization practices frequently entailed shaming and shame-related practices. For instance, in scene 3.13, when Ms. Jung addresses children who do not conform to the classroom rules as aka and peers also join this discourse on aka, it evokes feelings of shame in the targeted children who are being assigned a pejorative status for being improper. Similarly, when the teachers in scene 3.6 explicitly compare children's behaviors and state that "Minju won't like to be the last one either," the imaginative state of being the last one arouses feelings of shame for Minju and enforces her to amend her behavior to save face. For Somang teachers, shaming was clearly a major vehicle for normative moral socialization.

Shaming events were pervasive in multiple contexts of classroom socialization and ranged from explicit to implicit instances. The explicit ones involved arousing children's sense of shame through statements such as "How shameful," "You made me lose face," or "That's shameful behavior" as the following example illustrates.

SCENE 3.14: "SHIFTING TIME"

Participants: Ms. Shim (teacher), Ms. Um (teacher), Jungjin (boy, 2 years)

1. ((The Rainbow Room and the Green Room pass each other in the hallway))
2. Ms. Shim: ((to Jungjin)) How cute you are. How cute.

"WHY DON'T WE FIND A UNIQUE SELF CONCEPT"

3. Ms. Um: But he's not finished his banana yet.
4. Ms. Shim: How shameful. How shameful.

In this scene, the teachers collaboratively seek to arouse a sense of shame in the child who has not accomplished his task of finishing a snack. Ms. Um first tries to elicit shame by negatively assessing Jungjin's performance to an outside member, Ms. Shim, the teacher of the other classroom. Recruited by Ms. Um into shaming, Ms. Shim reinforces the shame-arousing framework by explicitly shaming the child and the situation, using the shame-related expression "How shameful." Here, the target child is asked to feel ashamed of his misbehavior and adjust himself to the classroom rule.

If a child's misconduct was framed as bringing shame on him- or herself in the example above, teachers also present themselves as feeling shame due to children's actions as the following case shows.

SCENE 3.15: "SHIFTING TIME"

Participants: Ms. Shim (teacher), Ms. Cha (director), Rainbow Room children

1. ((The Rainbow Room children and Ms. Shim run into Ms. Cha in the hallway))
2. Ms. Shim: Rainbow Room, good morning ((bows to Ms. Cha)).
3. Rainbow Room children: Good morning, Ms. Cha. ((bow to Ms. Cha))
4. ((The Rainbow Room comes back to the classroom))
5. Ms. Shim: You should greet Ms. Cha before I ask you to. I was a bit ashamed.

In this scene, as Rainbow Room children fail to greet the director of the preschool on their way back to the classroom, Ms. Shim prompts them through modeling a greeting expression and the embodied action of bowing (line 2). She later reprimands the children (line 5), negatively assessing their behavior and articulating the expected norm. The teacher inculcates the idea that shameful acts on the part of the children spread shame on others who are connected to them. This is similar to findings from other studies on the socialization of shame (Clancy 1986; Fung 1999; Lo and Fung 2012). At the same time, Ms. Shim's statement "I'm a bit ashamed" conveys not only her ashamed feeling but the implication that children should feel the same way. If one's feelings and emotions are expected to reside in an individuated self, having its own distinct and unique features in formal educational settings, here, feelings reside among connected selves, easily spread on others, and are considerably shaped by others' actions.

The shaming practices enacted in Somang everyday contexts were characterized by multiparty configurations. That is, Somang teachers often drew other people into a shaming scene to highlight the severity of the transgression as the following examples show.

66   BETWEEN SELF AND COMMUNITY

SCENE 3.16: "GROUP TIME"

Participants: Ms. Choo (teacher), Hyejin (girl, 5 years), Junghyun (girl, 5 years)

1. ((Hyejin and Junghyun chat during group time))
2. Ms. Choo: Hyejin, would you come up and show your younger brothers and sisters how shameful your behavior is?

SCENE 3.17: "LUNCHTIME"

Participants: Ms. Sung (teacher), Ms. Um (teacher), Sungmo (boy, 3 years), Jiju (boy, 2 years)

1. ((Ms. Um comes to the Arum Room with Jiju to borrow a thermometer and check his temperature))
2. ((Ms. Um and Jiju leave))
3. Ms. Sung: ((spoon-feeds meals to Sungmo)) Aka (baby), you should also go with them. How shameful. Tongsayng (younger brother or sister) was here.

In scene 3.16, upbraiding Hyejin who does not pay attention to Ms. Choo's speech during group time, Ms. Choo explicitly names Hyejin's behavior as shameful and invites four-year-old children in the classroom as witnesses to her misconduct. Her statement "Would you come up and show your younger brothers and sisters how shameful your behavior is?" prompts Hyejin to imagine herself as being seen by younger members of their classroom whose gazes intensify the targeted child's sense of shame. Similarly, in scene 3.17, Ms. Sung recruits Jiju, an outside member and a younger brother, as a witness to Sungmo's conduct. In negatively assessing Sungmo's performance in line 3, the teacher attempts to instill a sense of shame in Sungmo by conferring the pejorative role aka, alluding that he does not belong to the Arum Room, directing a shame-related term to him, and especially inviting an outside member, Jiju who is younger than Sungmo, as a witness. In both scenes, the teachers bring peers who are younger than the target child to the shaming scene as witnesses in order to arouse a feeling of shame in the misbehaving child. By asking the target child to imagine him- or herself as being seen by ones who are younger or socially inferior to oneself, this strategy creates the possibility of losing one's face in an age- and role-specified social hierarchy of peer relationships.

This idea of being gazed on by others, especially ones inferior to oneself, is more intensively enacted through what Lo and Fung (2012) called the embodied practice of shaming.[2] Somang preschool had a practice of taking a misbehaving child to another classroom and asking her or him to observe how members of other classrooms behave as the following scene exemplifies.

SCENE 3.18: "LUNCHTIME"

Participants: Ms. Jung (teacher, Arum Room), Ms. Um (teacher, Green Room), Jina (girl, 3 years)

"WHY DON'T WE FIND A UNIQUE SELF CONCEPT"

1. ((Ms. Jung approaches Jina who is lying down under the lunch table))
2. Ms. Jung: Aka (baby), let's go to the tongsayng (younger brother or sister) class. Let's see how they eat.
3. ((Ms. Jung takes Jina to the Green Room (the two-year-olds' classroom) and other children join them))
4. Ms. Um: Hi, Jina. Why are you here ((smiles))?
5. Ms. Jung: She came to see how tongsayng-dul (younger brother or sister, plural suffix) are eating.
6. Ms. Um: Oh! Would you come here?
7. ((Jina shakes her head and hides behind Ms. Jung holding her hands))

In order to have Jina conform to the classroom rule, Ms. Jung in this scene employs various strategies that arouse a feeling of shame in the child. She first confers a pejorative role, aka, to her and takes her to the two-year-old classroom referring to the Green Room as "tongsayng (younger brother or sister) class." As Jina and Ms. Jung step into the Green Room accompanied by some Arum Room children, Ms. Um playfully joins the shaming practice by asking Jina why she came here (line 4) and teasing her to join them (line 6). As Ms. Jung's statements in lines 2 and 6 illustrate ("Let's see how they eat," "She came to see how tongsayng-dul are eating"), the explicit purpose of this practice lies in having the misbehaving child observe how others behave, thereby evaluating one's behaviors in comparison to others' and feeling ashamed of the improperness of one's own behavior. Whereas the explicit purpose of this practice highlights the child's sense of shame developed through comparative observation of others' behaviors, the affective intensity of this practice lies in that it brings multiple parties as witnesses to the target child's wrongdoings and makes his or her misdeeds and shame public. When Ms. Jung takes Jina to the Green Room accompanied by other Arum Room children, the parties recruited in this shaming practice include not simply Ms. Um who actively participates as a co-shamer but also Green Room children and the accompanying Arum Room children who watch how Jina is disciplined and ashamed. Jina is publicly made an object of shame in ways that impose intense feelings and bring the gaze of others to bear on her.

The practice of taking children to other classrooms is also done in a reverse way—that is, in ways that younger children visit the classrooms of elder children to observe exemplary behaviors.

SCENE 3.19: "PLAYTIME"

Participants: Ms. Um (teacher, Green Room), Ms. Sung (teacher, Arum Room), Seomin (boy, 2 years)

1. ((Ms. Um comes to the Arum Room holding Seomin's hand))
2. Ms. Um: Ms. Sung, Seomin said he doesn't wanna play with his friends in the Green Room. So he came to see how *hyengnim-dul* (elder brother or sister, plural suffix) are doing.

3. Ms. Sung: ((goes around the classroom holding Seomin's hand)) Do you see any hyengnim fighting here? ((goes to the block area)) Look here, too. Hyengnim-dul get along very well.

In this scene, Ms. Um brings her two-year-old student Seomin to the Arum Room, a three-year-old classroom, to have him critically reflect on his own behaviors of fighting with friends in comparison to the exemplary ones of the older children—that is, getting along well. In this process, as in scene 3.18, Ms. Um and the co-shamer Ms. Sung intentionally arouse a feeling of shame in the target child by exposing his wrongdoings and immoralities to the gaze of others and constantly comparing his behaviors to other "well-behaved" and morally acting hyengnim-dul. In line 2, Ms. Um publicly announces Seomin's immoralities to Ms. Sung and to the Arum Room children, and Ms. Sung in line 3 reinforces this framework of exposure by taking the target child around the classroom. The teachers also collaboratively draw a comparative framework by making statements that enforce Seomin to evaluate his behavior in comparison to hyengnim's ("He came to see how hyengnim-dul are doing," "Do you see any hyengnim fighting here? Look here, too. Hyengnim-dul get along very well").

The practice of taking children to another classroom, as with other shaming practices, is enacted in ways that raise feelings of abandonment and ostracism in the target child. When teachers take the misbehaving child to other classrooms, it physically separates him or her from his or her own group. Even though the separation is temporally limited and the child is under the guidance of his or her teacher, the experiences of being out of the classroom and exposed to the gazes of strangers evoke a sense of fear that one could be expelled and abandoned by the group for his or her improper behaviors and immoralities. Teachers also reinforce the dread of abandonment and isolation through statements alluding to one's possible exclusion and expulsion from the group. For instance, in scene 3.18, Ms. Um provokes the state of estrangement by stating, "Oh! Would you come here?" to Jina who is brought to Ms. Um's classroom for failing to finish a meal. In a similar vein, when spoon-feeding the child who fails to eat by himself during lunchtime in scene 3.17, the teacher brings the younger brother who temporarily visited their classroom as a witness to his improper behaviors and says, "You should go with them." These statements provoke fears of being alienated from the group for failing to conform to societal norms and expectations. Somang teachers also employ utterances such as "You're the only one left. Aren't you lonely?" "You go out and play alone. Play alone outside the classroom," and "Yellow card. If you keep talking and not eating, I'll send you to the Green Room" to elicit the feelings of alienation from misbehaving children. This threat of abandonment and ostracism inculcates the idea that one needs to behave properly to fit into the group. Collectivity may be discredited for obstructing the development of children's individuated senses of selves in the explicit curriculum but is a value indispensable in encouraging a child to behave properly in everyday contexts. Failing to acquire this sensitivity has social consequences.

Conclusion: Some Possible Answers to Teachers' Agony

I opened this chapter with a teacher's agony over the difficulty of cultivating children's individuated senses of self, especially the discrepancies between her socialization efforts and the unsatisfactory outcomes in children's behaviors. The discourses on the difficulty of promoting children's selves prevail not only among Somang teachers but in public debates, media, and scholarly discussions of Korean early childhood socialization. Similar to Somang teachers' reactions to the perceived problem, these discourses are typically geared toward blaming children for failing to assimilate new socialization ideals and toward attributing unsatisfactory outcomes to the influence of settings outside the school. Teachers, therefore, typically ascribe failure to environments such as the home or larger Korean society while experts or reformers point to teachers' unfaithful enactment of the imported new ideals as major causes of failure.

Close observations of Somang everyday socialization practices in this chapter, however, suggest that the failure emerges not so much from the outside world or the unfaithful enactment of an imported curriculum as from a conflicting and contradictory socialization landscape in which incoherent, partial, and mutually contradictory socialization ideas intertwine, and these complexities and heterogeneities are masked for teachers by the ideological importance placed on newly imported educational values. Even though teachers work to cultivate children's selves through adoption of a Western curriculum, their conscious efforts falter as they clash with implicit cultural beliefs and practices, creating a highly fragmented and conflictual educational landscape. While teachers valorize the ideology of cultivating children's selves and aim to educate a child to know and have confidence in their own authentic needs, feelings, and thoughts, they also want children to be modest, reserved, and considerate in their expression of themselves as we have seen in cases like problematizing Nuri's excessive and self-absorbing expression or complex models of selfhood teachers hold in mind manifested in their evaluation of an individual child's character. Teachers explicitly disapprove of hierarchy, collectivity, competition, and comparison, associating them with older values that hinder development of children's selves. At the same time, they provide and reinforce these same values through embodied and implicit practices in the classroom and even through explicit instructions in the less formal arenas in their care of their pupils.

Teachers, however, rarely recognized, articulated, or conceptualized these intersecting and occasionally competing ideas of children's self-expression and ideal personhood mainly because working toward values of modesty, considerateness, uniformity, and collectivity were a part of their habitus (Bourdieu 1977). As Ms. Choo looked back on her school days in evaluating Nuri's behaviors or as Rainbow teachers spoke highly of Ayeon's harmonious character while dismissing Sowon's and Ara's individualistic characteristics as "strong" and "not belonging" without realizing the contradictions with stated socialization ideals, they demonstrated predispositions to perceive "good" personhood and social relations in terms of so-called traditional values rather than prioritizing the new values of individuality, self-confidence, or excellence. Moreover, the ideological importance placed on new values prevented teachers from articulating and even realizing the complexities and contradictions embedded in their socialization practices of self-expression and ideal personhood. Therefore, teachers' socialization consisted primarily of subtle dismissal of excessive expressions or scolding children for failing to express themselves appropriately as shown in the cases above. Ms. Choo, for instance, reprimanded children for pretentiously expressing their knowledge about the storybook she had chosen for reading or negatively assessed children's competitive aspirations to present their weekend stories during the weekend story time. Far less frequently do teachers directly address the complex, conflicting, and contradictory models of self-expression that children are actually expected to follow in everyday socialization contexts. As teachers seldom articulate the complex and heterogeneous aspects of their socialization practices and talk as if pupils simply need to abide by the explicit curriculum, children become frustrated with contradictions they experience between what is explicitly asked of them and what teachers actually expect in everyday educational contexts. The new explicit curriculum requires children to cultivate and express their authentic feelings and thoughts, but when they do so, they are likely to be scolded for being overbearing or self-absorbed. Children, for instance, would wonder why their desires to present weekend stories at the school activity exactly designed for that purpose are inconsiderate and undesirable. Teachers are also frustrated by children's inabilities to live up to their implicit and explicit expectations and typically attribute children's dissatisfactory behaviors to the pressures or values of the outside world as experienced in children's homes or the larger Korean society.

When the context moves to more mundane and "noneducational" ones, teachers tend to be oblivious to the contradictory and conflicting nature of their socialization practices because of the taken-for-granted quality of the habitus involving competition, comparison, uniformity, role, and status that continues in their practices unreflected despite the introduction of imported pedagogic goals (Bourdieu 1977). Moreover, teachers' tendencies to draw a clear distinction between official and informal school practices and their perspectives on the less formal contexts as "noneducational" create obstacles to critical reflection on their own embodied everyday socialization practices. Teachers, therefore, typically articulate their explicit curriculum in their efforts to establish pedagogic goals and consonant practices without being aware of their implicit strategic use of competition, comparison, uniformity, and shame in the classroom or their more explicit use of these techniques in managing students' mundane behaviors. When Ms. Choo is frustrated by children's obsession with roles and status in plays as introduced in the opening narrative, she simply criticizes children's play for not having any creative or unique content and reflects on the explicit curriculum and pedagogical styles but rarely pays attention to her embodied everyday practices of continuously bestowing particular roles such as hyengnim, aka, or tongsayng on children, asking them to behave in accordance with those assigned roles, and shaming them for not meeting appropriate standards. Many so-called traditional Korean educational ideas and values are transmitted through the workings of what Tobin, Hsueh, and Karasawa (2009) and Bruner (1996) refer to as "implicit cultural practices" and "folk pedagogy" despite teachers' conscious and active denials and their efforts otherwise.

The findings of this chapter, then, provide some tentative but practical answers to teachers' agony over the discrepancies between their educational efforts to promote children's selves and the socialization outcomes they observe. First, the findings suggest that more attention be paid to the tensions and contradictions that arise in the global circulation of socialization ideals. The hegemonic force of new socialization values blind teachers to the continuing inclusion of taken-for-granted aspects of everyday socialization in their interactions with students and to the "real" desires and expectations they have for their children. As a result, children are exposed to highly conflicted, fragmented, and inconsistent settings in their socialization landscape, which require them to follow mutually contradictory values. Children are verbally instructed to be unique, creative, and self-confident but are also asked to constantly be aware of the others' gaze, compare their behaviors with others, conform to group rules and expectations, and subordinate individual goals and satisfactions to those of the collectivity. As with Fong's (2007) study of Chinese parents' contradictory expectations for their teenagers, what Somang teachers actually expected of their children was, then, not simple replication of adult ideals but improvement in their self-concepts in ways that would go beyond the models held by adults, enabling them to succeed in a changing globalized world. Moreover, as the excessive ideological importance placed on new values hampers teachers from articulating or even recognizing the complex and contradictory desires they have for children, they talk as if they provide fairly unitary, consistent, and homogeneous ideas concerning children's selves and simply scold children for failing to meet their expectations. Children, therefore, are often confused and frustrated. If teachers had reflected on their own conflicting and inconsistent educational desires and developed ways to articulate the complex and situated models they have in mind for children, miscommunications that both teachers and children experienced in everyday socialization contexts might be reduced.

Second, the findings suggest that teachers need to create awareness of the power of implicit, unmarked, and situated socialization practices in the reproduction of core socialization beliefs and values. The findings of this chapter show that characteristically Korean or traditional core socialization ideas that teachers actively deny and strongly disapprove of are nonetheless transmitted through the workings of implicit, unmarked, and situated practices despite teachers' outspoken rejection of their tactics as outdated and obstructing the development of children's selves. Teachers rarely address what they might communicate implicitly or indirectly. In practice, they tend to sharply distinguish educational contexts from "noneducational" or informal ones and confine the scope of educational reforms primarily to explicit and formal educational contexts. More attention should be paid to the ways that educational efforts backfire through the workings of unreflected educational and socialization practices. Children's aspirations for uniformity, competition, comparison, hierarchy, and status that Ms. Choo in the beginning of this chapter found frustrating, for instance, resulted at least in part from the Somang informal and embodied socialization practices.

Third, the findings can be interpreted here as a foundation for urging teachers to critically reflect on the imagined dichotomy they hold toward socialization values and practices. Adopting the imagined dichotomy prevalent in recent Korean socialization discourse, Somang teachers typically regard Western socialization practices as exclusively loaded with "new" and "better" values of creativity, independence, and self-confidence in contrast to traditional Korean practices characterized by "old" and "backward" values of comparison, hierarchy, and uniformity. Therefore, in their efforts to recklessly dissociate themselves from any seemingly "traditional" or characteristically "Korean" values, teachers often overlook the intertwining of "new" values with "old" ones in actual socialization contexts. In scene 3.2, for instance, Ms. Shim misses out on creativity, uniqueness, and self-confidence deployed in a pun the children produce during competitive talk. As she looks at children's interactions only through a lens of the imagined dichotomy, children's pursuit of competition and uniformity appearing in competitive talk stand out and thus are identified as obsolete elements to be corrected. If she had not been bounded by the imagined dichotomy and were more lenient toward perceived "traditional" values, children in this scene would have more opportunity to further their emerging unique and creative linguistic competence. The dichotomous view, instead, made her heedless of the children's creativity and self-confidence deployed in otherwise competitive and uniformly oriented contexts and led her to interrupt and stop the children's talk.

Although the tensions and confusions that Korean teachers and children experience could be lessened through teachers' enactment of the critical reflection discussed here, socialization efforts to cultivate children's selves will continue to flounder unless larger structural and conceptual barriers surrounding the Korean early childhood socialization call for promoting children's selves are taken into consideration. Teachers might critically reflect on their mutually contradictory educational desires and rectify their tendency to claim wholeness and integrity of the curriculum. Even if teachers critically reflect on their conflicting and contradictory educational desires, their reflections will falter because of the excessive ideological importance placed on globally dominant socialization ideals and the imagined dichotomy imposed on Korean early childhood socialization discourses.

The challenge teachers face in achieving their goal for children is the unreflected and inconsistent demands they make of their preschool pupils at this historical juncture. How do these pupils perceive, view, and experience the inconsistent and contradictory demands bearing on them? The next chapter moves to children's experiences of the transforming Korean socialization landscape, especially their participation and engagement in the indigenization of globally dominant socialization ideologies and practices.

4

"I Want to Copy My Best Friend's Artwork"

Expressions and Social Relationships in Children's Peer World

In the artwork area in Arum classroom, Sungeun, Mira, Jungji, and Jisung are making artwork using wires Ms. Sung is distributing. Taking a blue wire from Ms. Sung, Sungeun says, "I'll make a spatula." Then Mira states to Ms. Sung, "I have to make ribbons. I have to make hundreds of ribbons. I'll make hundreds of ribbons." Mira starts making a ribbon and Sungeun looks at her for a while and then declares, "I'll make ribbons." Then Jungji and Jisung also say, "I'm making ribbons, too" and start making ribbons with wires. After a while, Mira shows her ribbon to Ms. Sung saying, "This is a ribbon" and Sungeun says, "It looks like a skeleton." Mira shouts, "Hey" in an angry voice and Sungeun responds by saying, "It can look like a skeleton to me." Mira expresses her discomfort again by shouting, "Hey," and Sungeun this time says, "It looks like a hat, too." Beside them, Jungji and Jisung argue over whose ribbon is bigger. As Jungji states Mira's ribbon is bigger than Jisung's, Sungeun joins them by saying, "Hey, mine is the biggest."

In the afternoon this interaction occurred, Ms. Sung expressed her uneasiness about it to me as follows: "One starts making something beautiful and everyone copies it. We can't see any diversity. In the morning today, as Mira says that she'll make hundreds of ribbons, everyone makes ribbons. While making them, they compare one another's and fight, so there's no progress."

Competitive talk and interaction like that quoted above are prevalent in Somang children's peer world. Children constantly compare and evaluate each other's skills, products, and performances and debate and argue over where they stand with one another in a wide variety of contexts. They also display keen concerns about what peers are doing and pursue the same activities, behaviors, and even feelings they see their peers around them engaging in in order to belong to the group. As reflected in Ms. Sung's narrative, children's pursuit of uniformity, comparison, and hierarchy in a scene like that above is viewed by teachers as a problematic situation that obstructs cultivation of "diversity" and "progress." Yet at the same time, teachers tend to regard children as simply boasting of trifling skills and fighting over trivial issues as Ms. Sung's definition of the interaction above as a "fight" illustrates. That is, teachers diminish the potential significance of the issues over which children quarrel.

This view of children as undeveloped, incomplete, and often concerned with what appear as trivial matters from an adult perspective is not only shared by Somang teachers but more broadly by adults in many contemporary societies. Some previous scholarship of children and childhood such as behavioristic and social learning theories (Bandura and McDonald 1963; Miller and Dollard 1941; Skinner 1957) or functionalistic approaches (Dahrendorf 1966; Parsons 1951) also share this view when they conceptualize socialization in terms of an adult shaping a child's behaviors through reinforcement, modeling, or soliciting imitation. Under this adult-centric view, children are visible but as incompetent and incomplete beings in the process of becoming fully developed social actors. Overwhelmingly concerned with the end point of development, children are typically regarded as targets of education, cultivation, and discipline and rarely seen as active partici-pants who engage in and contribute to the production of meanings crucial to cul-tural reproduction and transformation (Corsaro 1997; Corsaro and Miller 1992; Hirschfeld 2002; James, Jenks, and Prout 1998; Prout and James 2015). Ms. Sung in the above narrative does not view children as participating in the serious business of belonging or of constructing hierarchical social relationships but rather regards them as simply fighting over some trivial and unimportant issues in undesirable ways. However, when children's perspectives, voices, and experience are fully accounted for as emphasized by much recent scholarship on children and child-hood (Bluebond-Langner and Korbin 2007; Christensen and James 2008; Clark and Moss 2011; James 2007; Lancy 2008; Montgomery 2008; Sobo 2015), different con-tours of morality, sentiments, and social meanings appear.

From the perspectives and concerns of adults, children's interactions above are indications of their ongoing development, egocentricity, and a lack of uniquely established selves. From children's points of view, however, making sim-ilar artwork with their peers—that is, pursuing like tastes—is an act of belonging to a group and an effort not to be excluded from the group. Similarly, comparing and evaluating one another's artwork is not simply a fight but children's endeav-ors to gain authority and construct hierarchical social structures in which members constantly seek power and authority. Moreover, even though the teacher negatively assesses children's competitive and evaluative statements as "fights" in the interaction above, the children do express their own individuated thoughts as many Somang teachers desire in their explicit socialization goals. Sungeun, for instance, expresses her opinions about Mira's artwork by stating that it looks like a skeleton and a hat. While the purpose of these statements lies in confronting Mira's temporarily established or emerging authority, Sungeun's statements are also an expression of her own views and thoughts about her peer's artwork. When she states that "it can look like a skeleton to me" by rais-ing the pitch of her voice at "to me," she even alludes to the value of diversity and individuality. That is, she strategically appropriates the idea of diversity in addressing the peer world goal of gaining authority and occupying a better position in competitive talk. The depth and specificity of knowledge children display in the above scene, then, defy a common assumption held by teachers and found in some traditional studies of children and childhood—that is, the view of children as incomplete adults or adults in the making. Observing the competitive and individualistic orientation of children's talk should push scholars and teachers to pay attention to the agentive role children play in the reproduction and transformation of local cultural scenes as well as in the acquisition of cultural sensibilities.

In this chapter, I shift the focus from adult-centric views to children's voices, experiences, and perspectives to explore the contribution children make to their own socialization processes as well as to the production and reproduction of cultural meanings crucial to the changing Korean socialization landscape. Regarding children as complex and active participants inhabiting a specific cultural environment, this chapter aims to describe what it is like to live as a child in rapidly transforming Korean early childhood socialization environments. The chapter shows that children, rather than passively assimilating teachers' socialization inputs, creatively reconstruct and reinterpret heterogenous and conflicting socialization ideologies and values to construct their own culture-laden social world. Specifically, I focus on children's own uses, meanings, and interpretations regarding both explicit socialization inputs such as self-expression, creativity, or diversity and implicit ones of role, status, or hierarchy. For this purpose, I first describe major features and themes of Somang children's peer world and then examine how children construct meaning out of cultural practices and semiotic systems to which they are exposed in order to address themes of their peer world. The findings illustrate that children possess highly sophisticated knowledge regarding local socialization conditions around them and even sometimes unwittingly display penetrating and critical insights into the indigenizing processes and the global dominance of Western socialization ideologies.

Somang Children's Culture-Laden Peer World: Some Major Features and Themes

Studies of children's peer cultures have shown that children develop and maintain social practices, networks of relationships, and systems of meaning that are distinct to their own social and physical spaces, independent of the adult environments in which they are embedded (Adler and Adler 1998; Berentzen 1984; Best 1983; Corsaro 1985; Evaldsson 2005; Goodwin 1990, 2006; Hirschfeld 2002; Kyratzis 2004; Kyratzis and Guo 2001; Paley 1993). The studies, in particular, note conflicts, social differentiation, control of others' behaviors, and the pursuit of hierarchy and authority as main themes across many cultures and historical ages. Likewise, the culture-laden social world Somang children construct is characterized by two things: the pursuit of power and authority and constant shifts of alliance and exclusion. Somang children eagerly pursue establishing hierarchical social order in which members constantly seek power and authority. They, at the same time, incessantly solicit alliances and exert exclusions and utilize these alignment structures in pursuing specific ends.

Power, Authority, and Hierarchy

Somang children display ongoing concerns for gaining power and authority and constructing hierarchical social relationships in a variety of everyday activities and interactions. Children endeavor to gain control over the attitudes and behaviors of peers and constantly make comparisons and argue over where they stand with respect to one another in a variety of contexts. To address the goal of gaining power and authority, children employ various communitive and interactional skills such as producing competitive talk, offering personal toys or goodies, or transforming everyday routines or educational settings into contests. The following peer interaction, for instance, involves children's incessant interest in producing a stratified social structure in which participants work hard to occupy a better position in comparison to others.

SCENE 4.1: "LUNCHTIME"

Participants: Seoyun (girl, 3 years), Minseo (girl, 3 years), Haeun (girl, 3 years), Jungyoon (girl, 3 years), Sungeun (girl, 3 years), Hajun (boy, 3 years), Jiju (boy, 3 years)

1. Seoyun: ((picks up noodles in her bowl with a chopstick and holds it high)) Hey, Minseo, mine is bigger, right?
2. Minseo: ((holds her noodles higher than Seoyun's)) Wow, look at this.
3. Seoyun: We're same.
4. Haeun: Minseo wins.
5. ((Hajun, Jungyoon, and Sungeun compare the length of their spoons))
6. Jungyoon: I'm taller than my mom.
7. Hajun: I'm taller than my dad.
8. Jungyoon: Sungeun is taller than my house.
9. ((Hajun, Seoyun, and Jungyoon eat soup holding the end of spoons and laugh at one another's behaviors))
10. Jungyoon: I'm the first. ((points to Seoyun)) You're the second. ((to Hajun)) You're the third.
11. Seoyun: ((looks at Jungyoon)) No, you're also the first. ((turns to Hajun)) You're the first, too.
12. Hajun: No, let's have a match.
13. ((Hajun, Seoyun, and Jungyoon start eating and Jungyoon drinks up soup to finish her lunch))

78 BETWEEN SELF AND COMMUNITY

14. Hajun: Let's eat slowly.
15. Jungyoon: No, it's a race for eating fast.
16. Hajun: My mom says every day that I'll be a fool if I do bad things.
17. Seoyun: My mom says to me every day not to pee but to poop. She says to my baby brother not to pee but to poop.
18. Hajun: My baby says, "Why don't you share toys with me?" when I don't lend him a toy. . . . But my baby destroys my toys and . . .
19. Seoyun: My baby destroys toys. . . .
20. Hajun: By the way, when I give flowers to my baby, he says, "What is this?"
21. Seoyun: By the way, when I give flowers to my baby, he says, "What is this? Is this poo?" ((laughs))
22. Haeun: ((moves back to the table from the teacher's table)) I'm almost done. I'm almost done.
23. Jungyoon: Then you can't meet Santa Claus.
24. Haeun: If I do a spin, my skirt becomes large. If I do a pop, my skirt becomes large. Do I?
25. Hajun: Yes.
26. ((Haeun spins around to have her skirt flare out))
27. Hajun: Wow.
28. ((Seoyun stands up and spins around))
29. Haeun: ((to Hajun)) How's Seoyun?
30. Jungyoon: Look at me. Hey, look at me. ((stands up and spins around))
31. ((Haeun stands up and spins))
32. ((Jungyoon stands up and spins))
33. ((Haeun and Jungyoon come back to the lunch table))
34. Haeun: ((to Jiju)) Jiju, Jiju, whose skirts become bigger?
35. ((Jiju does not respond))
36. Haeun: I'm leaving.
37. Seoyun: It's okay. Losing is better.

The children in this scene produce competitive talk in which they compare and rank one another in terms of a wide variety of issues such as the length of their noodles and spoons (lines 1–5), their heights (lines 6–8), their eating speed (lines 10–23), and the skill of flaring out skirts (lines 24–37). The competitive structure first emerges as Seoyun compares the length of her noodles with Minseo's (line 1) and Minseo challenges her movement by finding a noodle longer than Seoyun's in her bowl and holding it high (line 2). Seoyun negates Minseo's temporarily established position by arguing that the lengths of their noodles are equal (line 3) and Haeun judges Minseo as the winner (line 4).

In this segment of interaction as well as the continuing competition- and comparison-oriented interactional structures, children argue over their relative social statuses and positions and use sophisticated linguistic and interactional skills to address their immediate social goals. In the segment from lines 9 to 21 wherein Hajun, Seoyun, and Jungyoon compete with one another over eating lunch, for instance, as Jungyoon ranks herself as the first and Hajun as the last (line 10), Hajun challenges this ranking and tries to attain a higher position by saying "No" and transforming the everyday routine of eating lunch into a contest (line 12), then negating a contest frame when he is behind the others (line 14), or switching the topic of the talk (line 16). In response to Hajun's strategy of switching the topic, Seoyun from line 17 participates in this shifted frame but implicitly challenges him by producing jokes. That is, Seoyun in lines 17, 19, and 21 produces statements similar to Hajun's in terms of their structures and contents but adds toilet words such as pee, poop, and poo to make them funny, thereby occupying a better position in this subtle competitive talk. Haeun, from line 22, also displays various interpersonal skills such as bringing a contest frame back (line 22), soliciting a new subject of the contest (line 24), inviting an outsider as referee to the contest (line 34), and controlling behaviors of others through retreating (line 36).

Children's eagerness to attain authority, power, and hierarchy is not confined to mundane and noneducational contexts like above but also prominent in educational settings. Children frequently transform an educational scene into a contest or employ a comparative and competitive framework in educational discourses. One can easily hear children making statements such as "Yay, I got the right answer," "Yay, I got two right answers," "I win," or "You're the last" through which participants evaluate one another with reference to a variety of skills and performances.

Replicating findings from children's peer cultures of other places (Corsaro 1997; Goodwin 1990, 2006; Kyratzis 2004), the social world created by Somang children through competitive verbal statements and contests is hierarchical. The social hierarchy and authority produced by children, however, are not identical to ones often found in adult social organizations and have their own peculiar characteristics. First, although children constantly evaluate one another in terms of various references, verbal arguments and contests rarely establish a clear winner and loser. None of the interactions in scene 4.1, for instance, resulted in clear rankings of the participants. Rather, as noted by Corsaro (1997, 154), children are preoccupied with process over structure in peer relations. That is, they are more interested in debating and negotiating where they stand with one another rather than establishing and maintaining a stable ranking. Second, the hierarchy and authority produced by children are not stable but constantly changing. The authority gained at a certain moment changes as the activity changes. Also, considering the fact that children value competition itself more than actually winning, authority is constantly sought and temporarily gained but never anchored in one person. Thus, it is not a type of social hierarchy in which one child can monopolize a position of authority (Goodwin 1990, 2006). Rather, it is a fluid and fragile one which bespeaks the reason children constantly jockey for positions. Third, just as the social world they organize is fluid and transitory, the criteria children use to attain power and authority also vary. The criteria might include anything children find relevant to the context such as the length of one's noodles, one's family members' heights, eating speed, or the skill of flaring out skirts as seen in scene 4.1. Thus, the criteria for evaluating one another's relative social status change as social context changes, even within one activity as shown in scene 4.1.

The tremendous effort children expend to gain power and the fluidity and fragility of children's social worlds mutually influence each other. Because authority in children's social world is unstable, this feature forces children to constantly jockey for position through a wide range of interpersonal and communicative skills. At the same time, as children's efforts to gain authority are focused more on the process itself rather than the structure produced by it, the social world they produce is fluid and complex rather than stable and fixed.[1]

Alliance Formation and Exclusions

Along with the goal of gaining power, authority, and hierarchy, alliance formation and exclusion are another central theme of Somang children's peer world. In their moment-to-moment interactions, children display keen concerns regarding who makes an alliance with whom and who is excluded from that relationship. They forge alliances and exclude others in everyday social interactions for particular ends, such as gaining access to existing games, recruiting playmates, obtaining particular toys, and protecting interactive space. To solicit collaborations and exert exclusions, they employ multiple interpersonal and communicative skills and resources such as utilizing social categories of gender, friends, or age, manipulating expressive means, or offering belongings. The following scene illustrates how children at the lunch table negotiate their alignment structures in which members constantly seek alliances and exclusions.

SCENE 4.2: "LUNCHTIME"

Participants: Seoyun (girl, 3 years), Minjun (boy, 3 years), Haeun (girl, 3 years), Jiwon (girl, 3 years)

1. ((Haeun comes to the table first, Minjun comes later and sits on the left side of Haeun))
2. ((Seoyun comes to the left side of Minjun))
3. Minjun: I'm not gonna sit beside you ((to Seoyun)). I'm gonna sit beside Jiwon.
4. Seoyun: ((to Haeun)) My friend, my friend.
5. ((Minjun looks at Seoyun))
6. Seoyun: ((to Minjun)) You're not my friend. ((to Haeun)) My friend, my friend, you and Miso are same.

In this scene, the children at the lunch table argue over who sits next to whom, which is an emblem of alliance in Somang children's peer world, and they display well-defined skills in this dispute. The conflict emerges as Minjun refuses to have

Seoyun sit beside him by explicitly stating that he does not want to sit with Seoyun and instead picks Jiwon as the one with whom he wishes to sit (line 3). Against Minjun's exclusive movement, Seoyun strategically uses the social category of friends in soliciting alliance with another child. In line 4, she calls Haeun who sits beside Minjun as her friend ("my friend, my friend"). Furthermore, as Minjun displays interest in her movement, Seoyun reinforces an alignment structure that forges an alliance with Haeun and excludes Minjun from their relationships by stating "you're not my friend" to Minjun while calling Haeun her friend again. Similar are the findings from the peer cultures of other places (Ahn 2011; Corsaro 1997, 2017), the concept of friendship, which is typically characterized by inclusions, affections, or putative goodness in adult conceptualization, is here creatively appropriated and transformed by children as a social category for realizing a differentiated social world.

Along with the social category of friends, Somang children also strategically utilize other resources such as expressive means, memberships, or sharing prohibited items as the following interactions illustrate.

SCENE 4.3: "OUTSIDE PLAY"

Participants: Yunseo (girl, 3 years, Penguin Room), Seoyun (girl, 3 years, Arum Room), Jeemin (girl, 3 years, Arum Room), Sua (girl, 3 years, Penguin Room)

1. ((Arum Room and Penguin Room children are wearing shoes and lining up to go outside and play))
2. ((Yunseo and Seoyun hold each other's hands))
3. Jeemin: ((approaches Yunseo and Seoyun)) I love you. I love you.
4. Yunseo: You love me, but I can't love you today.
5. Jeemin: ((stares at Yunseo and Seoyun)) I'm gonna be a *ccakkung* (a friend) with the teacher, Ahn. I'm gonna be a ccakkung with the teacher, Ahn. In here. ((comes beside me and holds my hands))
6. ((Yunseo and Seoyun hug each other and look at Jeemin))
7. ((Sua goes to Jeemin))
8. Sua: Jeemin, do you love me?
9. Jeemin: No, I can't be a ccakkung with [someone in the] Penguin classroom.
10. Yunseo: No.
11. ((Yunseo and Seoyun hug))
12. Jeemin: Okay, Penguins, you two become ccakkung. ((Pushes Sua beside Yunseo))
13. ((Jeemin holds Seoyun's hands))
14. Yunseo: No, Jeemin should be a ccakkung with someone she likes most.
15. Jeemin: ((to Seoyun)) I love you.
16. ((Yunseo comes beside Seoyun and hugs her))
17. Jeemin: ((takes the jelly out of her pocket and shows it to Seoyun)) Let's eat *mychoo* (jelly).

The children in this scene constantly negotiate over forming "two against one" structures wherein only two people get memberships and the third one is intentionally excluded. The three-year-old classrooms of Arum Room and Penguin Room jointly went to outside recess. The dynamics of alliance formation begin as Jeemin approaches Yunseo and Seoyun who already have forged a ccakkung relationship by holding hands together. A ccakkung, which literally means a partner, mate, or friend, is a pair of classmates who are close to each other and participate in everyday classroom routines such as playing, eating, or lining up together in the preschool context. As Jeemin attempts to join an alliance with Yunseo and Seoyun by displaying affection ("I love you, I love you," in line 3), Yunseo exerts exclusions by stating that she cannot love Jeemin today, even though Jeemin has affection for her ("You love me, but I can't love you today," line 4). Being excluded from the collaboration of Yunseo and Seoyun, Jeemin displays an alliance with me to challenge them, and Yunseo and Seoyun respond to Jeemin's movement by employing paralinguistic behavior of hugging. An alliance structure shifts as Sua appears in the scene in line 7 and the four children afterward incessantly negotiate over forging a dyadic alliance structure while excluding one child from that structure. In this process, the children manipulate a variety of linguistic and nonlinguistic emotional expressions such as statements regarding love and affection (lines 8, 15) and hugging and holding hands (lines 11, 13, 16), strategically employ the idea of membership ("No, I can't be a ccakkung with [someone in the] Penguin classroom," "Okay, Penguins, you two become ccakkung," lines 9, 12), and offer to share prohibited personal items with the one from whom they target to solicit collaboration ("Let's eat mychoo," line 17). A wide variety of interpersonal and communicative skills are adopted to construct a differentiated social structure wherein members constantly negotiate and argue over alliances and exclusions.

Although alliance and exclusion are highly valued and constantly sought in the children's world, as is the case for authority and social hierarchy, the social organization created through alliance formation and exclusion is rarely permanent and stable but highly fragile and fluid as Yunseo's statement in scene 4.3 that "you love me, but I can't love you today" nicely illustrates. Several factors contribute to this transitory feature of alliance and exclusion in children's social organization. First, the collaborative alliances children build represent a temporary convergence concerning a particular issue. Children rarely establish alliances based on the personal characteristics of group members. The motivation for forming an alliance more often depends on whether the members converge on a particular issue. As issues change, so does the social order (Maynard 1985, 217). In a similar vein, the criteria or resources for forging alliances and exclusions continuously change as the contexts shift. In scene 4.3, for instance, the criteria for forging alliances change from affection to one's classroom membership and later to sharing personal items. The structure of the preschool classroom itself also has to do with the fragility and fluidity of children's alliances. Except in group times, the curriculum is designed so that children are constantly asked to move around the room and make choices. Even during group times or lunch and snack times when everyone is participating in the same activity, children get to make choices for certain arrangements (e.g., seats), and these arrangements such as who sits with whom and who eats lunch with whom become an emblem of alliance. Therefore, when children move from one activity to another, it inevitably involves making new alliances and being excluded from alliances that have already been established. That is, the everyday routines themselves, to a certain extent, facilitate shifts of alliance formations and exclusions. In these respects, alliance and exclusion in children's culture rarely mean an establishment of stable core groups or constant exclusion of a particular child. Rather, they are part of children's everyday lives whose structures constantly shift as contexts change. In the next sections, I turn to the issue of how children address these themes and goals through their creative use and transformation of heterogenous and conflicting socialization inputs regarding their selves and personhood.

Copying or Belonging?: Expression as Means of Forging Alliances and Exclusions

Whereas Somang teachers make concerted efforts to have children express their own unique feelings, ideas, and thoughts and conceive of self-expression as a practice of cultivating children's individuated expressions, creativity, and diversity as reflected in teachers' frequent statements such as "We'd like to see diversity" or "Why can't we see diversity?," self-expression has completely different and somewhat opposite meanings in the Somang children's peer world. Children perceive expression as one of the resources they can employ to address goals of their peer world and therefore they strategically utilize and transform the meanings of expressions in a variety of interactional scenes with peers. In this process, an expression charged with globally dominating socialization ideologies of creativity and diversity in teachers' socialization inputs is reinterpreted and reconstructed as signifying social relationships of belonging, collaboration, and exclusion.

"Yay, We're the Same!": Expressions for Belonging and Collaboration

Even though much of Somang curriculum is set up to promote children's individuated self-expression, children rarely pursue individuality or creativity in their expressions but rather take avid interest in producing uniformity, oneness, or collectivity. Teachers typically criticize uniformity of children's expressions for lacking creativity and diversity and lament failing outcomes of their educational efforts. However, uniformity in children's social contexts rarely means a lack of development or failing but rather is a useful means or successful way to address goals of their peer world. The following interactions between two children in the message center illustrate the meanings children attribute to expressions.

84 BETWEEN SELF AND COMMUNITY

SCENE 4.4: "MESSAGE CENTER"

Participants: Seojin (boy, 3 years), Jiwoo (girl, 3 years)

1. ((Seojin and Jiwoo are drawing pictures in the message center))
2. ((Jiwoo draws a person with a purple crayon and Seojin looks at it standing beside her))
3. ((Jiwoo gives the purple crayon to Seojin and Seojin draws a person similar to Jiwoo's in his picture by looking at Seojin's picture))
4. Jiwoo: ((draws a yellow ribbon at the head of her person in the picture and gives the yellow crayon to Seojin)) Here.
5. Seojin: ((draws a yellow ribbon in his picture with the crayon)) Yay, we're same.
6. Jiwoo: ((draws a mountain with a green crayon and gives the crayon to Seojin)) Here you are.
7. ((Seojin draws a similar mountain in his picture))
8. Jiwoo: ((smiles)) Yay, we're same.
9. Seojin: ((smiles)) Yay, we're same.

In this scene, Jiwoo actively induces Seojin to copy her picture by handing the crayon she has used to him. Seojin copies Jiwoo's drawings with the passed crayon and similar interactions follow. Repeating these same procedures several times, these two children joyfully pursue "sameness" and are delighted at the same outcomes as their statements such as "Yay, we're the same" and the paralinguistic feature of a smile indicate. If only certain outcomes of these interactions are considered, children's interactions in the above scene could be interpreted as undesirable and hindering full development of children's creativity, expressiveness, and individuality as often criticized by teachers. When children's perspectives and contexts of interactions are fully taken into account, however, children in these interactions are found to be sharing their own thoughts and expressions with others and producing cooperative and communal outcomes. That is, to address the peer world goal of forging collaborations, children creatively and strategically transform the educational activity which is designed to promote children's individuated self-expression into a place where they make alliances through sharing of expressions and collaborative producing of communal outcomes.

Whereas the children in the above scene are fond of making alliances through expressions, children's interactions surrounding expressions entail not only collaborative relationships but also exclusive acts, thereby often producing conflicts in which some participants experience hurt feelings as the following scene illustrates.

SCENE 4.5: "CREATIVE READING CLASS"

Participants: Sujung (girl, 4 years), Haejin (girl, 4 years), Hyungjun (boy, 4 years), Yubin (girl, 4 years), Miso (girl, 4 years), Ms. Choi (teacher)

"I WANT TO COPY MY BEST FRIEND'S ARTWORK"

1. Ms. Choi: We're going to draw a picture based on the book we're reading today.
2. Sujung: Me rabbit.
3. Haejin: Me baby rabbit, too.
4. Junghyung: Me baby rabbit, too.
5. Yubin: I'd like to draw baby rabbit, too.
6. Haejin: No, only three can be rabbits.
7. Sujung: Me baby rabbit.
8. Hyungjun: Me baby rabbit.
9. Yubin: Me . . .
10. Sujung: Only two.
11. Yubin: I'd like to draw rabbit.
12. Sujung: Me baby rabbit.
13. Haejin: Me baby rabbit.
14. Miso: Me baby rabbit, too.
15. Hyungjun: Me baby rabbit, too.
16. Yubin: I . . .
17. Sujung: Only four.
18. ((Yubin covers her face with hands and shows angry and sad faces))
19. ((Ms. Choi reads the part about eating foods))
20. Yubin: Me chocolate cake.
21. Haejin: Me chocolate cake.
22. Miso: Me chocolate cake, too.
23. Sujung: I'll draw an ice cream.
24. Haejin: Me ice cream, too.
25. Yubin: Then you guys will get fat.

The children in this scene continuously argue over and debate regarding who depicts what in their drawings. As the title of the activity alludes, the creative reading class is a special program designed by Somang preschool to cultivate children's creativity and individuality. The outside specialist comes to each classroom once a week and leads an hour session wherein the teacher reads the storybook and does various activities based on the book. In the session above, Ms. Choi expects children to express their own unique ideas and feelings about the book through drawings. Children, however, show more interest in making same-theme pictures than in producing individuated self-expressions.

The movement for uniform expressions emerges as soon as Ms. Choi announces the topic of the activity (line 1) and Sujung declares the rabbit as the theme of her picture (line 2). The other two children claim a similar subject—that is, the baby rabbit—and Yubin in line 5 also expresses her wishes to have the baby rabbit as her topic. Haejin, however, in line 6 attempts to exclude Yubin from the alliance structure by stating that "only three can be rabbits." The alignment structure in which some members form alliances through same expression while others are excluded from that relationship is continuously produced several times afterward

86 BETWEEN SELF AND COMMUNITY

in lines 7–10, 11–18, and 20–25. In these segments of interactions, children eagerly pursue sameness to forge alliances and not be excluded from collaborative relationships.

Sujung and Haejin, in particular, subtly endeavor to exclude Yubin from alliance structures they are forging by limiting the number of those who can be members of the alliance whenever Yubin attempts to join the collaborative alignment (lines 6, 10, 17). Against their exclusive movements, Yubin also make efforts to challenge them and be part of the alliance by being the first one to declare the theme of the picture as in lines 11 and 20 or by conveying her despair through paralinguistic emotional expressions. When Sujung and Haejin cooperatively challenge Yubin's initiation of alliances through the new theme of chocolate cake in lines 23 and 24 ("I'll draw an ice cream," "Me ice cream, too"), Yubin opposes them by criticizing their taste as an unhealthy one that will make them fat ("Then you guys will get fat," line 25). Here, the statements about the topic of their drawings rarely reflect an individual child's own thoughts, ideas, or tastes but are an expressive means children strategically utilize to address their immediate social goals in the dynamics of coalition formation and exclusion. Whereas teachers imagine expressions as reflections of one's inner states, children perceive and utilize them as performative acts exerting certain effects on their relationships with others.

"I'm More Interested in My Friends' Tastes than Mine": Reflecting Others' Tastes for Alliances

In utilizing expressions as communicative means for creating and maintaining social relationships, Somang children not only pursue sameness and uniformity of expressions but actively adopt the tastes and opinions of peers into their expressions. In the following interaction, the children in the poem writing area produce poems that reflect preferences and thoughts of peers, not their own unique inner ones as desired by teachers.

SCENE 4.6: "POEM WRITING AREA"

Participants: Reehyun (girl, 4 years), Jihyun (girl, 4 years), Naeun (girl, 4 years), Ara (girl, 4 years)

1. Reehyun: ((writes a poem about Christmas)) Do in the same way. Do in the same way. You can do in the same way. You can write the same thing.
2. ((Naeun writes Christmas, twinkle in the poem))
3. ((Jihyun looks at Reehyun's poem and writes Christmas, twinkle in the poem))
4. ((Jihyun, Reehyun, and Naeun write poems about Christmas comparing one another's poems))
5. ((Jihyun writes Jihyun ♡ Reehyun in her poem))
6. Reehyun: Jihyun, would you like to have a ribbon or a headband?
7. Jihyun: Which one is the prettiest?

"I WANT TO COPY MY BEST FRIEND'S ARTWORK" 87

8. Reehyun: Either one.
9. Jihyun: Ribbon.
10. ((Reehyun draws a ribbon in her poem))
11. Reehyun: Is this pretty or not? Do you want me to combine these two?
12. Reehyun: What should I do in the back?
13. Jihyun: I'd like to decorate the back, too.
14. Reehyun: ((turns over the paper)) What do you like? ((shows the figure ruler to Jihyun)) Choose among these.
15. Jihyun: Diamond.
16. Reehyun: I'll draw a diamond for you.
17. Reehyun: You said a diamond, right? You have to choose one more.
18. ((Jihyun points to the waterdrop figure))
19. Reehyun: ((shows the figure ruler to Jihyun)) Next?
20. ((Jihyun points to the heart figure))
21. Reehyun: Heart?
22. ((Reehyun draws a heart using the figure ruler))
23. Ara: ((comes near the poem writing area and shows her artwork to children)) This is my computer.
24. ((Reehyun and Jihyun go to Ara, look on her computer, and come back))
25. Reehyun: What do you like? ((Jihyun decorates her poem and does not respond)) I said what do you like? You can choose the same one.
26. Reehyun: Do you want me to choose?
27. Jihyun: Yes.
28. ((Jihyun writes a poem on the back of the paper))
29. Reehyun: This is a letter, a letter. You have to show your letter when you do it.
30. Jihyun: Reehyun, what do you like in here? ((shows the figure ruler))
31. Reehyun: Star.
32. Jihyun: You can only choose small ones. Three small ones.
33. Reehyun: This one.
34. Jihyun: Ice cream?
35. Naeun: ((gives her poem to Reehyun)) Here you are.
36. ((Reehyun looks at Naeun's poem))
37. Jihyun: What do you like more? You have to choose again. You have to keep choosing.
38. ((Reehyun looks at Naeun's poem and does not respond))
39. Jihyun: Reehyun, which figure do you like? Which figure do you like?
40. Reehyun: You choose for me.

The poem writing is one of the activities Somang teachers list as representing the unique and special aspects of their curriculum in that it aims to promote children's creativity and self-expression through encouragement of expressions free of pre-designated forms, means, or structures. Even though it is named as "poem writing," teachers do not impose conventional forms for the poems but expect children to express their unique selves using a variety of means including drawings, figures, and letters. Contrary to teachers' educational goal, however, children, as shown in this scene, produce poems that highly reflect the tastes and preferences of peers.

The movement starts by Reehyun who solicits an alliance with Naeun and Jihyun by prompting them to write a poem identical to hers (line 1) and Naeun and Jihyun write poems about Christmas following Reehyun's (lines 2–4). Even though the alliance formed through the Christmas poems included three children at first, the alignment structure shifts to a dyadic one as Jihyun writes about her relationships with Reehyun in her poem ("Jihyun ♡ Reehyun," line 5). In Jihyun's explicit attempts to make an alliance with Reehyun, Reehyun responds by making a poem that considers preferences and thoughts of Jihyun. From line 6, Reehyun closely consults with Jihyun in writing her poem by continuously asking for Jihyun's tastes and preferences. When a move that signals loosening of her coalition with Jihyun appears as in line 25, Reehyun tries to retain the collaborative alignment by forcing Jihyun to express her preferences. Furthermore, Reehyun defines their activity as "writing a letter" wherein they are expected show and share their expressions as reflected in her statement "This is a letter, a letter. You have to show your letter when you do it" in line 29. Here, the "poem writing" becomes an activity of "writing a letter." Reehyun's articulation of the activity as "writing a letter" successfully restores an alliance as reflected in Jihyun's constant asking of Reehyun's preferences in lines 30–34. The established coalition, however, soon shifts as Naeun offers her poem to Reehyun and Reehyun pays more attention to Naeun's poem than Jihyun's solicitation of alliance. Against Reehyun and Naeun's coalition, Jihyun from line 37 consistently asks Reehyun to present her preferences and tastes. For Jihyun, expressions in her poem are resources she employs in the dynamics of the two-against-one structure in which Reehyun and Naeun forge alliances while Jihyun herself is excluded.

Reehyun's statement that "this is a letter, a letter" clearly shows that expressions in this activity are not so much about manifesting one's inner thoughts, feelings, and ideas as they are about constructing an alignment structure that forges alliances with someone while excluding others from those relationships. That is, children strategically and creatively transform and reinterpret the activity designed to promote globally dominating socialization ideologies such as self-expression, creativity, or diversity into one that displays relationships with others and exerts social forces in the peer world. While teachers typically evaluate expressions in these activities as lacking creativity and being swayed by others, for children, expressions that reflect only their inner states rarely get valued in the children's social world as they do not exert any influence on children's societal and political spheres.

"I Drew You in My Picture": Reflecting Relationships in Expressions

If children in the above section produce expressions that reflect tastes and preferences of peers, they sometimes even explicitly represent their establishing and established relationships in expressions. The following interactions in the message center show how children actively use expression as a medium through which they display their collaborative and exclusive relationships with others, thereby utilizing their work to manipulate their fluctuating social relationships.

SCENE 4.7: "MESSAGE CENTER"

Participants: Nuri (girl, 4 years), Jiwon (girl, 4 years), Ayeon (girl, 4 years), Jihyun (girl, 4 years)

1. ((Nuri and Jiwon draw pictures in the message center))
2. ((Ayeon looks at them and brings small decorations from another table))
3. ((Nuri and Jiwon attach decorations to their pictures))
4. ((Ayeon looks at their pictures standing beside Jiwon and puts her arms around Jiwon's shoulders and looks at Jiwon's picture))
5. ((Nuri draws three persons in her picture and writes "Nuri baby" and "Ayeon mom" to mark two of them))
6. Nuri: ((to Ayeon)) Look, look! You're a mom.
7. ((Ayeon looks at Nuri's picture and moves beside Nuri))
8. ((Jiwon draws two persons similar to Nuri's in her picture and writes "Jiwon" and "mom" to mark them))
9. Nuri: ((to Ayeon)) Mom, you should look after this. ((Goes to the other table to get color pencils))
10. Jiwon: ((to Ayeon)) Mom, mom, mom. ((looks at Ayeon's picture)) Mom, what is this?
11. Nuri: ((comes back)) Ayeon, I'll be your sister.
12. ((Nuri erases "Nuri baby" and writes "Nuri sister"))
13. Nuri: Jiwon, you're a baby, right? I'll be a sister.
14. ((Nuri writes "Jiwon baby" on the person without name, to mark her))

In this segment of interactions, children strategically utilize expressions in their pictures to construct the "two against one" coalition in which two forge alliances while one is excluded from that relationship. The "two against one" dynamics begin when Ayeon in line 4 moves close to Jiwon, puts her arms around Jiwon's shoulders, and shifts her attention from pictures of Nuri and Jiwon to exclusively Jiwon's picture. Against Ayeon and Jiwon's emerging coalition, Nuri from line 5 draws a picture in which Ayeon and herself appear as main characters. By drawing two persons in her picture and identifying these two persons as "Nuri baby" and "Ayeon mom," Nuri actively attempts to forge alliances with Ayeon. The pretend frame of mom and baby that presupposes caring and affective relationships reinforces the collaborative structure that Nuri initiates.

As Nuri's strategy successfully forges alliances with Ayeon as indicated in Ayeon's behavior in line 7, Jiwon in line 8 adopts a similar strategy to Nuri's to challenge Nuri and Ayeon's alliances. That is, Jiwon draws two persons similar to ones in Nuri's picture and names them as a mom and herself. At the moments when

FIGURE 4.1A Transformation of Nuri's pictures

alignment structures are susceptible to change such as in line 9 when Nuri briefly leaves the table, both Nuri and Jiwon employ the pretend frame and utilize expressions in their pictures to negotiate the dynamics of the "two against one" structure. The "two against one" structure, however, also shifts as Nuri changes her role from baby to sister in lines 11 and 12 and identifies the third person as "Jiwon baby" in lines 13 and 14. That is, Nuri's inclusion of Jiwon in her picture initiates an alignment structure that embraces the three children instead of two. As before, Nuri strategically appropriates the contents of her picture in manipulating her relationships with the other two children.[2]

The message center[3] is an activity defined by Somang teachers as aiming to foster children's creativity and diversity. In contrast to the teachers' goal, however, children here transform it into a place in which they display, manipulate, and negotiate shifting social relationships. Similar interactions appear in the ensuing scenes.

15. Ayeon: ((holds the glue)) I grabbed this first, so I can lend . . .
16. ((Nuri snatches the glue from Ayeon))
17. ((Ayeon goes to the other table to get decorations))
18. Jiwon: Mom! Where's the mom?
19. ((Ayeon comes back and distributes decorations to Jiwon and Nuri))

"I WANT TO COPY MY BEST FRIEND'S ARTWORK"   91

FIGURE 4.1B Transformation of Nuri's pictures (lines 12, 14, Scene 4.7).

20. Jiwon: ((to Ayeon)) Please, please give me the glue, mom. ((Pretends to cry))
21. Ayeon: I need glue, Jiwon.
22. ((Nuri takes the glue))
23. Ayeon: Mom also needs the glue. ((Takes the glue and sticks the decorations on her picture))
24. Nuri: ((Jiwon)) Baby, look at this. ((Shows her picture))
25. Jiwon: Sister, yours are pretty.
26. Nuri: You are pretty, too. ((Points to Jiwon in her picture))
27. Jiwon: Yours are pretty, too. ((Points to Ayeon's picture))
28. Ayeon: Is my flower beautiful?
29. Nuri: ((to Jiwon)) You're an elementary school student and I'm a middle school student. You became a sister, right?
30. Jiwon: Am I five years old now, then?
31. Nuri: Ta-da. ((Shows her picture again))
32. Ayeon: Why is the cloth here so long?
33. Jiwon: ((points to Nuri and Jiwon in Nuri's picture)) Blue, blue ((points to blue colors of Nuri and Jiwon in the picture)). We two have beautiful things, so you ((Ayeon)) can't have a beautiful one.

Whereas interactions from lines 1–14 center on Nuri and Jiwon's competitive efforts to forge alliances with Ayeon, in this segment of the interactions, the focus shifts

FIGURE 4.2 Jiwon's picture is similar to Nuri's (lines 8, Scene 4.7).

to subtle conflicts between Ayeon and Nuri and their tensions around forging alliances with Jiwon. The shift emerges from lines 15 and 16 wherein Ayeon claims ownership of the glue and Nuri ignores this by grabbing the glue. Unlike Nuri who confronts Ayeon's possession of the glue, Jiwon acknowledges her ownership. In lines 18 and 20, Jiwon asks Ayeon for the glue by employing the previously established pretend frame in which Ayeon is a mom and Jiwon is a baby. However, as Ayeon refuses to lend the glue to Jiwon (line 21) and Nuri initiates a collaboration with Jiwon (line 24), the alignment structure that forges alliances between Nuri and Jiwon and excludes Ayeon from them emerges. From line 24, Nuri and Jiwon confer the roles of sister and baby to themselves following the characters of Nuri's picture and build an alliance through strategic appropriation of expressions in Nuri's picture. In line 26, for instance, Nuri praises Jiwon in her picture ("You are pretty, too") in response to Jiwon's favorable assessment of Nuri's picture. Jiwon even reinforces the "two against one" alignment structure in line 33 by pointing out that the dresses of Nuri and herself in the picture have parts colored blue while Ayeon's dress is void of the blue color. The expressions in children's productions are evidently a means of arranging, manipulating, and negotiating the fleeting collaborative and exclusive alignment structures of their peer world.

This is further evidenced in the ensuing interactions. In the following segment of interactions, the alignment structure that forges the alliance between Nuri and

"I WANT TO COPY MY BEST FRIEND'S ARTWORK"

FIGURE 4.3 Children pointing at pictures to negotiate alignment structure (lines 26, 27, 33, Scene 4.7).

Jiwon while excluding Ayeon from it shifts as a new member, Jihyun, enters into their interactive space.

34. Nuri: Let's play mom and dad.
35. Jihyun: ((comes to the message center)) I'd like to play, too. Let me in. Let me in.
36. Jiwon: ((to Jihyun)) You can't be a mom because it's already taken.
37. Nuri: Then how about we live in different countries?
38. Jihyun: Okay, I'll be a mom ((points to a mom in Nuri's picture)).
39. Jiwon: I'm a sister.
40. Nuri: Jihyun, which one is prettier? ((Points to her picture))
41. ((Jihyun points to Nuri in the picture))
42. Jiwon: Which one is prettier, Jihyun? ((Points to her picture))
43. ((Jihyun does not respond))
44. Jihyun: I'll be with Nuri, Bora, and Yuji.
45. Jiwon: I'll be with Nuri and Ayeon.
46. ((Jihyun hugs Nuri))
47. Nuri: Am I your mom? ((Smiles))
48. ((Jihyun keeps hugging Nuri))
49. Nuri: Jihyun, please. ((Flees from Jihyun smiling))
50. ((Jihyun follows Nuri by crawling and pretending to cry))

94 BETWEEN SELF AND COMMUNITY

51. ((Jiwon looks at Jihyun and Nuri and holds Ayeon's hands))
52. Nuri: ((to Jihyun)) I hung up this in this way. ((Puts her picture up)) So you can see it whenever you want.
53. ((Jihyun looks at Nuri's picture standing beside Nuri))
54. ((Nuri goes to bathroom))
55. ((Jihyun crawls to Jiwon and pretends to cry))
56. ((Jiwon does not respond))
57. ((Jihyun goes back to her seat))
58. Jiwon: ((to Ayeon)) Would you like to play princess?
59. Ayeon: No.
60. Jiwon: ((to Nuri)) We two were together, right? Not Ayeon, right?
61. ((Nuri draws a picture with the figure ruler and writes Jihyun in the picture and gives it to her))

The new alignment structure arises as Jihyun comes to the message center expressing her wishes to join the play in line 35. Unlike Jiwon who tries to protect their interactive space by arguing that the role of mom is already taken (line 36), Nuri provides room for Jihyun to join by employing another pretend frame—that is, the frame of living in different countries ("Then how about we live in different countries?" line 37). Through Nuri's offer, Jihyun successfully enters into the play, and the alliance of Jihyun and Nuri afterward gets strengthened as Jihyun asymmetrically responds to Nuri and Jiwon's strategic utilizations of their productions. For instance, Jihyun affirms Nuri's pretend frame and appropriation of pictures by employing paralinguistic behavior of pointing to the mom in Nuri's picture, willingly taking the role of mom in line 38, and pointing to Nuri as prettier than Jiwon in Nuri's picture in line 41. On the other hand, in line 43, Jihyun refuses to forge alliances with Jiwon by not responding to Jiwon's solicitation of making an alliance through utilization of her own picture.

Both Nuri and Jihyun continuously endeavor to maintain their alliances in the ensuing interactions. In lines 46–50, Jihyun actively adopts the pretend frame and the accompanying emotional behaviors such as hugging and crying to make caring relationships with Nuri clear. Nuri also endorses Jihyun's attempts and further reinforces their relationships by reminding them of the pretend frame constructed through her picture. In line 52, Nuri states that "I hung up this in this way. So you can see it whenever you want" and holds up her picture. Jiwon who has been excluded from Nuri and Jihyun's alliance attempts to solicit an alliance with Ayeon in lines 51 and 58 and also with Nuri in line 60, but her attempts are limited by Nuri's movement to reinforce her collaboration with Jihyun by creating the picture in which Jihyun appears as a main character and offering it to Jihyun.

The alignment structure later shifts again as Nuri adopts another frame of playing princess and attempts to forge alliances with Jiwon by conferring the role of sister to Jiwon while Nuri herself takes the role of princess. Nuri's picture in

"I WANT TO COPY MY BEST FRIEND'S ARTWORK" 95

FIGURE 4.4 Final product of Nuri's picture (Scene 4.7).

figure 4.4 shows how her expressions changed reflecting their fleeting and fluctuating social relationships.

These interactions, which lasted for forty-five minutes, demonstrate that expressions in these children's social worlds rarely reflect their inner states primarily as desired by teachers but are resources children as social actors utilize, appropriate, and manipulate to exert certain effects on their political and societal spheres. Children's adoption of the pretend frame in their pictures as well as in their interactive space, in particular, facilitates and elaborates the strategic use of expressions as the pretend frame provides more room for children to creatively arrange and negotiate alignment structures. As noted by other studies on children's pretend play (Griswold 2007; Sheldon 1996), the pretend frame blurs the distinctions between children and their characters, therefore taking some of the responsibilities away from the child for what he or she is saying. Likewise, under the pretend frame, the children in the above scene navigated a variety of alignment structures without being constrained too much by social relationships existing in the real peer world. The strategy of utilizing expressions in one's pictures rather than directly expressing one's thoughts and intentions toward others also mitigates the burdens and risks one might experience in direct confrontations and oppositions. When the pretend frame is combined with the appropriation of expressions in one's works, it further eases children from strains, responsibilities, and worries ensuing from their opposing and exclusive utterances and behaviors toward peers.

96 BETWEEN SELF AND COMMUNITY

If interactions in the scene above involved subtle confrontations and oppositions, children also make more explicit movements as the following interaction
between Yubin and Misoo illustrates.

SCENE 4.8: "ARTWORK AREA"

Participants: Yubin (girl, 5 years), Misoo (girl, 5 years), Jihoon (boy, 5 years), Haejin
(girl, 5 years), Ms. Choo (teacher)

1. ((Children are drawing and writing on papers))
2. Misoo: ((to Jihoon)) I'm drawing you in my picture.
3. ((Jihoon looks at Misoo and smiles))
4. ((Haejin stretches her body to look at Misoo's picture))
5. Misoo: ((to Haejin)) You're here, too. ((Points to a girl in the picture))
6. ((Misoo draws a person in the picture))
7. Misoo: ((to Ms. Choo)) I'm drawing a picture about Yubin. She's peeing.
8. Yubin: Why are you doing it only to me? ((Cries))
9. Haejin: Why is Yubin crying?
10. Misoo: No, that's how I want to draw.
11. Yubin: But your friend does not like it.
12. Ms. Choo: ((in a stern voice)) Yubin.
13. Misoo: Is it okay if you wash your hands?
14. Yubin: Yes ((nods)).

In this scene, Misoo actively builds alliances with Jihoon and Haejin by drawing
them in her picture. She first forges collaboration with Jihoon by stating that Jihoon
is in her picture (line 2) and then also drags Haejin into their alliance as Haejin
displays interest in their collaboration through bodily movement (line 4). Whereas
Misoo includes Jihoon and Haejin into her alliance structure, she excludes Yubin
from the alliance by drawing her as a ridiculous figure in her picture. In line 7, she
states to Ms. Choo that she is drawing Yubin in her picture as behaving absurdly
("I'm drawing a picture about Yubin. She's peeing"). As Yubin's emotional behavior of crying and complaining in line 8 suggest, Misoo's drawings in her picture
are an enactment of exclusion that exerts effects on their social relationships. Even
though Misoo invokes the frame of artwork and individuated expression ("No,
that's how I want to draw," line 10) to defend her movement of exclusion, the ensuing interactions that involve Misoo and Yubin's negotiations of Yubin's appearance
in Misoo's picture demonstrate that Misoo's expressions in her picture are rarely
a reflection of individuated thoughts, feelings, or preferences but a performative
act that creates an exclusive relationship in their social sphere.

"Yours Look Strange": Evaluation as Collaborative and Exclusive Acts

If children in the cases so far presented strategically appropriated expressions of
their creations such as artwork, pictures, or poems to negotiate and manipulate

"I WANT TO COPY MY BEST FRIEND'S ARTWORK" 97

social relationships, they also actively used evaluation of their products as a means for forging alliances and exclusions. As discussed in chapter 3, teachers typically criticize evaluative practices prevalent in children's peer interactions for hindering cultivation of children's authenticity and creativity and attribute them to the influences of the outside world wherein characteristically Korean traditional socialization practices such as standardization and uniformity linger on. The evaluative practice in children's worlds, however, rarely means assessing one's performance based on the standardized or uniform criteria as often regarded by teachers but frequently acts as a communicative means for creating social inclusions and exclusions.

In the following scenes, for instance, children speak highly of others' creations to address their immediate social goals of entering into existing play and building collaborative relationships with peers.

SCENE 4.9: "MESSAGE CENTER"

Participants: Minsu (boy, 4 years), Hajin (boy, 4 years), Jungjin (boy, 4 years)

1. ((Minsu sits in one corner of the message center and makes artwork using stickers))
2. ((Hajin and Jungjin come near Minsu))
3. Jungjin: Wow, it's pretty.
4. Hajin: Wow, it's pretty.
5. ((Hajin and Jungjin sit beside Minsu and make their artwork))
6. Hajin: I'm gonna attach a national flag sticker.
7. Jungjin: I'm not gonna attach a national flag sticker.
8. Hajin: Wow, I found the sticker ((picks up the national flag sticker)).
9. Jungjin: Minsu, we live together right?
10. Minsu: Yes.
11. ((Jungjin decorates his artwork with the stamp))
12. Hajin: Let me use it, too.
13. ((Jungjin refuses to give the stamp to Hajin))
14. ((Hajin puts his hand on Jungjin's hand and pushes the stamp))
15. Jungjin: No.

SCENE 4.10: "ARTWORK AREA"

Participants: Jihoon (boy, 5 years), Lin (girl, 4 years)

1. ((Jihoon comes to the artwork area and approaches Lin))
2. Jihoon: ((looks at Lin's picture)) Lin's is pretty. Lin's is pretty. Lin's is pretty.
3. Lin: ((touches Jihoon's face)) You're pretty, too. You're pretty, too.
4. Jihoon: ((smiles)) Lin's is pretty.

In scene 4.9, Hajin and Jungjin compliment Minsu's artwork to enter into the interactive space Minsu already occupies (lines 3–4). Given that the ensuing interactions rarely involve Minsu's active participation but rather center on Hajin and Jungji's conflicts, their compliments "Wow, it's pretty" is one of the access skills they employ to meet their momentary social goal of entering into play. Similarly, in scene 4.10, Jihoon abruptly applauds Lin's picture to join the activity and build a collaborative relationship with Lin. Lin's response to Jihoon's compliments clearly shows that evaluative remarks on others' creations and toward others themselves bear the same meanings and functions in the children's social world. That is, in line 3, Lin states to Jihoon that "you're pretty, too. You're pretty, too" in response to Jihoon's praise of Lin's artwork. Here, Jihoon's "Lin's is pretty" and Lin's "You're pretty" are deployed with the same intentions and effects— that is, to create an alliance for play. Lin's paralinguistic behavior of touching Jihoon's face, along with her compliments, especially demonstrates that complimentary remarks toward others' creations are actions of alliance and collaboration in children's social world. The meanings and functions evaluative remarks have in the children's social world are also manifested in the following interaction between two best friends.

SCENE 4.11: "RUBBER BAND PLAY"

Participants: Sungeun (girl, 3 years), Jeemin (girl, 3 years)

1. ((Children are linking rubber bands at the boards))
2. ((Sungeun and Jeemin come to the table))
3. ((Sungeun takes the last board left and links rubber bands at her board))
4. ((Jeemin, without a board, plays with rubber bands))
5. Jeemin: ((puts rubber bands on her wrist and shows to Sungeun)) Is this pretty?
6. Sungeun: No.
7. Jeemin: Is this pretty?
8. Sungeun: No.
9. Jeemin: Is this pretty?
10. Sungeun: No.
11. Jeemin: ((raises voice)) I'm saying is this pretty? I'm saying is this pretty?
12. Sungeun: No.
13. Jeemin: ((raises voice)) No, I'm saying is this pretty?
14. Sungeun: No.
15. Jeemin: ((shouts)) Hey, I'm saying is this pretty?
16. Sungeun: Don't be my friend.
17. Jeemin: What? What did you just say?
18. ((Sungeun does not respond))
19. Jeemin: ((in an angry voice)) I'd like to make a red ring.
20. Sungeun: Okay.
21. Jeemin: ((puts the red rubber band on her finger and shows to Sungeun)) How is this?
22. Sungeun: Gorgeous.

Jeemin and Sungeun are close friends who tend to go through everyday routines side by side in the Arum Room. In this scene, Jeemin and Sungeun participate in the rubber band activity together and Jeemin continuously seeks compliments about her rubber band artwork from her best friend Sungeun. Jeemin employs various strategies such as raising her voice and expressing frustration to get Sungeun's recognition, but Sungeun continuously refuses to compliment her work. As Jeemin's demand for compliment escalates, Sungeun in line 16 withdraws her friendship with Jeemin by stating, "Don't be my friend." Sungeun's statement, here, indicates that complimentary remarks are not so much an opinion one has toward others' creations as a performative act of maintaining and negotiating social relationships. As Jeemin confronts Sungeun's withdrawal of friendship by having her articulate the intention of ending their relationships once more ("What? What did you just say?" line 17), Sungeun finally recedes and applauds Jeemin's new creation by evaluating it as gorgeous. For these two close friends, compliments are emblems of friendships that confirm and reinforce their intimacy and closeness.

If these two children negotiate their social distance through the issue of giving compliments, children also make an exclusive movement by providing negative evaluations toward others' creations. In the following scene, the five-year-old children challenge Sowon's attempts to join their group by consistently giving negative assessments of Sowon's picture.

SCENE 4.12: "ARTWORK AREA"

Participants: Sowon (girl, 4 years), Misoo (girl, 5 years), Soojung (girl, 5 years), Suji (girl, 5 years), Jihoon (boy, 5 years)

1. Misoo: Transform to chicken!
2. Jihoon: Transform to chicken!
3. Soojung: Let's eat chicken.
4. Jihoon: Let's eat chicken.
5. Sowon: ((gives her picture to Misoo)) Sister, here you are.
6. ((Sowon leaves to go to the other side of the classroom))
7. Misoo: Isn't this picture weird?
8. Soojung: It looks completely ridiculous.
9. ((Sowon comes back))
10. Suji: The head is pretty, but except the head, everything else looks weird.
11. Misoo: What is this? What is this? It looks like a cat. ((Laughs))
12. Misoo: ((points to the person in the picture)) Sowon, why is this woman's nose in this way?
13. Soojung: Why does the eye look like a shining hamster?
14. Jihoon: It looks like a witch. ((Laughs))
15. Suji: It looks like a witch. ((Laughs))
16. ((Sowon leaves))

In this scene, Sowon seeks to access the interactive space five-year-old children occupy by offering her picture to Misoo (line 5). Misoo, on the other hand, signals refusal to forge a collaborative relationship with her by appraising Sowon's picture as "weird." The other children in the artwork table afterward sequentially and collaboratively produce negative assessments of Sowon's picture and Sowon finally leaves at the end of this interaction. Children's evaluative remarks themselves seem to be straightforward and open thoughts and opinions they have toward their peer's performance. The statements even contain very detailed and specific assessments of Sowon's picture. Moreover, the expressive forms children utilize in the evaluations above are the ones expected to be displayed in formal educational contexts. Children, for instance, are asked to provide detailed descriptions of their artwork or weekend experiences using expressive forms similar to the ones in the above scene during group times or weekend story time. Utilizing similar forms of expressions, however, children seek to exert exclusions in their social sphere. As much as Sowon's offer of her creation to Misoo is a means of seeking affiliation, the other children's negative appraisals of Sowon's picture are acts of ostracization. Given that the children adopt the expressive form expected in the explicit curriculum, it is not the case that children do not yet possess self-expressive forms and other accompanying values such as self-confidence, creativity, or diversity as often criticized and assumed by teachers, but they are already equipped with these and even have abilities to strategically appropriate and transform them to address their social goals.

Expressions as Power, Authority, and Hierarchy

Expressions in children's social world are not only means of constructing a collaborative and exclusive social structure but also resources for pursuing social hierarchy, another major theme of Somang children's culture-laden social world. Whereas teachers endeavor to persuade children of the value of diversity in expressions, children rarely perceive expressions as having distinct and equivalent qualities but as semiotic resources that enable them to gain power and authority in the fluctuating local social order. Children, therefore, display keen interest in comparing, competing, and ranking expressions of one another and make use of expressions in coconstructing stratified social organization.

"Mine Is Better than Yours": Expressions as Competition and Authority

The meaning of expressions as semiotic resources for pursuing power and authority in children's peer world are often manifested in ways children transform the official curriculum designed to promote self-expression and creativity into a place of competition and hierarchy as the following interactions in the wire play area illustrate.

SCENE 4.13: "WIRE PLAY AREA"

Participants: Jina (girl, 3 years), Sol (girl, 3 years), Jin (girl, 3 years), Seoyun (girl, 3 years), Haeun (girl, 3 years), Yujung (girl, 3 years), Ms. Chung (teacher)

1. Jina: ((to Seoyun)) Yours are not pretty. Mine is prettier than yours.
2. Jina: ((to Yujung)) Yours are not pretty.
3. Seoyun: ((to Yujung)) Mine is pretty, right?
4. ((Yujung nods))
5. Seoyun: You have to say pretty, right? You have to say pretty to your friends, right?
6. Seoyun: ((to Ms. Chung)) Seoyun got hurt, right?
7. ((Ms. Chung nods))
8. Jina: ((touches Haeun's wire)) Hey, what is this?
9. Sol: ((to Jina)) I'm gonna make this and give it to you.
10. ((Sol throws several wires with heart shape on the table))
11. Seoyun: ((picks up the heart-shaped wire and takes it)) Yo-ho, Yo-ho!
12. Jina: ((looks at Seoyun)) What's yo-ho, yo-ho all about?
13. ((Haeun takes a heart-shaped wire and adds more shapes to it by twisting the other side of the wire))
14. ((Seoyun gazes at Haeun))
15. ((Jina gazes at Haeun and twists the wire following Haeun))
16. Haeun: ((shows her wire)) Look. Look.
17. Seoyun: You make it well.
18. ((Haeun gives it to Seoyun))
19. Haeun: ((takes the wire from Seoyun)) Wait, I have to decorate it more. ((Goes to the other side of the classroom))
20. Seoyun: I have to decorate it more. ((Follows Haeun))
21. Haeun: ((comes back and holds her wire up)) Who wants to have this?
22. Jina: Me. ((raises her hand))
23. Haeun: ((gives the wire to Jina)) Then who wants to have it next?
24. ((Sol raises her hand))
25. Jina: ((makes a heart shape using wire)) This is what I made. Who wants to have this?
26. Seoyun: Me ((raises her hand)).
27. ((Ms. Chung makes her own wire artwork and puts it on her wrist))
28. Seoyun: Teacher, I made this.
29. Ms. Chung: Seoyun, look at mine ((shows her wrist)).
30. ((Seoyun goes beside Ms. Chung and winds her wire around Ms. Chung's finger))
31. ((Jin stares at Seoyun and Ms. Chung))
32. ((Jin comes to me and winds her wire around my wrist))

Participants in this scene pay keen attention to others' expressions, make concerted efforts to compare expressions of one another, and aim to gain dominant positions in these comparative and competitive interactions. Argumentation about social status mediated through expressions starts from Jina who evaluates Seoyun's and Yujung's wire artwork in a degrading manner ("Yours are not pretty," lines 1–2) and compares her own work as superior to theirs ("Mine is prettier than yours," line 1). Seoyun challenges Jina's claim by eliciting an affirmative response from Yujung (lines 3–4) and assessing Jina's negative appraisal of her peers' artwork as morally wrong ("You have to say pretty to your friends, right?" "Seoyun got hurt, right?" lines 5–6). In the subsequent interactions, Jina continues to speak of others' artwork in downgrading ways to occupy a better position in competitive interactions (lines 8 and 12).

If the competitive structure initially centered on children's incessant jockeying for a better position, the dominant status starts to anchor in one child from line 13, as Haeun displays her skill of adding more shapes to the wire by twisting the other side of the wire. The other children steadily and admiringly gaze at Haeun's adept hand movements and endeavor to make the same shape by copying Haeun's hand gestures (lines 14–15). Haeun, at the same time, claims and reinforces her dominant status by producing ritualistic statements that have an effect of temporarily occupying an authoritative status in the children's authority structure established during their competitive talk and interactions. Haeun states, "Look, look," "Who wants to have this?" and "Then who wants to have it next?" and exhibits her artwork to peers in lines 16, 21, and 23. These statements "Look" and "Who wants to have this?" which occur prevalently in children's peer talk draw the attention of peers to one's own artwork and position that work as desirable so that others wish to possess it. Here, Haeun also adopts these ritualistic routines to achieve authority. The attempts to establish authority through these statements get accomplished as other children affirmatively respond to her as shown in lines 17, 22, and 24.

As Jina and Seoyun similarly produce these ritualistic routines in lines 25 and 28, Ms. Chung who has cut wires and provided them to children sitting at the corner of the table without intervening in the children's interactions, playfully participates in these authority-seeking interactions. In line 29, she states to Seoyun, "Seoyun, look at mine" and shows her own artwork to Seoyun who showed off her wire to Ms. Chung. Ms. Chung's participation soon arouses another competitive structure in which Seoyun and Jin competitively decorate Ms. Chung's finger and my wrist with their own wire works (lines 30–32). As Seoyun decorates Ms. Chung's finger with her wire, Jin gazes at it for a while and then utilizes me as a decorating object to compete with Seoyun.

In this segment of interactions, power asymmetry among children rapidly fluctuates. It starts from participants jockeying for authority and status through evaluative and comparative commentaries, shifts to a hierarchical structure in which one child occupies a relatively dominant status, and finally moves to children's competition over drawing adults into their creations. As the hierarchical social relationships and structures fluctuate, children's expressions also change. If everyone makes heart-shaped wire works from lines 1 to 12, participants' attention shifts to Haeun's creation which adds more shapes to the previous one from lines 13 to 26 and then to decorating adults' hands from lines 27 to 32.

Although Ms. Chung playfully showed off her wire work to Seoyun in the scene above, her participation in children's competitive interactions was, at the same time, an expression of frustration. As Ms. Sung, the other teacher of Arum Room approached Ms. Chung right after the scene above, Ms. Chung told her, "Maybe we need something more here. Something more difficult or some other materials. They're all making the same things again." As alluded to in this statement, Ms. Chung, dissatisfied with the educational outcomes of this activity, self-mockingly joined children's uniformity-seeking and competition-oriented interactions. She then decides to modify the activity to correct children's practice of "making the same things" and to properly instigate children's diversity and creativity. Although children's pursuit of competition, comparison, and uniformity is a problematic outcome for teachers as shown in Ms. Chung's reaction, children's expressions are bound to these values because expressions gain meanings only when they can be utilized as resources for negotiating one's relative status with one another in the stratified peer world. Also, even though the final products might look identical to teachers as reflected in Ms. Chung's statement "They're all making same things again," close observations of children's creations show the changes of expressions along with the pursuit of uniformity in expressions. That is, children's expressions transform reflecting their fluctuating hierarchical local social order. Although transformation of expressions in the above scene is not an individuated creative self-expression as desired by teachers, children nonetheless do exhibit diverse forms of expressions in the process of evaluating and comparing statuses of one another.

The children in the following scene also produce diverse forms of expressions and strategically utilize them in competition and comparison-oriented interactions.

SCENE 4.14: "ARTWORK AREA"

Participants: Yubin (girl, 5 years), Nuri (girl, 4 years), Bora (girl, 4 years), Sowon (girl, 4 years)

1. Yubin: Hey, if you go to Kim's club . . . You have four five hundred coins? Coins? There's the one like this ((points to her picture)). If you push there, the one like this comes out ((shows her jewel box to Nuri)).
2. Nuri: Really?
3. Yubin: Yes, but you have to find the jewel box there.
4. Nuri: Sister, how many jewel boxes do you have?
5. ((Yubin does not respond))
6. Nuri: Only this one?

104 BETWEEN SELF AND COMMUNITY

7. Nuri: I have six. Then I have five more ((shows her five fingers)).
8. Nuri: I like drawing only one piece of hair.
9. Yubin: I'll draw this one in this way. Would you like to have this?
10. ((Nuri does not respond))
11. Nuri: Sister, which princess would you like to have?
12. Yubin: Heart princess.
13. Yubin: I'll dress up this. ((Dresses up the character of her picture))
14. Nuri: ((gazes at Yubin's picture)) In fact, I'll do dressing up, too. ((Draws a dress in her picture))
15. Yubin: Nuri, look at mine ((shows her picture)).
16. Nuri: Okay.
17. ((Yubin writes Nintendo on her picture and shows it to Nuri))
18. Nuri: ((to Bora who sits next to Nuri)) Bora, which of us did better? Yubin sister or me?
19. ((Bora does not respond))
20. Nuri: ((to the researcher)) Teacher, I made this flower with Mom last weekend. ((Shows the paper flower to me))
21. Researcher: Wow, that's pretty.
22. Nuri: This is a carnation.
23. Sowon: Belly button, Belly button. Ha, ha, ha. ((Points to the belly button of the person in her picture))

In this scene, the two children construct an opposing and confrontational social relationship in which they incessantly negotiate their relative social status and positions. Yubin draws the picture about her weekend experiences and explains the details of her picture, especially about the jewelry box she received from a toy vending machine in the supermarket during the weekend and brought to school, to Nuri. In response to Yubin's description of her picture and the jewelry box, Nuri in line 4 turns the interaction into competitive talk by asking Yubin, "How many jewel boxes do you have?" As Yubin does not answer her question, Nuri attempts to occupy the higher position by affirming the number of Yubin's jewel box(es) as "only one" ("Only this one?" line 6) and claiming hers as six ("I have six. Then I have five more," line 7). Against Nuri's move, Yubin in line 9 employs the ritualistic statement "Would you like to have this?" to gain authority in this competition. Nuri then refuses to approve of Yubin's position by ignoring her question and instead producing a question that presumes and enforces Yubin's taking of Nuri's picture, thereby positioning Yubin lower than Nuri ("Sister, which princess would you like to have?" line 11). In the subsequent interactions, Yubin continues to explain details of her picture along with adoption of ritualistic routines such as "Look at mine" to occupy a dominant position in her competition with Nuri. Nuri also attempts to gain a higher status by copying Yubin's picture and inviting others as referees of their competition. In line 18, Nuri states to Bora, "Bora, which of us did better, Yubin sister or me?" Later, as Bora refuses to judge their expressions,

"I WANT TO COPY MY BEST FRIEND'S ARTWORK" 105

Nuri draws me into the competition and shows the artwork she made during the weekend to me.

In these competitive and authority-seeking interactions between two children, the children not only produce similar pictures and use them as resources to evaluate each other's skills but also employ various forms of expressions to compete and gain higher status in the competition. Although teachers often criticize children's expressions created in contexts like that above as uniform, children produce both uniform and diverse expressions and employ the one that suits better their immediate social goals. For instance, Nuri in line 14 argues that she is dressing up the character in her picture as Yubin does and draws her character similarly to Yubin's to compete with her. However, when Nuri invites me as a referee of their competition in line 20, she utilizes a different expression from Yubin's as a resource to occupy a higher status. That is, she shows the paper flower she made with her mom during the weekend to compete with Yubin's jewelry box. Similarly, in line 23, Sowon joins these competitive interactions by making use of her picture which is dissimilar. Sowon even tries to get attention from the others by drawing a comic character and making fun of her picture ("Belly button, belly button. Ha, ha, ha"), a strategy distinct from that of Yubin and Nuri who tend to claim the superiority of their expressions based on an aesthetic viewpoint and qualities such as prettiness. The distinction of uniformity and diversity, then, does not have the meanings in the children's social world that they do in the teachers' stratified socialization ideologies. The expressions, whether uniform or diverse, gain meaning only when they can be used to exert certain effects in the children's social sphere where members constantly jockey for power and authority.

"You're the Last": Pursuing Explicit Rankings of Expressions

Children's hierarchical and stratified social structure is frequently achieved through explicit ranking of their expressions. Although teachers endeavor to persuade children of the meaninglessness and impossibility of standardized evaluation of their self-expressions, children enjoy and display keen interest in ranking their own expressions themselves. In the following scene, the children in the poem writing area rank their performances and argue over where they stand with respect to one another in terms of various features of poem writing.

SCENE 4.15: "POEM WRITING AREA"

Participants: Soojung (girl, 4 years), Misoo (girl, 4 years), Jihoon (boy, 4 years), Ms. Shim (teacher)

1. Misoo: If I finish this one, I'll be three.
2. Jihoon: I wrote two.
3. Soojung: I wrote four (*neykay*). I'm the first. I win. You're the last ((points to Jihoon)). You're the second.

106 BETWEEN SELF AND COMMUNITY

4. Misoo: But you said *leykay*.
5. Misoo: But you said leykay.
6. Misoo: Leykay, leykay, leykay. ((Laughs))
7. Soojung: ((in a crying voice)) Teacher, Misoo said . . .
8. Jihoon: If you cry about it, you can't be a Rainbow Room member.
9. Ms. Shim: Did you feel bad? You might feel bad, but it's not such a bad incident.

The move for ranking emerges as Misoo declares the number of poems she will be finishing, and Jihoon responds to her attempts by announcing the number of his poems as two. Soojung then claims that she wrote four poems and ranks the relative positions of Misoo, Jihoon, and herself. Soojung explicitly states that she occupies the highest position while Misoo and Jihoon follow her as the second and the last. Against Soojung's construction of a stratified social structure in which Soojung herself holds the highest status, Misoo challenges Soojung's ranking by producing a series of evaluative commentaries on Soojung's remark of "I wrote four." In lines 4–6, Misoo points out Soojung's slurred pronunciation of "four" (neykay) as "leykay" and mocks her pronunciation to negate the legitimacy of the ranking Soojung declared. Jihoon also takes an opposing stance toward Soojung by problematizing Soojung's emotional behavior of crying as inappropriate for members of the Rainbow Room. Here, Jihoon tries to control the emotional behavior of Soojung by creatively adopting teachers' socialization discourses that utilize age, role, and membership in disciplining children as discussed in the previous chapter.

In a similar context, the two children in the following scene argue over the ranking of their expressions and adopt a variety of skills and resources to achieve better positions in the ranking.

SCENE 4.16: "ENGLISH CLASS"

Participants: Jungyoon (girl, 3 years), Yujung (girl, 3 years)

1. ((Children put small ornaments in their English workbooks))
2. Jungyoon: You're the last. You're the last.
3. Yujung: No.
4. Jungyoon: ((points to small ornaments)) You have this much left. ((Points to places in the English workbook)) You don't have any here. You have too many empty places here.
5. Jungyoon: Would you like to see mine? Would you like to see mine? Would you like to see mine? This is a *saca* (lion). A saca (lion) ((shows her English workbook to Yujung)).
6. Yujung: Not a saca ((in Korean)). It's a lion ((in English)). A lion ((in English)).
7. Jungyoon: I'm wearing a skirt. ((Stands up and turns around holding her skirt))
8. Yujung: I'm wearing a skirt, too.
9. Jungyoon: That's a dress.
10. Yujung: It's also a skirt.

Argumentation over ranking emerges as Jungyoon asserts Yujung is the last one to finish the English class activity by explicitly stating "You're the last." As Yujung negates Jungyoon's ranking, Jungyoon affirms the ranking by pointing out the incompleteness of Yujung's performances in detail (line 4). Furthermore, she adopts a comparative framework and seeks higher status by employing the ritualistic statement "Would you like to see mine?" several times in line 5. Against Jungyoon's ranking, Yujung pinpoints Jungyoon's naming of the lion in her English workbook in Korean (saca) as incorrect and states, "A lion" in English. Here, Yujung actively makes use of her knowledge of English vocabulary to attain a better standing in the competition. Along with the ensuing interactions in which Jungyoon and Yujung employ their outfits to challenge each other, the overall focus of interactions centers on ranking their expressions, performances, and knowledge and debating where they stand relative to each other in terms of these issues. Similarly, the children in the following scene transform educational activity into a site of competition and ranking.

SCENE 4.17: "CREATIVE READING CLASS"

Participants: Haejin (girl, 5 years), Sujung (girl, 5 years), Ms. Kim (teacher), Ms. Shim (teacher)

1. Haejin: Yay, I got it right.
2. Sujung: Yay, I got it right twice.
3. Haejin: So what?
4. Ms. Kim: Why do you think the mom screamed?
5. Sujung: Because the cat ran away.
6. Ms. Kim: Yes. The cat ran away.
7. Sujung: I got all the right answers.
8. Haejin: No, you didn't get all the right answers.
9. Sujung: Yes, I did get all the right answers. I'm the first, Junhuyk is the second, and you're the last.
10. Haejin: So what?
11. Sujung: Teacher, I think Mom will run after the cat because she
12. Haejin: Cats will . . . Cats will
13. Ms. Shim: Hey, guys. If you speak at the same time, we can't hear. It's not important who does more. Let's wait till others finish.

In these interactions, Haejin and Sujung argue over who got more right answers and rank themselves in terms of the number of answers they gave. Ms. Kim, the creative reading class teacher, constantly asks questions about the storybook while reading the book to children to have them express their thoughts and feelings about the story. Whereas Ms. Kim uses this pedagogical method to provide opportunities for children to express their authenticity and creativity, children conceive of their comments as a competition in which they can establish peer hierarchy through ranking. For children, educational activities like the above are places wherein they jockey for power and authority and rank their performances and accomplishments rather than sites of self-expression and creativity.

"Copying Expressions" and "Copying Behaviors": No Distinctions of Educational and Mundane Contexts in Children's Peer World

As seen so far, expressions in children's phenomenal social world are resources for building differentiated, stratified, and hierarchical social relationships. Distinct from meanings teachers typically attribute to expressions in ideational and educational contexts, children coconstruct their own meanings for expressions loaded with values of collaboration, exclusion, authority, and power. Along with these highly contrasting values and meanings children and teachers respectively attach to self-expression, another salient feature that distinguishes expressions in the children's peer world from expressions in the world the teachers aim to construct is children's systemic and coherent pursuit of these values in both educational and mundane contexts. That is, whereas teachers practice contradictory ideas regarding children's self-expressions depending on the contexts of enactment as seen in chapter 3, children tend not to distinguish educational and mundane contexts and rather pursue homogenous and consistent values in both contexts. Children develop their own sophisticated interactional routines and practices for expressions and employ them consistently in both noneducational and educational realms.

Eating Rituals and Seeking Communality and Hierarchy

The eating ritual Somang children develop on their own nicely illustrates how children develop their own interactional routines for constructing a differentiated and hierarchical social structure and invariably use them in both formal educational and everyday mundane realms. Similar to findings of ritualized communicative acts in other peer cultures (Boggs 1978; Goodwin 1980; Katriel 1987; Morgan, O'Neill, and Harré 1979; Mishler 1979), this eating ritual called *ttala meki* has its own sophisticated communicative rules, structures, and act sequences. The term *ttala meki* is a compound word composed of the verbal root of *ttala-hata* (follow or copy) and the noun form of *mek-ta* (eat) and therefore literally means "following or copying others' eating." In practice, it is enacted in ways such that one follows various features of others' eating practices including selection of food items, procedures, or methods as the following scene illustrates.

SCENE 4.18: "LUNCHTIME"

Participants: Jiwhan (boy, 5 years), Seunghoon (boy, 4 years), Wobin (boy, 4 years), Yeonu (boy, 4 years), Minseo (boy, 4 years), Jihyuk (boy, 4 years), Yunwoo (boy, 5 years), Ms. Park (teacher)

"I WANT TO COPY MY BEST FRIEND'S ARTWORK" 109

1. Jiwhan: ((to Seunghoon and Wobin) Let's eat together with other boys.
2. ((Seunghoon and Wobin nod and sit at the table))
3. Seunghoon: ((Yeonu, Minseo, and Jihyuk approach the table)) Let's eat together with our friends, these boys.
4. Wobin: Let's eat together with friends, these boys.
5. Jiwhan: We boy friends will do ttala meki, right?
6. ((Seunghoon and Yeonu nod))
7. Wobin: Let's leave Yunwoo brother out.
8. Ms. Park: Friends, Yunwoo brother will be very sad if he hears it.
9. Wobin: Teacher, we boy friends eat together.
10. Ms. Park: Good for you.
11. Jiwhan: We're gonna do ttala meki, right? I'll do first.
12. Yeonu: ((points to Jiwhan and Seunghoon)) Jiwhan, Seunghoon.
13. Wobin: No, Jiwhan, me, and Seunghoon.
14. Jiwhan: No ((points to Minseo)), he has to go first. He has to go.
15. Jiwhan: I'm the first. Eat eggs.
16. Jiwhan: ((takes a spoon from his lunch box and makes a funny gesture)) Oh, oh, oh, oh.
17. ((Others all laugh))
18. Jiwhan: Eat eggs.
19. ((Other children pick up eggs and eat them))
20. Wobin: Put anchovies on the rice.
21. ((Other children put anchovies on the rice))
22. ((Wobin eats anchovies and rice))
23. ((Others eat anchovies and rice))
24. Seunghoon: Eat soup.
25. ((Seunghoon eats a spoonful of miso soup))
26. ((Others eat a spoonful of miso soup))

As children's interactions in this scene show, Somang children's eating ritual typically consists of four steps of interactional sequences; recruiting members (lines 1–10), deciding turns of commands (lines 11–14), issuing an order (lines 15–18, 20, 22, 24–25), and carrying out the order (lines 19, 21, 23, 26). From the beginning of the scene, Jiwhan solicits collaborations with other children by referring to them as boys and friends and offering to eat lunch together. The other children consolidate the emerging collaborative structure by repeating Jiwhan's statement and identifying the social categories of friends and boys in lines 3 and 4. Jiwhan announces the intention of beginning the ritual in line 5 ("We boy friends will do ttala meki, right?") and the children afterward negotiate who will be included in and excluded from the collaborative alignment structure formed through the eating ritual (lines 6–10). The children then debate the turns for commanding in lines 11–14. By announcing himself as the first, Jiwhan occupies the role of issuing an order and commands everyone to eat eggs (lines 15–18). Following Jiwhan's command, the other children then eat eggs all together. The same interactional structures appear in what follows (lines 20–23, 24–26). In these segments of interactions, the children attune their eating items, speed, order, and procedures to follow the leader's directions, thereby fitting into the group. In lines 20–23, for instance, Wobin divides the eating procedure into the two processes of putting anchovies onto the rice and eating them afterward. Following Wobin's commands, the children choose the same foods, wait until other members all put anchovies onto their rice, and hold their appetite and eating speed until Wobin issues the next order.

In this eating ritual, the main themes of the children's social world—that is, the shifts of alliance formation and exclusions and the pursuit of power and authority—are intricately intertwined and actively sought. The first interactional sequence of the ritual—that is, the recruitment of members—is an act of constructing an alignment structure in which members who are recruited to participate in the ritual forge alliances while others are excluded from those relationships. As the recruitment aims to build a differentiated social relationship, its process frequently involves disputes over participation as Wobin's intention of excluding Yunwoo in the above scene exemplifies. The other three steps of interactional sequences center on building a hierarchical social structure in which certain members temporarily occupy a higher status in relation to others. The member who takes the role of issuing an order attains a dominant position and the others who follow the command are accorded relatively lower status. The turn for giving a command, therefore, becomes a critical issue in which children strive to get turns as the debates in the above scene illustrate. The authority and power accorded through the role of the commander, however, never anchors on a particular member but is constantly sought and temporally gained, reflecting the fluid and transitory character of Somang children's overall hierarchized social organization. Moreover, even though children endeavor to get the first turn, they, at the same time, equally distribute turns for the leader. In line 14, for instance, as other members leave out Minseo who recently came to the Rainbow Room, Jiwhan includes him in the turn. In negotiating turns, Yeonu in line 12 also looks after Seunghoon who sits next to him. The hierarchical social order children produced in this eating ritual, then, is not so much a reckless pursuit of power and authority as a constant negotiation of relative social status which requires considerable collaboration on the part of each individual member.

Even though the eating ritual is highly patterned as the above scene illustrates, it also involves constant negotiations, disputes, or conflicts over the patterned script. In the following scene, for instance, some members attempt to monopolize the dominant position and manipulate social distances among themselves to address immediate social goals while at the same time conforming to the basic pattern of the ritual.

"I WANT TO COPY MY BEST FRIEND'S ARTWORK" 111

SCENE 4.19: "LUNCHTIME"

Participants: Jeemin (girl, 3 years), Sungeun (girl, 3 years), Sol (girl, 3 years), Jin (girl, 3 years), Seoyun (girl, 3 years), Jiju (girl, 3 years)

1. Sungeun: Hey. ((Points to the empty table))
2. ((Sungeun and Jeemin go to the empty table together))
3. Sungeun: ((to Sol and Jin who sit at another table)) Sol and Jin, I'll be here.
4. ((As Sol and Jin do not move, Sungeun and Jeemin go to Sol and Jin's table))
5. ((Jiju comes to the table))
6. Sungeun: Hey, we're full. We're full.
7. Jeemin: Over there. ((Points to the empty table))
8. ((Jiju leaves))
9. ((Jeemin and Sungeun go to the front table with their lunch box to get food from the teachers))
10. Jin: Hey, Jiju, I like you. I like you.
11. ((Jiju comes back and goes beside Jin dragging Jeemin's chair))
12. Seoyun: Jeemin will scold you.
13. ((Jiju moves beside Seoyun with Jeemin's chair))
14. Seoyun: Hey, I'm gonna hit you.
15. Jiju: It doesn't hurt me.
16. Seoyun: ((holding her toy)) Hey, I'll hit you.
17. Jiju: It doesn't hurt me.
18. ((Jiju leaves))
19. ((Jeemin and Sungeun come back with their lunch. Seoyun leaves to get lunch))
20. Jeemin: We're gonna do ttala meki.
21. ((Sungeun nods))
22. Jeemin: ((to Sol and Jin who mix their side dishes and rice in the lunch box)) After you finish mixing, you have to eat when I order to eat.
23. Jeemin: Eat. ((Takes a spoonful of mixed food))
24. ((Sungeun, Sol, and Jin take a spoonful of mixed food))

Like the case before, the eating ritual in this scene also emerges from arranging seats for lunchtime. From lines 1 to 18, the children constantly argue over who sits where with whom, which is an emblem of friendship and collaboration in the children's peer world. By announcing the beginning of the ritual in line 20 ("We're gonna do ttala meki") and asking Sol and Jin to follow her direction in line 22 ("After you finish mixing, you have to eat when I order to eat"), Jeemin recruits members to participate in the ritual and at the same time claims her turn for the leader. Jeemin then initiates the order and other children comply with her command by eating as Jeemin directs (lines 23–24). In this short span of interactions, children enact the four steps of act sequences constituting the eating ritual.

25. Jeemin: Eat once more. ((Takes a spoonful of mixed food)) Oh, it's hot.
26. ((Sungeun takes a spoonful of mixed food))
27. Sol: Guys, look at me. ((Holds the lunch box up and sips miso soup))
28. Jeemin: You guys eat when I suggest to eat. Let's eat.
29. Jin: No, we're not eating yet.
30. Jeemin: ((to Jin)) Then you count twenty, hundred. Then I'll do very fast.
31. Sungeun: We had a big piece of beef yesterday. And I ate it, right?
32. Jeemin: ((to Sol)) Which side dish do you like most?
33. ((Seoyun comes back with food in her lunch box))
34. Sol: Chicken.
35. Jeemin: ((digs into the mixed foods, finds chicken, and eats it)) Guys, eat chicken.
36. ((Sol, Jin, Sungeun, and Seoyun find chicken and eat it))
37. ((Jiju comes to the table with an empty lunch box))
38. Seoyun: ((in a mocking tone)) You haven't mixed food yet. You don't even have food in your lunch box.
39. Jiju: If you keep doing that, I'll then never get food from the teachers. I'll eat. With my mom and dad.

The interactions afterward configure differently from the typical ones like scene 4.18 as Jeemin intends to monopolize the leader position by issuing the second order in line 25. Whereas Sungeun complies with Jeemin's dominance, Sol counters her attempts by not following Jeemin's direction and instead drawing others' attention to her own independent eating. That is, rather than taking a spoonful of mixed food, Sol holds the lunch box up and sips miso soup (line 27). Against Sol's movement, Jeemin tries to retain the leader position by articulating her position and issuing an order ("You guys eat when I suggest to eat. Let's eat," line 28), but this time, Jin obstructs Jeemin's attempts by explicitly stating, "No, we're not eating yet." Here, Sol and Jin problematize Jeemin's dominance in the leadership position which goes against the equity rule embedded in the typical patterned eating ritual practice. Jeemin, however, strives to monopolize the dominant position by negotiating the speed with Jin ("Then you count twenty, hundred. Then I'll do very fast," line 30) and reflecting Sol's tastes in her direction ("Which side dish do you like most?" line 32). The command that reflects Sol's preference successfully elicits participants' compliance and enables Jeemin to maintain her authoritative status. Even though the interactional sequences do not follow the typical idealized pattern of the ritual, children in this scene also address main themes of their peer culture through the ritual by incessantly negotiating their relative social status and social distances among themselves.

Similar to the eating ritual, Somang children also contrived the ritual of following others' behaviors named *ttala haki*. As the following scene illustrates, the main interactional structure of this ritual consists of the recruitment of members, the commander's issuing of an order, and other participants carrying out the order.

"I WANT TO COPY MY BEST FRIEND'S ARTWORK"

SCENE 4.20: "PLAY TABLE"

Participants: Nuri (girl, 4 years), Bora (girl, 4 years), Jiwon (girl, 4 years)

1. Jiwon: ((to Nuri and Bora)) Let's play ttala haki. Let's play ttala haki.
2. Jiwon: Stretch legs. ((Stretches her two legs))
3. ((Nuri and Bora stretch their legs))
4. Jiwon: Fold legs. ((Folds her legs))
5. ((Nuri and Bora fold their legs))
6. ((Jiwon gives commands to stretch and fold legs alternatively eleven times and Nuri and Bora follow her commands))
7. Jiwon: Stretch legs. ((Stretches her two legs))
8. ((Bora stretches her legs, but Nuri does not))
9. Jiwon: Stretch legs. ((Stretches her two legs))
10. ((Bora stretches her legs, but Nuri does not))
11. Jiwon: Stretch legs. Stretch legs. Stretch legs. Stretch legs.
12. Bora: I'm the tallest in the world. Now it's Jiwon's turn.
13. Nuri: No, Jiwon already had a turn.
14. Bora: No, kisses . . . and hearts . . . Unfold one leg. ((Unfolds her right leg))
15. Nuri: No, no, it's my turn.
16. Bora: No, I'll do. Eenie, meenie, miney, mo. ((Points to herself)) Me. Ready for ttala haki.
17. Bora: Tutututu, hello. ((Stretches her right leg onto her right ear and pretends to answer the phone)) Tutututu, hello.
18. ((Nuri and Jiwon stretch their right legs onto their right ears))
19. Bora: Now let's call people's names. Tutututu, Bora. ((Stretches her left leg onto her left ear))
20. Nuri and Bora: Tutututu, Bora. ((Stretch their left legs onto their left ears))
21. Bora: Tutututu, Nuri. ((Stretches her right leg onto her right ear))
22. Nuri and Bora: Tutututu, Nuri. ((Stretch their right legs onto their right ears))

The ttala haki ritual in this scene starts with Jiwon's offer to play the ritual with Nuri and Bora. Jiwon then promptly occupies the commander's position by issuing an order in line 2, and the other two children stretch and fold their legs several times following Jiwon's continuous commands (lines 2–9). The tension over the turns of the commander emerges as Nuri refuses to follow Jiwon's direction in line 10 and then Nuri and Bora jockey for the commander position thereafter until Bora occupies the position. From line 17, Bora commands other children to follow the somewhat grotesque behavior of pretending to answer the phone with their legs. She makes several different versions of this command of answering the phone on foot and the other two children faithfully follow her directions. Similar to the cases of the eating ritual, these three children forge alliances by participating in the ritual and doing the same behaviors and at the same time construct hierarchical relationships through the roles of a commander and followers.

These rituals of ttala meki and ttala haki denote that children pursue uniformity and sameness in both educational and noneducational contexts. The interactional routines and strategies children employ as well as the values they pursue in the rituals exemplified above parallel the ones used in formal educational realms. As much as children are fond of producing similar artwork or strive to write poems with similar themes to solicit collaboration and fit into the group, they also endeavor to select same items of food, eat with the same procedures, speeds, and methods, and follow others' behaviors in order to belong to the group. For children, copying or following consistently means collaboration, alliance, and belonging in both noneducational and educational contexts. Moreover, children use similar interactional routines and strategies in both realms. For instance, the interactional structure in scene 4.4 wherein Jiwoo directs Seojin to copy her drawing and Seojin continuously draws as Jiwoo does is almost identical to the last two interactional sequences of the two rituals in which the leader issues an order and others follow the leader's directions. Through these interactional routines in both cases, children build a hierarchical social structure in which the one giving an order temporarily occupies a higher position and the others following a direction attain relatively lower status and also establish collaborative social relationships in which participating members forge cooperative alliances. Similarly, as children actively reflect the tastes and preferences of their peers in their artwork to build alliances, they also issue orders that reflect the tastes of peers in the eating ritual as shown in the scene above (scene 4.19) in which Jeemin asks Sol's tastes and reflects the answer in her order. Unlike teachers who restrain children from copying or following others' expressions in educational contexts while urging them to constantly adjust their behaviors to others in mundane noneducational contexts, children apply highly consistent meanings to copying or following and strategically utilize these behaviors as means to address peer world goals of constructing a differentiated, hierarchical, and stratified social organization regardless of its situated contexts.

Ritualized Communicative Activities and Ranking Practices

Children's pursuits of consistent goals and values in both educational and noneducational realms are also apparent in other interactional routines and practices. Children, for instance, frequently employ the ritualistic expression "Who wants to have this?" in both mundane and educational contexts to address goals of their peer world. In the following scenes, the children at the lunch table participate in ritualized communicative practices through which they negotiate their social status and social distances among themselves.

SCENE 4.21: "LUNCHTIME"

Participants: Haeun (girl, 3 years), Sungeun (girl, 3 years), Hajun (boy, 3 years), Jihyuk (boy, 3 years), Byungju (boy, 3 years), Sungmo (boy, 3 years)

1. Sungeun: Who wants to have this? ((Holds up her chopsticks))
2. Other children: Me. ((Raise their hands))
3. Haeun: Who wants to have this? ((Holds up her water bottle))
4. Other children: Me. ((Raise their hands))
5. Sungeun: Who wants to have this? ((Holds up the lid of her lunch box))
6. Other children: Me. ((Raise their hands))
7. Sungeun: Who wants to have this? ((Holds up the small charm attached to her bag))
8. Other children: Me. ((Raise their hands))
9. Haeun: Who wants to have this? ((Holds up her chopsticks))
10. Other children: Me. ((Raise their hands))
11. Sungeun: Who wants to have this? ((Holds up the cover of her lunch box))
12. Other children: Me. ((Raise their hands))

SCENE 4.22: "LUNCHTIME"

Participants: Jina (girl, 3 years), Seoyun (girl, 3 years), Jeemin (girl, 3 years), Jihyuk (boy, 3 years), Sungmo (boy, 3 years)

1. Seoyun: Who wants to have this? ((Shows her spoon))
2. Other children: Me. ((Raise their hands))
3. Seoyun: Jina, you win.
4. Jina: I win.
5. Jina: Who wants to have this? ((Shows her spoon))
6. Other children: Me. ((Raise their hands))
7. Jina: Seoyun, you win.

In these ritualized communicative activities, children coconstruct a collaborative and stratified social structure by using a ritualistic expression, "Who wants to have this?" This ritualistic expression grants authority to the one who employs this statement by having him or her offer his or her belongings and thereby attaining the right to choose a beneficiary. The ones who raise their hands, on the other hand, temporarily occupy relatively lower status as the decision of who would get the belongings is under the control of the announcer. In both scenes above, children constantly produce a series of hierarchical social structures in which some members jockey for power and authority by using this ritualistic expression and others cooperatively occupy lower positions by employing another ritualistic expression— that is, the bodily behavior of raising hands with the statement of "Me." Reflecting the overall characteristics of Somang children's social organization, the hierarchical social structures constructed through ritualized activities constantly shift as participants vie for an authoritative position. For instance, Sungeun and Haeun competitively maneuver for the presenter's position in scene 4.21 and Seoyun and Jina take turns for the position in scene 4.22. Also, unlike the announcement implying the offer of one's own possessions, the giving rarely takes place as in the cases of scenes 4.21 and 4.22. In scene 4.21, the ritualized interaction does not even entail the sequence of choosing a member of the group to give one's possession to, and in scene 4.22, the sequence of choosing is included but does not lead to the actual giving. The two children instead choose each other as the beneficiary of their offers, thereby forging alliances in scene 4.22. Then the focus of the ritualized interactions lies less on establishing a stable social hierarchy but on pursuing the hierarchy itself which reflects a general feature of Somang peer social organization. That is, children are engrossed in the process over the outcome of social hierarchy.

The ritualized communicative activities in informal settings employing the statement "Who wants to have this?" have similar interactional routines, goals, and effects to the ones occurring in educational contexts. In scene 4.13 discussed before, for instance, Haeun and Jina produce the ritualistic expression "Who wants to have this?" (lines 21, 23, 25) to present their artwork as desirable, thereby achieving authority, and other children respond to these attempts by employing another ritualistic expression—that is, raising their hands. These coconstructed social hierarchies constantly shift and rarely result in concrete outcomes of giving as in the cases of everyday and mundane contexts. These similarities, then, attest that children create their own culturally situated and ritualized communicative activities and consistently apply them to address goals of their peer world regardless of its contexts.

Children's consistent seeking of their own virtues and goals is also extensively found in their ranking and competition-oriented practices. As children strategically transform educational activities into a place of competition and ranking, they also strive for competitive and stratified social relationships in mundane noneducational contexts. In the following scenes, for instance, children turn eating, which could be pursued as an individual act, into contests and evaluate one another in terms of their eating speed.

SCENE 4.23: "LUNCHTIME"

Participants: Jeehyung (boy, 3 years), Hyunwoo (boy, 3 years), Hajun (boy, 3 years), Jiho (boy, 3 years)

1. Jeehyung: We're gonna win. We're gonna finish this one, too. So we'll be the first.
2. Hyunwoo: We're gonna win.
3. Hajun: ((to Jeehyung)) We do exercise, right? So we're gonna win.

SCENE 4.24: "LUNCHTIME"

Participants: Hyunwoo (boy, 3 years), Wooju (boy, 3 years), Seoyun (girl, 3 years)

1. Hyunwoo: Yay, we won.
2. Wooju: Yay.

"I WANT TO COPY MY BEST FRIEND'S ARTWORK" 117

3. Seoyun: It's not about winning.
4. Hyunwoo: ((goes to the other table)) Wooju and I won.

In scene 4.23, Jeehyung transforms eating into a match in which he and Hajun can win as a team. Against Jeehyung's movement, Hyunwoo declares that he and Jiho will win as a team. Hajun then substantiates their winning by stating, "We do exercise, right? So we're gonna win." Similarly, Hyunwoo and Wooju in scene 4.24 turn eating into a competition and declare their winning and Seoyun tries to subvert the emerging hierarchy by negating the contest frame. Here, competition involves building hierarchical and differentiated social relationships in which members as a team seek winning against others.

Children also pursue explicit ranking of everyday behaviors and performances as the following scenes illustrate.

SCENE 4.25: "OUTSIDE PLAYTIME"
Participants: Jihoon (boy, 3 years), Jihyuk (boy, 3 years), Jiho (boy, 3 years)

1. Jihoon: ((stands in front of the building door and points to children coming to the door)) You're the first. You're the second and the third.
2. Jiho: How about me?
3. Jihoon: You're the fourth.
4. Jihyuk: How about me?
5. Jihoon: You're the fifth.

SCENE 4.26: "LUNCHTIME"
Participants: Junghyun (girl, 5 years), Haejin (girl, 5 years), Misoo (girl, 5 years), Hyungjoon (boy, 5 years)

1. ((Children at the lunch table rank one another while having lunch. Some children finish their lunch and leave. Junghyun, Haejin, Misoo, and Hyungjoon are at the table))
2. Junghyun: Haejin wins. Misoo is the last.
3. Haejin: The last one is *tong* (bronze) medal. The last one is *ttong* (poo) medal.
4. Junghyun: I'm gonna feed Haejin-*ssi* (Ms. Haejin) ((picks up the spoon and feeds Haejin)).
5. Junghyun: Oh Haejin-ssi wins.
6. ((Junghyun finishes lunch and leaves))
7. Misoo: A loner. A loner ((in a singing tone))
8. Misoo: ((to Haejin)) Would you like to be a loner?
9. ((Haejin does not respond))
10. Misoo: Would you be a mate with Yongjin?
11. Haejin: No.
12. Misoo: Would you be a loner, or would you be a mate with Yongjin?

In scene 4.25, Jihoon, coming back from outside play, ranks peers in terms of their orders of coming into the school door. The explicit ranking is constructed through his ordering and other children's collaborative participation in the ranking frame. The children in scene 4.26 also rank one another in terms of their eating speed. Unlike scene 4.25 in which children cooperatively produce a clear ranking, rank-pursuing interactions in scene 4.26 involve subtle manipulations and negotiations of social distances among themselves. In ranking one another in terms of eating speed, the children construct an alignment structure in which two members forge an alliance while one is excluded from that relationship. For instance, Junghyun, acting as a referee of the contest, constantly judges Haejin favorably ("Haejin wins," line 2; "Oh Haejin-ssi wins," line 5) and even supports Haejin's eating ("I'm gonna feed Haejin-ssi," line 4), thereby forging strong alliances with Haejin. Misoo, on the other hand, gets excluded from their coalition as Junghyun consistently judges Haejin above Misoo and Haejin produces a pejorative comment toward Misoo's performance. In line 3, affirming Junghyun's judgment of Misoo as the last, Haejin states that Misoo gets a bronze medal as the last one and then repeats the same statement, this time changing the consonant "t(tong)" to "tt(ttong)." By making a fortis consonant, the meaning of the term changes from bronze to poo, which has an effect of conferring a pejorative status on Misoo. Misoo does not confront their exclusive movements, but as Junghyun finishes lunch and leaves, she expresses her discomfort toward Haejin and tries to isolate Haejin from the group. She sings the part of a pop song with the lyric "a loner, a loner" and implicitly bestows the identity of loner on Haejin first by asking her whether she would like to be a loner and then pairing her with Yongjin who is considered a troublemaker in the Rainbow Room. Ranking practice here entails coalition- and exclusion-seeking acts as well as the pursuit of social hierarchy, all of which are major themes of Somang children's social world.

The prevalence of ritualized communicative activities employing expressions such as "Who wants to have this?" and ranking practices like the above in both educational and noneducational realms demonstrate that the distinction of educational and mundane has no significance in children's phenomenal social world. Furthermore, the parallel of interactional structures of ritualized communicative activities and ranking practices enacted in educational and noneducational contexts suggests that children's transformation of self-expression is not a momentary response but a systemic and sophisticated cultural practice codeveloped to address goals of their phenomenal peer world.

"I Know That Not All Expressions Get Praised": Penetration and Critical Insights into Globalizing Socialization Practices

The way Somang children collaboratively construct and reconstruct their own practices and meanings of self-expression seen so far attests that they have highly sophisticated and elaborated understandings of socialization spheres around them

"I WANT TO COPY MY BEST FRIEND'S ARTWORK"   119

and possess cultural abilities to create situated and ritualized cultural practices that fit into the social themes of their peer world. Children's cultural sensibilities are not confined to strategic appropriation of available cultural resources but even penetrate socialization ideologies and practices thereby transforming them. That is, the close observations of children's reinterpretations and reconstructions of their self-expressions as well as their pursuit of consistent values in their interactional realms make clear that children have penetrating insights into the heterogenous, conflicting, and contradictory nature of the transforming Korean socialization landscape and respond to the contradictions and disruptures based on their own penetrations and understandings.

Children's responses to heterogenous and conflicting socialization inputs regarding self-expression nicely illustrate this point. As discussed in chapter 3, teachers make concerted efforts to inculcate new socialization values of self-expression, individuality, and creativity in their pupils by continuously provoking children to express their authentic thoughts, desires, and feelings in everyday educational contexts. The efforts included praising any expression children produce by using an unconventional communicative repertoire such as "Wow, that's super" and "How great it is" or asking details of the productions by employing utterances like "Wow, what's the name of your artwork?" "How did you make it?" and "What's that picture about?" At the same time, however, teachers unwittingly provide information about the unequal value of children's expressions when they choose some expressions over others to be presented or shared in group activities. Somang children seem to recognize the conflicts and contradictions involved in socialization inputs and strategically respond to them in their own ways. In the following scene, children complain about the teacher's implicit evaluation of their artwork and try to steer the evaluation favorably toward themselves.

SCENE 4.27: "GROUP TIME"

Participants: Ms. Sung (teacher), Jihoon (boy, 3 years), Jeemin (girl, 3 years), Seoyun (girl, 3 years), Jungyoon (girl, 3 years)

1. ((Ms. Sung introduces Jihoon's wire artwork to the class))
2. Jungyoon: It looks like a spacecraft when it stands up.
3. Ms. Sung: Oh, really?
4. Jihoon: No, it's not.
5. Jeemin: Teacher, why didn't you bring mine? The one I made yesterday.
6. Ms. Sung: Yeah?
7. Jihoon: ((comes up to the front and transforms his wire artwork)) It's a saw shark.
8. Ms. Sung: Oh, he says it has suddenly been transformed to a saw shark. Which part is the saw?
9. ((Jihoon transforms the wire artwork))

10. Ms. Sung: The shark seems not finished yet. He will show us later when it is finished.
11. ((Jihoon goes back to his seat))
12. Ms. Sung: ((shows Jihoon's artwork again)) These are all fish. This one is a fish. This one is a fish. This one is a fish, too. Then why do you think I brought these three fish? Jihoon, what kind of fish is this?
13. Jihoon: ((comes up to the front)) This is a transformable fish. ((Stands toward Ms. Sung and transforms the fish))
14. Ms. Sung: Why don't you show to your friends how you make it? ((Makes Jihoon stand toward the children))
15. Jiju: I can make better wire work.
16. Ms. Sung: Oh, you can also make it. A good one?
17. Seoyun: I can make a better one with a wire.
18. Ms. Sung: Wooju, would you see how your friend makes a great wire work? Look here, he says he made a hole here.
19. Seoyun: Teacher, I can make a hole, too.
20. Children: I can make a hole, too.
21. Ms. Sung: I'm sorry, Jihoon, but your friends want to know what you made before, not how you transform it.

In this scene, a typical group time of Somang classroom, Ms. Sung picks up one of the artworks she regards as fitting into her socialization goals of creativity and diversity and presents it to the whole class. Following the Reggio curriculum, her intention here is to cultivate children's self-expressions and creativity by sharing a creative artwork with the whole class and providing chances for a selected child to present his or her ideas and thoughts about the artwork. Apart from the teacher's pedagogical goals, children view this scene as a place in which their creativity and self-expressions are evaluated by an authoritative figure. In line 5, Jeemin asks Ms. Sung why she did not bring the artwork she made yesterday. Although Jeemin's utterance is framed as a question, it is based on her awareness that their individual artwork is not valued for itself but is assessed according to certain criteria, and her artwork is ranked lower than Jihoon's. Based on these understandings, she opposes the teacher's evaluation and decision. Children's insights into teachers' evaluation of their creativity and self-expression are also manifested in the later development of this scene. From lines 15 to 20, Jiju, Seoyun, and other children sequentially produce comparative statements in which they assess their own artwork and skills as superior to Jihoon's, thereby implicitly challenging the teacher's appraisal of Jihoon's artwork as better or more creative than their own.

Children's awareness of teachers' evaluations of their self-expressions is not conscious knowledge but an embodied understanding that they have acquired through everyday exposure to and engagement with Somang pedagogical practices. By being exposed to contradictory socialization inputs, children come to realize that

"I WANT TO COPY MY BEST FRIEND'S ARTWORK"

under the surface of teachers' effusive praise, there exist continuous evaluations and appraisals of their self-expressions and creativity. This then often leads to children's keen interest in achieving recognition from teachers. Children frequently show their productions to teachers with statements like "Teacher, look at mine," "Teacher, this is what I made," or "Teacher, this is my masterpiece" and articulate their thoughts and ideas about artwork, pictures, or play to teachers. Children's expressions here exist not so much for their own sakes but mostly to influence teachers. In Somang classrooms, showing and explaining one's productions to teachers even exists as a situated cultural practice which constitutes a crucial part of children's expressive behaviors as the following scenes illustrate.

SCENE 4.28: "FREE CHOICE TIME"

Participants: Jungyoon (girl, 3 years), Seoyun (girl, 3 years), Ms. Sung (teacher), Ms. Chung (teacher)

1. ((Jungyoon finishes her picture and approaches Ms. Sung))
2. Jungyoon: Teacher, look at this.
3. Ms. Sung: Wow, that's great. How great it is.
4. ((Jungyoon leaves and goes to Ms. Chung))
5. Jungyoon: Teacher, this is what I drew. Look at this.
6. Ms. Chung: Great! What kind of picture is it?
7. Jungyoon: Mom and Dad. They are doing their hair.
8. ((Seoyun looks at them from the other side of the table and comes to show her picture to Ms. Chung))
9. Jungyoon: Hey, you don't draw well.

SCENE 4.29: "WIRE ARTWORK AREA"

Participants: Eunseo (girl, 3 years), Jeehyung (boy, 3 years), Ms. Sung (teacher)

1. ((Ms. Sung comes to the wire artwork area))
2. Ms. Sung: Eunseo, what's that?
3. Eunseo: It's pants.
4. Ms. Sung: Oh, pants?
5. Jeehyung: Teacher, this is grass. ((Holds up his wire work and shows to Ms. Sung))

In scene 4.28, Jungyoon actively seeks recognition of her picture from teachers by sequentially showing it to Ms. Sung and Ms. Chung. The teachers compliment her picture, and Ms. Chung further prompts Jungyoon to verbally articulate the contents. Similarly, in scene 4.29, Jeehyung also tries to draw the attention of the teacher by showing his wirework to Ms. Sung and naming it. As indicated in Jungyoon's statement toward Seoyun "Hey, you don't draw well" in line 9 and Seoyun's and Jeehyung's movement of showing their products in contrast to teachers' acknowledgment of Jungyoon and Eunseo, the children participate in a competitive structure in which they vie with one another for teachers' recognition. As much as children enjoy and display keen interest in comparing, evaluating, and ranking their own expressions, they are, at the same time, keen to challenge evaluations made by teachers which are often implicit but clearly do exist underneath ostensible compliments. Children's self-expressions acquire their full meanings and are completed through teachers' acknowledgment of their value.

Children's responses to teachers' implicit evaluations through the invention of showing and articulating practices like the above demonstrate that they provide penetrating insights into transforming socialization ideologies and practices. Unlike teachers who are oblivious to contradictions involved in their everyday socialization practices of self-expression, children do recognize inconsistencies and incongruities in teachers' practices and strategically respond to them in their own ways. These penetrating insights and understandings are similar to, even though not identical to, what Willis (1977) conceptualizes as "penetration" in his study of working-class students' counter–school culture. That is, much as English boys recognize the illusions of teaching paradigms, especially capitalism's promises of advancement through education, Somang children penetrate the illusion of wholeness and integration that teachers claim for their socialization ideologies and practices and recognize subtle but pervasive evaluations existing behind ostensible emphases on diversity and creativity. Children, here, are insightful critics of Korea's transforming socialization landscape as well as strategic actors who shape their own developmental spheres.

Creative Embellishment of Cultural Models of Social Hierarchy: Role and Status in Children's Peer Relationships

Children's cultural abilities and sensibilities are found not only in their strategic engagement with newly imported socialization ideologies and practices as seen so far but in their creative embellishment of so-called traditional ideologies and practices which are implicit but strongly transmitted through teachers' everyday and mundane practices. Somang children, in particular, display keen interest in cultural ideas of role and status and creatively utilize and appropriate them in addressing goals of their peer world. As discussed in the previous chapter, Somang teachers heavily relied on positional socialization (Douglas 1970) in inculcating socially appropriate behaviors and emotions in children. Discourses on hyengnim (elder brother or sister) and aka (baby) (or tongsayng [younger brother or sister]) employed in this context provide two related pieces of cultural information regarding social hierarchy and status. First, by constantly instilling rules of conduct vested in a role and position that the child is expected to hold, these discourses stress the importance of role propriety and role obligation. Second, although the discourses are used in the context of emphasizing role-appropriate behaviors, they also provide information about social hierarchy invested in hyengnim and aka (or tongsayng). That is, when teachers confer honorable and authoritative identity to hyengnim and pejorative, shameful, and incompetent status to aka, this creates a social hierarchy in which hyengnim possesses authority and power over aka (or tongsayng).

Along with the discourses on role propriety, teachers also socialize children into cultural models of conduct expected between peers of different ages. Like the conduct of social hierarchies in other places such as Thailand (Howard 2007, 2012), hierarchical social relationships are sustained through the bidirectional flow of benefits and services as well as through authority and obedience. Extending the social conduct of the elder and the younger sibling relationships to peers, teachers emphasize the importance of generosity and compassion on the part of elders toward their younger counterparts, and the younger's respect for the elder. Teachers, for instance, often make statements such as "You should speak nicely to a younger sister when she does things incorrectly," "You should care for your younger brother as you're an elder sister to him," "How about yielding it to the younger sister?" and "You don't hit your elder brother. You should respect him" in resolving conflicts among peers. If teachers' discourses on hyengnim and aka provide information regarding the authority of the superior over the subordinate and the subordinate's obedience, these utterances stress mutual dependency in which the generosity of the superior is reciprocated by the respect of the subordinate.

Exposed to these cultural models of social hierarchy, children creatively appropriate and embellish them as semiotic resources to build their own social world. That is, they strategically employ teachers' discourses on hyengnim and aka (or tongsayng), creatively use the pretend frame and role-appropriate behaviors, and identify and debate their relative social status in order to manipulate social distances and hierarchies among themselves, control and direct behaviors of others, and criticize moralities of their peers.

Strategic Use of Hyengnim and Aka Socialization Discourses

As much as the discourses on role propriety prevail in everyday socialization contexts, children widely utilize and appropriate the discourses on hyengnim and aka in various contexts of peer interactions. In the following scene, for instance, children strategically employ the discourse on aka to negotiate social distances among themselves and monitor and police behaviors of others.

SCENE 4.30: "LUNCHTIME"

Participants: Jungho (boy, 4 years), Ara (girl, 4 years), Bora (girl, 4 years), Dongju (boy, 4 years), Ms. Choo (teacher)

1. ((Ara, Bora, Jungho, and Dongju are at the lunch table and Ara and Bora eat lunch doing ttala meki together))
2. ((Jungho, who sits beside Ara, moves close to Ara and clings to Ara))

124   BETWEEN SELF AND COMMUNITY

3. Ara: You're like an aka (baby). You're like an aka (baby).
4. Bora: Let's go to the Pine Room. Let's go to the Pine Room.
5. Ara: ((in a coddling tone to Jungho)) You don't need to go, right?
6. Bora: Wait, Ara. Okay?
7. Bora: Hey, you have to wait after finish eating, okay?
8. Bora: Ara. After cleaning up your lunch box, you have to wait.
9. Ara: ((cleans up her lunch box)) Let's see who wins. Jungho or Bora? It's Bora.
10. ((Bora and Ara leave and Jungho and Dongju are at the table))
11. ((Ms. Choo comes and feeds Jungho))
12. Dongju: Hey, Jungho, you're not gonna get a top. You're not gonna get a top.
13. Ms. Choo: Why?
14. Dongju: Ara and I told him that we're gonna give him lots of tops if he eats well.

The children at this lunch table actively employ the discourse of aka in arranging social relationships among themselves. Among the four children at the lunch table, Ara and Bora forge collaborative relationships by enacting the eating ritual of ttala meki and the other two children individually eat lunch while sporadically speaking with Ara and Bora. The collaborative alignment structure of Ara and Bora formed through the eating ritual falters as Jungho expresses his affection toward Ara through bodily movements. In attempts to protect their alliance and exclude Jungho from it, Bora and Ara cooperatively confer the pejorative identity of aka to Jungho in lines 3–4 through utterances of "You're like an aka (baby)" and "Let's go to the Pine Room." By identifying Jungho as an aka and then shaming him as belonging to a younger-age classroom, these two children successfully exclude Jungho from their alliance. If teachers used discourses on aka and shaming practices of taking children to other classrooms to discipline their behaviors, children here selectively adopt the exclusive effects of these discourses and practices and construct a two-against-one alignment structure.

Children also use discourses of hyengnim and aka in criticizing peers' inappropriate behaviors and problematizing the moralities of peers as the following examples illustrate.

SCENE 4.31: "IN THE BUS ON THE WAY TO AN EXCURSION"
Participants: Suyong (boy, 4 years), Jungho (boy, 4 years), Junwoo (boy, 4 years), Jungwoo (boy, 4 years)

1. Junwoo: Stupid Jungho. Stupid Jungho. Idiot Jungho.
2. Suyong: That hurts Jungho's feeling.
3. Junwoo: Stupid Jungho.
4. Suyong: That hurts Jungho's feeling.
5. Suyong: ((to Jungho)) You are sad, right? You're very sad, right? Say that to them. Say you're sad.
6. Jungwoo: Bag-dropping Jungho. Bag-dropping Jungho.

"I WANT TO COPY MY BEST FRIEND'S ARTWORK" 125

7. Jungwoo: ((looks at the apartments through the bus window)) Apartment Jungho.
8. Jungho: ((in angry voice)) Stop, piggies.
9. Suyong: Stop talking to him, Junwoo and Jungwoo. Hahaha.
10. Junwoo: Piggy Jungho.
11. Suyong: Stop talking to him, tongsayng-dul. Hahaha.

SCENE 4.32: "IN THE BATHROOM"

Participants: Jina (girl, 3 years), Sungeun (girl, 3 years), Seoyun (girl, 3 years)

1. ((Jina, Sungeun, and Seoyun brush their teeth in the bathroom after finishing lunch))
2. Jina: ((pulls Sungeun's slipper)) I wore it first.
3. Sungeun: I wore it first.
4. Jina: ((pulls Sungeun's slipper)) I wore it first.
5. Seoyun: It's because Jina is an aka. It's because Jina is an aka. It's because Jina is an aka. Aka Jina.
6. ((Jina snaps Seoyun's face))
7. Sungeun: Phew, aka Jina.
8. ((Sungeun sighs and gives one side of her slipper to Jina))

In scene 4.31, as a group of children teases Jungho calling him names, Suyong continuously points out the inappropriateness of the children's linguistic behaviors. Suyong asks the children to imagine the feelings of Jungho and at the same time urges Jungho to actively express his hurt feelings. As Junwoo and Jungwoo continue bullying Jungho, Suyong directly asks them to stop harassing Jungho by stating, "Stop talking to him, Junwoo and Jungwoo. Hahaha," "Stop talking to him, tongsayng-dul. Hahaha" in lines 9 and 11. Here, Suyong implicitly criticizes Junwoo's and Jungwoo's behaviors toward Jungho by conferring the pejorative identity of tongsayng-dul to them. Similarly, in scene 4.32, in their conflict over the slipper in the bathroom, Seoyun and Sungeun accuse Jina of forcibly taking others' belonging by employing discourses of aka. Seoyun identifies Jina as an aka by repeating the utterance "It's because Jina is an aka" several times and problematizes Jina's behaviors. Sungeun finally yields part of her slipper to Jina but demotes Jina as an aka and criticizes the immaturity and inappropriateness of her behaviors by stating, "Phew, aka Jina." If teachers use discourses of role propriety to facilitate classroom routines and have children conform to group rules, children in these cases strategically appropriate them to censure others' behaviors and criticize the moralities of their peers.

Achieving Legitimacy through Role and Status

Somang children's strategic use of role and status also involves the unconventional employment of kin terms among peers. The person reference and address of peer

126   BETWEEN SELF AND COMMUNITY

groups of these ages generally follow linguistic rules used in sibling relationships. That is, the younger refers to and addresses the elder using fictive kin terms such as brother and sister and the elder refers to and addresses the younger using first names and pronouns. In terms of self-reference, children tend to use status-neutral and intimate pronouns to refer to themselves in playgroups. Somang children usually conform to these linguistic rules in interactions with peers but employ unconventional forms when they try to manipulate and negotiate social distances and hierarchies among themselves. Children, in particular, use fictive kin terms rather than pronouns to refer to themselves in addressing their immediate social goals as the following scene illustrates.

SCENE 4.33: "PLAYING WITH TOPS IN THE HALLWAY"

Participants: Jungwoo (boy, 4 years), Kangjun (boy, 4 years), Junwoo (boy, 4 years), Hyungjun (boy, 5 years), Junghyun (girl, 5 years)

1. ((Jungwoo, Kangjun, Junwoo, and Hyungjun play tops in the hallway. Junghyun watches them without participating in the game))
2. Junghyun: My elder brother spins it very fast. My elder brother spins it very fast. You guys get lost.
3. Junwoo: We have a very strong top between these two anyway.
4. Jungwoo: I found it, right? On the playground.
5. Junghyun: *Enni* (elder sister) has the stronger top at home. Enni (elder sister) has the stronger top at home.
6. Kangjun: I have the stronger top.
7. ((Junwoo and Jungwoo win against Hyungjun))
8. Junwoo: We won.
9. Hyungjun: I'm happy because I lost.
10. Junwoo: Why?
11. Hyungjun: Because I'm *hyeng* (elder brother) anyway.

In this competitive talk, a group of children compare skills of one another using a variety of resources. As Junghyun, the only girl in the group, fails to participate in the top-spinning game, she instead joins the competitive talk and attempts to occupy a dominant position by utilizing the skills of her own older brother. Against her talk, the four-year-old boys argue the excellence of their gadget by stating, "We have a very strong top between these two anyway." Junghyun then challenges their argument by claiming the superiority of the top she owns and has at her home. In line 5, she states, "Enni (elder sister) has the stronger top at home. Enni (elder sister) has the stronger top at home." Here, Junghyun refers to herself as "elder sister" rather than the typical use of "I," thereby marking the status asymmetry between herself and the four-year-old boys. In a similar vein, after being defeated by the four-year-old boys, the five-year-old Hyungjun states that he is satisfied with his defeat because he is the elder brother regardless of the result ("Because I'm

"I WANT TO COPY MY BEST FRIEND'S ARTWORK" 127

hyeng (elder brother) anyway," line 11). By articulating his status as an elder brother, he tries to turn over the hierarchy constructed through the game and restore his authority demoted by defeat in the game with the younger boys. The elder and the younger sibling relationship invoked through unconventional use of kin terms and the claim of elder brother status enables these two children to temporarily gain authority and occupy dominant positions in the fluctuating hierarchical peer order.

The unconventional use of the person reference and address occurs not only in building hierarchical social relationships but also in controlling behaviors of others and expressing a negative stance toward peers. The following conflict among three children exemplifies this usage.

SCENE 4.34: "PLAYTIME"

Participants: Rihyun (girl, 4 years), Ayeon (girl, 4 years), Yongjun (boy, 3 years)

1. ((Rihyun and Ayeon play house in the play area and leave to get paper from the artwork table))
2. ((Yongjun comes to the house and plays with toys))
3. Yongjun: ((picks up the bed and makes it fly through the air)) The bed is flying.
4. Rihyun: ((comes back)) Don't do it. Don't do it to enni (elder sister).
5. Yongjun: I don't like *ne* (you).
6. Rihyun: Don't dislike the elder sister.

The conflict among the three children emerges as Yongjun occupies the play area Rihyun and Ayeon temporarily left. Rihyun, coming back to the play area and finding Yongjun playing with the toy Rihyun and Ayeon consider as theirs, demands Yongjun stop playing with their toy by stating, "Don't do it. Don't do it to enni (elder sister)." Rihyun's demand comes in the form of a directive, but she also uses the kin term enni (elder sister) to refer to herself to mark the status asymmetry between herself and the three-year-old Yongjun. Against Rihyun's movement, Yongjun also conveys his discomfort toward Rihyun by baldly stating, "I don't like ne (you)." In expressing his unpleasant feelings, Yongjun refers to Rihyun as ne (you), the addressee reference used by the superior toward the subordinate addressee or by interlocutors of equal status, instead of the kin term expected to be used as the younger toward the elder. By employing this status-lowering reference, Yongjun attempts to subvert the power asymmetry between himself as the younger and Rihyun as the elder and display his uncomfortable feelings and grievance toward Rihyun. Rihyun then, again, refers to herself as enni (elder sister) in a bald directive to Yongjun to remind him of the status asymmetry between herself and Yongjun, thereby criticizing and controlling his behavior. Children's strategic uses of kin terms as self-reference and status-lowering reference toward an elder in this scene illustrate that the children not only have highly sophisticated knowledge of kin term usage and cultural ideas associated with them but also create their own routinized cultural practice of person reference to address goals of their peer world.

Pretend Frame and Role-Appropriate Behaviors

If children use unconventional person reference in multiage group interactions to mark and sometimes subvert power asymmetries, they frequently employ the pretend frame in interactions with peers of the same age. Same-age playgroups generally exchange nonhonorific and status-neutral forms of person reference and address with peers and thereby are devoid of resources available to members of multiage groups. In a situation wherein they cannot invoke age differences and entailing power asymmetries existing in the real world, children in the same-age interactions employ a pretend frame and strategically use linguistic rules and associated cultural models of role and status constructed through social relationships. The following scene shows how children of the same age negotiate social distances among themselves utilizing a pretend frame of familial relationships and accompanying cultural models of conduct.

SCENE 4.35: "WATCHING VIDEO"

Participants: Eunseo (girl, 3 years), Jeehyung (boy, 3 years), Haeun (girl, 3 years), Jungyoon (girl, 3 years), Hyunwoo (boy, 3 years)

1. ((Children are watching a video together))
2. ((Eunseo crawls to Jeehyung and Haeun who sit together side by side))
3. Eunseo: ((crawls)) *Eng. Eng* ((pretends to cry like a baby)).
4. ((Jeehyung and Haeun do not respond))
5. Eunseo: ((to Jeehyung)) *Appa* (Daddy), appa ((in a crying voice))
6. Haeun: He's not your appa. He's not your appa. You're not aka (baby), too. You're not aka. Jeehyung, don't take care of her.
7. ((Eunseo stares at Haeun and crawls to Jungyoon and Hyunwoo))
8. Eunseo: *Eng. Eng.*
9. ((Jungyoon and Hyunwoo do not respond))
10. ((Eunseo stops crawling and watches the video))

In this narrative, Eunseo positions herself as aka (baby) in her efforts to forge alliances with other children. She first employs the pretend frame by producing aka-like bodily and emotional behaviors of crawling and crying in line 3. As Jeehyung and Haeun implicitly refuse to include Eunseo in their relationships by not responding, Eunseo reinforces the pretend frame by referring to Jeehyung as appa (daddy) and producing the speech style of aka, speaking in a crying voice (line 5). The kin term address of appa and affective and linguistic features indexing aka invoke cultural models of conduct related to the superior and the subordinate relationship. In this way, Eunseo portrays herself as younger, less powerful, and more in need of help while hoping to obligate the other children to be kind, caring, and generous toward her as her superior. Haeun's ensuing utterances purporting to ignore the pretend frame, especially the statement "Jeehyung, don't take care of her," attests that Haeun also understands Eunseo's strategic use of the kin term and the

"I WANT TO COPY MY BEST FRIEND'S ARTWORK" 129

underlying cultural model of conduct that the superior has responsibility to be caring and generous toward the subordinate. Even though Eunseo fails to enter into a dyadic relationship, her use of kin terms and a pretend frame and other children's reactions show that the children have sophisticated knowledge regarding role- and status-related expressive means and can creatively utilize them to mobilize their social relationships.

Similarly, in the following scene, Eunseo constitutes an age-based hierarchical structure by employing a pretend frame and actively induces the addressee's beneficence.

SCENE 4.36: "LUNCHTIME"

Participants: Jina (girl, 3 years), Eunseo (girl, 3 years), Hyungjun (boy, 3 years), Sol (girl, 3 years)

1. ((Eunseo shows her spoon to Jina))
2. Jina: ((turns her head)) It's not pretty. It's not pretty. It's not pretty.
3. Eunseo: I won't buy you a princess dress.
4. Jina: I won't buy you a cavity medicine. I won't buy you a cavity medicine.
5. Hyungjun: How about me, Eunseo?
6. Jina: I'll buy you a cavity medicine.
7. Eunseo: I'll tell my mom.
8. ((Jina leaves the table to get food))
9. Eunseo: *Eng. Eng.* ((Leans her head toward Sol))
10. Sol: Would you like to play with enni (elder sister) meanwhile? ((Strokes Eunseo's head))
11. Eunseo: Yes, *eng. Eng.*

After a conflictual interaction with Jina, Eunseo in this scene seeks emotional comfort from Sol by employing bodily demeanors and emotional behaviors signifying aka in line 9. By portraying herself as helpless, younger, and in need of care, Eunseo coerces the addressee Sol to display feelings of compassion and kindness toward herself. As Sol's utterance "Would you like to play with enni (elder sister) meanwhile?" and accompanying bodily behavior of stroking Eunseo's head in line 10 signify, Sol ratifies Eunseo's pretend frame and enacts the behaviors expected for the status of enni as the elder. Here, Eunseo and Sol coconstruct the pretend sibling relationships and invoke cultural models of mutual dependence related to the senior-junior relationship to make an alliance amid conflicts with peers.

Children's strategic use of the pretend frame and kin terms is deployed not only in the contexts of forming alliances but also in exerting exclusions as the following case illustrates.

SCENE 4.37: "LUNCHTIME"

Participant: Junghan (boy, 4 years), Nayun (girl, 4 years), Jungyoon (girl, 4 years), Jiwon (girl, 4 years)

1. Junghan: Eat all of the *pwulkoki* (barbecue).
2. Nayun: ((with a sigh)) Ugh.
3. Jiwon: ((with a sigh)) Ugh.
4. Junghan: Are you guys from the Pine Room? Why are you eating badly like tongsayng-dul (younger brothers and sisters)?
5. Junghan: Who wants to have me?
6. Jungyoon: ((points to flowers on her T-shirt)) Who wants to have flowers?
7. Junghan: Me.
8. Jungyoon: No, you can't. Boys can't.
9. Junghan: I have many flowers in my home and I won't give [them to] you. I have many flowers in my home.
10. ((Jungyoon points to the flowers on her T-shirt and pretends to give them to Jiwon and Nayun))
11. Jungyoon: ((to Jiwon and Nayun)) *Aka-dul-a* (babies), aka-dul-a.
12. Junghan: I'm an aka (baby), too.
13. Jungyoon: No, you're not an aka.
14. Jungyoon: These are snake flowers.
15. Junghan: I'm okay with snake flowers.
16. Jungyoon: Aka-dul-a. Eat lunch.
17. Junghan: Me, too.
18. Jungyoon: No, you said you're a hyenga (elder brother).

This scene starts with the conflict between Junghan and other children at the lunch table who engage in the eating ritual of ttala meki. Against Nayun and Jiwon who complain about Junghan's command to eat all of the side dishes, Junghan confers the pejorative identities of tongsayng-dul (younger siblings) and one-year-old Pine Room members to criticize their incompetence. As Junghan strategically employs teachers' discourses on tongsayng and shaming practices here, the opposition between Junghan and other children emerges. Jungyoon especially tries to forge alliances with Nayun and Jiwon to confront Junghan. In this process of constructing an alignment structure in which Nayun, Jiwon, and Jungyoon make alliances while Junghan is excluded from it, Jungyoon utilizes various resources such as the social category of gender (line 8) and gestures of offer (line 10) and the employment of the pretend frame along with kin term which stands out as the major strategy. That is, Jungyoon repetitively addresses Nayun and Jiwon as aka (lines 11 and 16) to invoke mutual dependence between the speaker and addressees while refusing to identify Junghan as aka (lines 13 and 18) despite Junghan's continuous claims of aka identity (lines 12 and 17). Even though it is not clear from Jungyoon's statement alone whether her utterance "No, you said you're a hyenga (elder brother)" is related to Junghan's previous statements in line 4, it at least reminds him of his strategy of bestowing pejorative identities on the three girls and establishing authority through this. If the superior status of hyeng grants power and authority in pursuing interactions, the subordinate statuses of aka and tongsayng-dul become valuable resources in the contexts of forging alliances and creating exclusions.

While children utilize the cultural conduct of mutual dependence in manipulating social and personal proximity among themselves as shown in the examples above, they also appropriate the authority-obedience dimension of the elder-younger relationship to control others' behaviors. The following scene exemplifies this usage.

SCENE 4.38: "PLAYING HOUSE"

Participants: Haeun (girl, 3 years), Minju (girl, 3 years), Suji (girl, 3 years), Sungeun (girl, 3 years)

1. ((Minju approaches the play area))
2. Haeun: You're aka (baby).
3. Suji: ((to Minju)) You're aka. You can't do because you're aka.
4. Minju: ((in honorifics)) I'll do many things.
5. Sungeun: ((to Minju)) Minju is a good aka. Minju is a good aka, right? Stay there, okay?

In this scene, Haeun and Suji actively try to protect their interactive space from the intrusion of Minju who approaches the play area to enter the house play. In an effort to restrict Minju's participation, these two children employ a pretend frame and confer the status of aka on Minju. As Suji's statement "You can't do because you're aka" attests, the younger-elder relationship constructed through referring to Minju as aka portrays Minju as incompetent and in the position to be obedient toward her elder. Minju rectifies her subordinate position by shifting her utterance to honorifics, the speech level indexing respect and deference toward the superior but not ordinarily used in peer interactions among children of these ages wherein reciprocal exchange of nonhonorific forms with peers is the norm (line 4). By employing an unconventional form of speech, Minju conveys deference toward Haeun and Suji and at the same time tries to persuade them of her right to enter the existing play by claiming her abilities ("I'll do many things"). Sungeun, another child occupying the play area, then provides inducements for Minju to comply by referring to Minju as a "good aka" but simultaneously conveys the elder's authority by conferring the subordinate identity aka and giving a directive and making a demand ("Stay there, okay?" line 5). Here, Sungeun appropriates both mutual dependence and authority-obedient dimensions of the superior-subordinate relationship to control behaviors of her peer.

The pretend frame and kin terms are also employed in subverting hierarchies of the real world and controlling behaviors of the superior as the following interactions between four-year-old children and a five-year-old child illustrate.

SCENE 4.39: "PLAYTIME"

Participants: Misoo (girl, 5 years), Ara (girl, 4 years), Ayeon (girl, 4 years)

1. ((Misoo approaches Ara and Ayeon who are making cakes using blocks))
2. ((Misoo touches the block and puts it on the top of the cake))
3. Ara: We're making cakes. ((Ara moves and gives Misoo a seat to join them))
4. ((As Misoo joins them and makes cakes, Ayeon makes a sad face to Ara))
5. Ara: ((to Ayeon)) Enni (elder sister), enni won't ruin it. Enni won't. It's okay.
6. ((Ayeon makes a sad face to Ara))
7. Ara: Doggy, doggy. Let's stop. Let's stop. ((Pats Misoo)) That makes *emma* (mommy) angry.

In this scene, the conflict starts as Misoo, who is a year older than Ayeon and Ara, enters into the existing play. Whereas Ara accepts Misoo's entrance by explaining their play to Misoo with accompanying bodily movement (line 3), Ayeon opposes Misoo's joining and appeals to Ara by making facial expressions indexing sadness and refusal (line 4). Ara persuades Ayeon implying that Misoo's entrance will not destroy their alliances (line 5). However, as Ayeon keeps expressing sadness, Ara contrives a strategy that controls Misoo's behavior without explicitly confronting her. Both the way Ara refers to Misoo in line 5—that is, referring to her as an elder sister—and the fact that Ayeon does not directly express opposition to Misoo but appeals to Ara to shun their elder sister, reflect that Misoo is an authoritative figure these younger sisters cannot easily confront. Ara, who is between Ayeon with whom she wants to maintain an alliance and Misoo with whom she cannot engage in a direct challenge, creatively employs the pretend frame and kin term to subvert the hierarchy existing in reality. She addresses the elder sister Misoo as doggy and refers to herself as emma (mommy), thereby constructing a pretense relationship in which she as the superior has rights to give commands toward the subordinate Misoo, and Misoo as the subordinate needs to comply with her wishes. In particular, as Sheldon (1996) notes in her study of preschool girls' negotiation for power in pretend play, the pretend frame here blurs the distinctions between children and their characters, therefore taking some of the responsibilities away from the child for what she is saying. Here, Ara creatively appropriates the pretend frame and her sophisticated understandings of cultural models of conduct in hierarchical relationships to control behaviors of peers and manipulate social orders of the peer world.

Conclusion: Children as Fully Developed Postmodern Fragmented Subjects

Viewing children as complex and active agents inhabiting specific cultural environments, this chapter describes what it is like to be a child in a globalized and globalizing Korea wherein rapid change of socialization ideologies and ideals for personhood create a conflicting and contradictory socialization landscape. Unlike teachers and previous adult-centric views of children and childhood as peripheral to the adult world and undeveloped yet subject to influences from adult norms in the outside world, the detailed ethnographic descriptions of children's social worlds from their point of view indicate that children possess highly sophisticated understandings of the heterogenous and conflicting nature of the socialization milieu, reconstruct and reinterpret competing and contradictory cultural inputs, and sometimes even provide critical and penetrating insights into socialization environments they are exposed to.

The children in this chapter are found to be creating their own meanings and practices of self-expression which are not only distinct from but contrast sharply with the ones teachers provide for them. Whereas self-expression in teacher's socialization practices refers to one's individuated expressions entailing values of creativity and diversity, children reconceptualize and practice self-expression as competition, hierarchy, and relationality. That is, children display keen interest in producing identical expressions to those of their peers to signal belonging to the group, reflect peers' ideas in their own creations to build alliances, and evaluate and rank expressions of one another to create hierarchical social order. Although teachers view children's pursuit of uniformity, ranking, and competition in enacting self-expression as lacking creativity and diversity and therefore signs of the failure of their pedagogical goals, children do intuitively understand the social nature of expression and selectively choose and transform available cultural resources regarding self-expression to address themes of their peer world. Here, unlike teachers who treat self-expression as unfolding in a social vacuum and discuss it in simple terms despite its complex and contradictory enactment in actual socialization contexts, children unconsciously and consciously realize that every expression occurs in a social sphere. Therefore, from children's points of view, every expression is inevitably social and creatively and strategically appropriate for constructing their own culture-laden social world. As shown in children's reactions to teachers' unwitting evaluation of children's creativity, children even have penetrating insights into conflicts and contradictions within the changing socialization landscape and strategically respond to these in their own ways. Children here are never passive recipients of globalizing socialization inputs but rather active participants shaping and reshaping their own rapidly changing socialization landscape.

Furthermore, the model of self-expression children construct on their own is highly systemic and coherent, unlike teachers' conflictual and inconsistent models. That is, whereas teachers adhere to different ideas of self-expression depending on context, children pursue complex but consistent and coherent ideas of self-expression regardless of educational or noneducational/informal contexts. In her study of postmodern fragmented selves, Strauss (1990, 1997) discusses multiple strategies a person could use to deal with heteroglossia and names three different responses as horizontal containment, vertical containment, and integration.

According to her discussion, horizontal and vertical containments work such that one compartmentalizes contradictory cultural models and holds conflicting beliefs in separate and noninteracting compartments. Horizontal containment occurs such that each set of beliefs is more or less equally theorized. Vertical containment differs from horizontal in that one set of vertically contained beliefs is learned more as theory, and hence is verbalized with greater ease, than is the other, which is more implicit (Strauss 1997, 315). Integration is a strategy one uses by selectively choosing parts from each of several contradictory cultural models and integrating them in a new internally consistent one.

Applying Strauss's three different types of responses to contradictory models of self-expression enacted in Somang classroom, Somang teachers and children use strategies of vertical containment and integration, respectively. That is, Somang teachers compartmentalize contradictory models of self-expression. They follow explicit and ideologically dominating models in educational contexts and implicit traditions in other noneducational and mundane occasions. On the other hand, children, exposed to contradictory models of self-expression, selectively choose parts fitting into their peer goals of building a differentiated and stratified social structure and construct a new coherent schema equally easy to articulate and express in a single consistent voice. Moreover, children create their own rituals and ritualized communicative activities and apply them consistently both in educational and noneducational contexts to enact this newly constructed, coherent model of self-expression. The way children use the strategy of integration in dealing with heteroglossia of socialization inputs clearly demonstrates the depth of cultural knowledge they possess regarding conflicting socialization ideologies and the rich cultural abilities used to cope with the conflicts and contradictions. Children are fully developed "postmodern fragmented subjects" (Strauss 1997) as much as teachers are. In the next chapter, we will see how these children as "postmodern fragmented subjects," especially with respect to their transformation and reinterpretation of global imports, significantly change adults' socialization and pedagogical practices, thereby influencing the globally transforming South Korean early childhood socialization landscape.

5

"Maybe We're Not Wrong"

Communal Creativity and Multidirectionality of Learning

It was a hot summer day, about two months after Rainbow Room teachers anxiously expressed to me the difficulty they experienced in providing encouragement for children to find and develop unique senses of self. I entered the Rainbow Room as usual and found that the architecture of the classroom had drastically changed. The tables and play areas once occupying the center of the classroom have been moved into the corner and were taken over by the huge empty space. Ms. Choo approached me and said, "We're doing Scouts this week. Scouts are said to be good for fostering children's senses of cooperation and collaboration. So, for a week, we're doing Scout activities that everybody does things all together." Naming their Scout activity as "Nature Expedition," Rainbow Room teachers designed the curriculum composed mainly of teamwork and explicitly educating children about the importance of collectivity, cooperation, and harmony. Teachers divided the whole class into several groups, asked children to collectively produce outcomes as a team, and sometimes even scolded children for claiming their own opinions in decision-making processes. To accommodate the new curriculum, the free-play areas once set up to have each child individually make play choices were removed and the empty space was instead provided to have more group times and team play. Children who were expected to express their authentic needs, feelings, and thoughts a week ago are now asked to suppress their individuality for the sake of the group and show collectivity, collaboration, and harmony. It was not just the architecture of the classroom but explicit curriculum and socialization goals that had been dramatically changed.

This chapter examines transformations of the socialization landscape to discuss multidirectional learning in globalized contexts. The way children creatively reinterpret and reconstruct heterogeneous and conflicting cultural inputs to build their own culture-laden social world shown in the previous chapter, demonstrates that socialization is never a process of passive internalization or orderly change moving to a definable goal of maturity, but an "uneven and spasmodic process that responds to internal and external stimuli and transforms social experiences into complex systems of meanings" (Van Ausdale and Feagin 2001, 23). In this chapter, I develop this argument further by examining how children's strategic reconstruction and reinterpretation of cultural meanings contribute to the production, extension, and elaboration of adult culture, especially adult socialization practices. Studies highlighting the interactional, negotiated, and dynamic character of learning have argued for the complexity and dynamic fluidity of the expert-novice relation and shown children's direct influence on adults' actions (Cross 1979; Dunn 2013; Jacoby and Gonzales 1991; Kaye 1982; Resnick et al. 1997; Rogoff and Lave 1984; Waksler 1986). These studies have illustrated that children do not simply react to adults' initiatives and directives, but their actions constrain, facilitate, and encourage adults' activities and practices. Rogoff (1990), for instance, articulates the multidirectional nature of socialization through an "apprenticeship model" and the notion of "guided participation." Empirical research such as Pontecorvo and colleagues' (2001) study of Italian families' dinner table talk which details children's discursive contributions to the structure and thematic content of parental talk also substantiates the idea of "mutual apprenticeship."

Like children in these studies, the children in this chapter, as competent cultural beings, do not only coconstruct their own phenomenal social sphere but wield influence in the larger socialization landscape. In the case above, teachers modified and redirected their socialization goals and practices in the process of reacting to children's transformations which they viewed as undesirable and unsatisfactory. That is, as children produced their own meanings of self-expressions loaded with values of uniformity, hierarchy, exclusion, or competition and displayed highly competitive and exclusive demeanors in this process, teachers regarded these transformations as failures of their education and started to revise their curriculum in ways they believed would better obtain socialization goals. Ironically, as indicated in the new curriculum above, teachers, in the process of responding to children's strategic transformations, came to emphasize taken-for-granted local socialization values and beliefs such as communality and relationalities rather than the new ideals of self-expression, creativity, or diversity they explicitly and eagerly pursued.

By closely examining microhistories of activities and curricula enacted in Somang classrooms, this chapter traces the details of those transformations and shows that children's strategic appropriation of classroom activities and accompanying socialization values does not remain restricted to their peer world but exerts influence on teachers' enactment of and views on socialization practices. In particular, I explore how local socialization values undermined in globalized South Korean education due to the ideological emphases given to imported ideas and practices come to constitute major parts of newly revised socialization practices. The microhistories described in this chapter illustrate that children, through their active participation in the globalized socialization landscape, incite teachers to reflect on globally dominant socialization practices they persistently pursue and then make them articulate and practice implicit local socialization values rarely enunciated in dominant socialization discourses. Based on these observations, the chapter argues for the importance of acknowledging the interplay between children's social worlds and the worlds of adults and theorizes socialization as a multidirectional process wherein both children and adults as participants mutually attune, collaborate, and shape learning experiences for one another. The mutual involvement and interplay of children and teachers in indigenizing processes not only furthers the notion of multidirectional learning but also provides empirical materials to discuss children's agency in the meeting of the global and the local in globalizing socialization spheres.

In the following, I discuss multidirectionality by examining four specific activities in Somang preschool: message center, nature expedition, weekend stories, and *tongkuk* (children's drama). These four activities were chosen as the focus of analysis for two related reasons. First, these activities constituted core parts of the Somang curriculum and everyday classroom activities. The message center and tongkuk were practiced across all Somang classrooms and were also popular among children. Children liked to participate in these activities and utilized them in their own ways which often led to drastic transformations of the activities. Teachers also viewed all four activities as key pedagogical areas wherein they could foster their major educational goals and paid attention so that these activities would work as planned. Second, as popular activities among children, these activities were often substantially transformed by children, therefore becoming the central focus of teachers' reform efforts. During my stay in Somang preschool, I could frequently hear teachers having intensive debate and discussion about these activities among themselves, sometimes with outside experts and even with me. As the most debated and discussed and transformed activities, they are ideal places to investigate children's shaping of the globalizing socialization landscape and multidirectionality of learning.

Message Center: From My Expression to Our Expressions

Indigenization of the Message Center

In every classroom of Somang preschool, there is an activity area called the message center in which children are asked to express their own ideas, thoughts, and feelings using a variety of expressive means such as letters or pictures. In implementing the Reggio Emilia approach, Somang preschool not only adopted Reggio's basic philosophies and pedagogies but actively copied specific activities of the original Reggio preschools in Italy. The message center is one of those activities. As with any borrowing of educational forms and ideas, Somang adoption of the message center also entailed selective adoption and transformation rather than straightforward copying of an original form.

The message center, in its original form, is an area in the Reggio Emilia classrooms where children write or draw messages with provided materials such as papers, pens, or pencils. Along with small tables and chairs, the message center typically has small mailboxes with children's names on each box wherein children can send messages created in the center to other children. Educational practices of the Reggio Emilia list development of literacy, communication skills, and social relationships as major goals (Cadwell 2002; Fraser and Wien 2001; Gandini 2005). Gandini (2005) defines the message center as a prominent feature in the classrooms in Reggio Emilia that promotes children's relationships and their desire to communicate in a "hundred languages." Similarly, Cadwell (2002) mentions that the original idea of the message center in Reggio Emilia stems from Italian educators' desire to provide a place where connections and relationships could grow through communication and exchange. Introducing the message center as an effective way of fostering children's literacy and communication, Fraser and Wien (2001) state that children become aware of the need to use conventional symbols as a means of communication and develop abilities to read and write in an authentic way. These goals reflect the sociocentric aspects of the Reggio philosophy which emphasizes good citizenship, community support, and children's learning through their relationships and collaboration with peers, teachers, and community (Gandini 1993).

When the message center came to Somang preschool, however, its overall contours—that is, its educational goals and ways of enactment—were substantially changed to meet local demands. In particular, the sociocentric trends of the original form were stripped off and seemingly expressive and individuated components highlighted and inflated. The following narrative by a Rainbow Room teacher illustrates how the message center was indigenized to reflect local demands and contexts: "What I expected (in this activity) was finding diversity. I wanted to see children drawing bicycles, animals, or airplanes. I mean whatever they have in their own minds. Express their own thoughts in there. Not just copying others." In this comment, Ms. Park conceives of the message center as a place in which children express their own inner thoughts. Contrasting copying others' work with expressing one's own thoughts, she explicitly states that the goal of the message center lies in promoting children's diverse expressions. Similarly, in the following interview, Ms. Choo, another teacher of the Rainbow Room, mentions that she planned the message center as a place in which children express and cultivate their authentic inner feelings and thoughts. Expressing dissatisfaction with children's lack of originality, she compares the purposes of the message center to a rainbow and highlights the phrase "hundred languages," all of which imply that she perceives self-expression, creativity, and diversity as main goals of this educational activity: "I can't understand why everyone is drawing the same thing in the message center. We planned the message center as a place where kids can express their real thoughts. They can also express their feelings in there. Everyone has different colors, right? Reggio calls it 'hundred languages.' We wanted to see rainbows, not just one color."

Although the message center in the Reggio approach originally has multiple educational goals as mentioned before, the adopted format practiced in Somang preschool focuses primarily on promoting children's self-expressions and their individuality. The sociocentric purposes important in the Reggio philosophy, such as relationships, exchange, or communications, get removed and the expressive dimensions are highlighted.

The tendency to reinterpret the message center as a place for promoting self-expression, creativity, and diversity while undermining sociocentric dimensions is also reflected in the spatial arrangement of the message center in the Somang preschool. The original form of the message center includes small mailboxes wherein children can exchange messages created from the center. Although mailboxes are typically located close to or within the message center in their original format, mailboxes in the Somang preschool are separated from the center and located in another area of the classroom. Children, therefore, rarely conceive of the mailbox as connected to the message center, nor do they produce messages for others there. Rather, children usually used the mailbox as an individual locker in which they put their own artwork. This spatial arrangement reflects Somang teachers' lack of interest in communicative and relational aspects of the original message center.

Moreover, even though the original format rarely defines the message center as a place for cultivating children's individual expressions, Somang teachers reinterpret passages such as "developing authentic ways of reading and writing" or "the desire to communicate in a hundred languages" as signifying values of "self-expression," "creativity," or "diversity." That is, even though the passage "the desire to communicate in a hundred languages" includes the importance of communication, Somang teachers rarely pay attention to the communicative aspects of the activity and mostly focus on the phrase "in a hundred languages" which they interpret as implying the development of an individual child's own and distinctive ways of expression. For instance, in the comment above, Ms. Choo quotes only the phrase "hundred languages" from the original, "the desire to communicate in a hundred languages," and uses the analogy of rainbow to highlight diversity and creativity. The phrase "a hundred languages" in Reggio philosophy implies many expressive means belonging to children and the importance of providing an environment in which children can express themselves through diverse symbolic systems such as language, art, music, or dance. Although the phrase "a hundred languages" implies expressiveness, it does not necessarily mean an individual child's creativity and diversity as interpreted by the teachers in the interview. Rather, as shown in the original passage "the desire to communicate in a hundred languages," the message center as well as other Reggio activities view children's learning as interactive and collective outcomes wherein peers, teachers, and parents collaboratively think, negotiate, and revise. Similarly, in the passage "developing authentic ways of reading and writing," teachers focus primarily on the word "authentic" and reinterpret it as implying children's creativity and diversity.

Somang teachers' transformations of the message center reflect recent changes of the larger South Korean socialization landscape, in particular, the way globally dominant socialization ideologies and practices are indigenized in South Korean early childhood education. As I discussed in chapter 3, South Korean early childhood education typically employs a dichotomous and hierarchical framework in implementation of Western or globally popular educational ideas, practices, or curricula. Under this framework, Western or imported socialization curricula are viewed as not only superior to Korean ones but also consist exclusively of globally dominant values considered new, good, and worthy of emulation. Somang teachers, therefore, regarded the Reggio approach and specific activities of the Reggio curriculum, like the message center, as loaded solely with new socialization values and ideologies such as creativity, individuality, or diversity. The sociocentric aspects of the message center such as its emphasis on relationalities and communications were erased and the elements seemingly related to new socialization ideologies amplified to meet the local demand of raising a creative and expressive child. Through these indigenizing processes, the message center became a place for cultivating children's expressivity, creativity, and diversity.

Children's Strategic Transformations

As alluded to in Ms. Choo's interview "I can't understand why everyone is drawing the same thing in the message center" as well as in children's engagements with the message center partly presented in chapter 4, Somang children rarely conceive of the message center as a place for expressing individuated feelings and thoughts as desired by teachers. Children instead strategically appropriate and reinterpret the message center as a site for building, consolidating, and negotiating peer social relationships. Children, in the message center, make similar artwork with peers not to be excluded from the group, fondly draw similar pictures with peers and reflect peers' preferences rather than their own in their drawings to build alliances (see scene 4.4, chapter 4). They include peers as main characters of their artwork to negotiate social distances among themselves (see scene 4.7, chapter 4) and consistently compare and evaluate products of one another to construct social hierarchy as well as to forge coalitions (see scene 4.9, chapter 4).

The message center, in particular, was one of the most popular activities and play areas in Somang classrooms. The Rainbow Room children, for instance, gathered at the message center upon their arrival in the classroom and enjoyed drawing pictures and making artwork in the company of peers at the center. One could easily find children, especially girls in the Rainbow Room, wearing similar outfits and drawing pictures with similar themes such as princesses, hearts, or stars. The following two cases are typical scenes of the message center that show how children participate in and engage with this activity. Scene 5.1 illustrates the way children transform the message center as a place for pursuing social power and authority, one of the major goals of Somang peer world.

"MAYBE WE'RE NOT WRONG" 141

FIGURE 5.1 Drawing similar pictures in the message center.

SCENE 5.1: "MESSAGE CENTER"

Participants: Nuri (girl, 5 years), Sujeong (girl, 5 years), Ayeon (girl, 4 years), Jiwon (girl, 5 years), Dain (girl, 5 years), Seoa (girl, 5 years), Hayun (girl, 4 years), Sein (girl, 5 years)

1. Nuri: ((After finishing making a princess book in the message center, Nuri shows the book to Sujeong and Ayeon)) Princess book, Princess book.
2. Nuri: Would you like to see what's inside? ((unfolds the book)) Ta-da. Ta-da.
3. ((Sujeong and Ayeon do not respond))
4. Nuri: ((shows her princess book to the girls at the table)) You want to have this, right?
5. ((Dain raises her hand))
6. Ayeon: No. ((shakes her head))
7. Jiwon: No. ((shakes her head))
8. Jiwon: Mine is better than yours.

In this scene, a group of girls in the message center jockey for positions in their peer world by evaluating each other's works. The competitive structure emerges as Nuri shows off the princess book she made (lines 1–2) and Sujeong and Ayeon challenge her by ignoring her statements (line 3). Nuri further attempts to position herself as a skillful authoritative figure whom other children envy by producing a rhetorical question "You wanna have this, right?" (line 4). This ritualistic expression that temporarily establishes asymmetries between the questioner and the respondent depending on the responses of the respondent constructs a hierarchical relationship with Dain who positions herself as low in expertise by showing her aspiration for getting Nuri's princess book (line 5). By contrast, Ayeon and Jiwon explicitly oppose Nuri's attempts to gain power by refusing Nuri's offer (lines 6–7) and making a statement that Jiwon's book is better than Nuri's (line 8).

In the subsequent exchanges, similar interactional structures emerge. The children competitively decorate their princess books and incessantly attempt to establish hierarchical rankings by producing rhetorical questions (lines 9–10, 12–14, 15–18).

9. Jiwon: ((decorates her princess book)) You guys want to have mine, right?
10. ((Children at the table do not respond))
11. ((Nuri decorates her princess book more by adding hearts to the book cover))
12. Nuri: ((shows her princess book)) You guys want to have mine, right?
13. ((Dain raises her hand))
14. ((Seoa raises her hand))
15. Nuri: You want to hear how I made the book? ((shows the inside of her book)) I draw this in here and here. And this is the heart. I draw the eyes here and color it with blue pencil.
16. Nuri: You guys want to see the inside? ((shows her book))
17. Nuri: ((looks at Dain)) Who wants to have this?
18. ((Dain raises her hand))

Furthermore, in the following subsequent interactions, Nuri, who is most active in these interactions, utilizes the social category of age in debating where she stands relative to other children in terms of expertise.

19. Dain: ((to Hayun)) Hayun, this ((Nuri's book)) is really pretty.
20. ((Hayun does not respond and draws her book))
21. Nuri: You guys want to have this, right? Who wants to see inside? I'll show you only inside.
22. ((Sujeong, Ayeon, and Jiwon look at Nuri but do not respond))
23. Nuri: I'm five years old in American age.
24. Dain: Right. Right.
25. Nuri: ((to Hayun)) Are you five, too?
26. ((Hayun looks at Nuri and does not respond. She decorates her book))
27. Nuri: Nahee is still four years old. Her birthday is summer.
28. Nuri: ((looks at Sein who is decorating her princess book with Jiwon)) Hey, Sein. You have to draw by yourself.

29. Nuri: ((to Dain)) They don't draw better than me, right?
30. Dain: Jiwon draws better than you.
31. Nuri: You're saying that Jiwon doesn't do better than seven years old? Seven-year-olds draw eyes in this way . . . and . . .

In the above interactions, as Hayun, Sujeong, Ayeon, and Jiwon tacitly oppose Nuri's attempts to gain power and authority by ignoring Nuri's moves (lines 20, 22), Nuri states that she is five years old in American age (line 23) and asks Hayun whether she is the same age as Nuri (line 25). Even though the children in this scene are all six years old in Korean age which is counted as one year old when one is born and one becomes two years old on January 1 of the next year, their American ages differ depending on the birthday of each child. Here, Nuri tactically uses the idea of American age to articulate hierarchies and gain authority among the children. She points out the age of Hayun who is four years old in American age and also brings up Nahee's age as a topic of the talk in her efforts to challenge Hayun's and other children's deliberate disregard for Nuri's statements. Moreover, as Dain appraises Jiwon's drawing as superior to Nuri's (line 30), Nuri downgrades Jiwon's drawing based on the rationale that a six-year-old's drawing—that is, Jiwon's drawing—cannot be better than a seven-year-old's (line 31). The children, in this scene, turn the message center into a place for evaluating one another in terms of skills, arguing over rankings, and gaining authority through competitions.

Children transform the message center not only to construct social hierarchy but also to establish differentiated social structure, another major goal of the Somang peer world. The following scene illustrates how the children negotiate social distances among themselves by drawing pictures of one another in the message center.

SCENE 5.2: "MESSAGE CENTER"

Participants: Ayeon (girl, 4 years), Nahee (girl, 4 years), Nuri (girl, 5 years), Dain (girl, 5 years)

1. ((Ayeon, Nahee, Nuri, and Dain are in the message center))
2. Ayeon: Who should I draw in the mini book?
3. ((Nahee, Nuri, and Dain raise their hands))
4. Ayeon: Eeny, meeny, miny, moe. Nahee.
5. ((Nuri and Dain give a sigh of disappointment))
6. Ayeon: I'll give a Hello Kitty to the one who I draw the last. Who wants to give way?
7. ((Nahee, Nuri, and Dain raise their hands))
8. Ayeon: I'm gonna start from Dain, then.
9. ((Ayeon draws Dain on the paper))
10. Ayeon: You two give way to Dain, so I'll draw you guys later.

144   BETWEEN SELF AND COMMUNITY

11. Ayeon: ((after finishing Dain)) Dain, do you like it? I'm done with Dain. Who should I draw next?
12. Nuri: Raise your hand if you'd like to look after this. ((picks up the picture she has been drawing))
13. ((Ayeon, Nahee, Dain raise their hands))
14. Nuri: ((to Ayeon)) You look after this. ((Nuri leaves the table to get a pen))
15. Ayeon: Raise your hand if you'd like to take a picture at my birthday party.
16. ((Nahee and Dain raise their hands))
17. Ayeon: Eeny, meeny, miny, moe.
18. Ayeon: Now I'm gonna draw Nahee.

In this scene, Ayeon actively recruits the members to be drawn in her mini book and negotiates with three other children over their turns to be the character of her mini book. Here, the four children produce the repetitive interactive structure in which Ayeon asks questions using the phrase starting with "who . . ." and "raise your hands . . ." and other children raise their hands (lines 2–3, lines 6–7, lines 15–16). Along with the questions "You wanna have this, right?" or "Who wants to have this?" in scene 5.1, Somang children, in their everyday peer talk, frequently produced this interactive structure which has an effect of forging alliances between the questioner and the respondent as well as building power asymmetries between them. By continuously producing these questions and actively drawing other children in her mini book, Ayeon attempts to form alliances with other children and also temporarily attains the power of controlling other children. The alliance structure formed at this particular moment, however, constantly fluctuates, and the children actively utilize the message center, especially the strategy of drawing other children, in these constant shifts of alliance and exclusion as the following subsequent interactions illustrate.

19. Ayeon: Now it's over if I finish Nahee. How should I draw Nahee?
20. ((Ayeon draws Nahee on the paper))
21. Nahee: Color here with pink, Ayeon.
22. Ayeon: No. ((colors the crown with yellow))
23. ((Nahee stares at Ayeon))
24. Nuri: I'm done with Nahee. Who wants to go next? ((Nahee moves her seat from Ayeon to Nuri))
25. Nuri: Eeny, meeny, miny, moe. Dain.
26. Nuri: Dain, which color would you like me to draw you? Pink?
    . . .
27. Ayeon: This is just for me. I'm not gonna draw anyone. I'm gonna draw a friend you guys don't know. I'm gonna draw a friend you guys don't know at all.
28. Nuri: How about here?
29. Dain: Like Nahee's.

30. Ayeon: This is Nahee. I'm gonna make it really, really pretty. ((touches Nahee's head in the picture)) How would you like this to be colored? Which color? Or a crown?

31. Dain: ((to Nahee)) Which one do you think is prettier? Mine or yours?

Here, the alliance formed between Ayeon and Nahee in the previous interaction falls apart as Ayeon refuses to draw Nahee in ways requested by Nahee (lines 19–23) as Nahee's paralinguistic behaviors in lines 23 and 24 demonstrate. Nuri, on the other hand, uses this fracturing moment as a chance to form coalitions with Nahee and Dain by making a statement that she finished drawing Nahee (line 24) and also by drawing Dain in her princess book through close consultation with her (line 26). Against Nuri's move, Ayeon first withdraws her commitment to draw Nahee to influence and curb Nahee's stances (line 27) but later resumes previous strategies of drawing Nahee by making a statement that she will draw Nahee very prettily and actively asking Nahee how she wants to be drawn in Ayeon's mini book (line 30).

This interaction lasted for forty-six minutes, and the oppositional and competitive structure made between Nuri and Ayeon over making alliances with Dain and Nahee in the above scene soon shifted as Nuri chose Ayeon to be drawn in her book and then drew Ayeon as requested by her. The coalition between Nuri and Ayeon, however, later broke off again as Ayeon attempted to restore an alliance with Nahee by choosing her as the partner to share her work and reaffirming her commitment to draw Nahee in her book. Drawing a friend in the princess book, especially drawing as requested by a friend, is an emblem of friendship and thereby has an effect of forging alliances among peers. Strategically using drawing as a resource for soliciting alliances and enforcing exclusions, children mark and police social and personal distances among themselves. In this process, the message center activity becomes one of the resources children utilize to negotiate and confront everyday dynamics of coalition formation within the peer world.

Children's engagement with the message center activity seen so far parallels the way Somang children redefine and reconceptualize self-expression as relationality, competition, and power in other educational contexts, issues discussed in chapter 4. Children in the message center display keen interest in personal expressions as desired by teachers. However, the meanings, motivations, and outcomes of children's expressions diverge sharply from teachers' initial educational goals. Although teachers expect to find children's creative and diverse expressions in the message center, children pay more attention to where they stand vis-à-vis one another in terms of expertise, thereby typically producing highly uniform expressions such as princess drawings or princess mini books in the scenes above. At the same time, unlike teachers' expectations to cultivate individual children's unique preferences, thoughts, and ideas through message center activity, children's drawings there are highly influenced by peers' preferences and needs as means of negotiating social distances among the children in their peer world. For Somang children, the message center is a site for constructing hierarchical rankings and alliances within friendship groups through competition, copying, and comparison.

Teachers' Redefinition of the Message Center

Somang teachers were highly critical of the way children strategically utilized and appropriated the message center. Their criticisms were multifold, but the first and explicit reaction lay mostly in problematizing children's pursuits of uniformity and hierarchy. Children's princess drawing in the message center was the target of particular criticism in the Rainbow Room. Rainbow teachers' explicit goal for the message center was promoting children's diverse expressions as reflected in Ms. Park's narrative in which she "wanted to see children drawing bicycles, animals, or airplanes." However, as shown above, what teachers encountered in the message center was children competitively drawing princesses highly influenced by peers' standards and requests. Confronted with the discrepancies between socialization goals and outcomes, teachers criticized children's activities for not being creative, authentic, or diverse enough. In particular, teachers interpreted children's longings for uniformity, hierarchy, and competition found in the message center as negative aspects of Korean traditional educational practices that hinder development of true and authentic expressions expected of children in globalizing South Korea. Teachers, therefore, closely scrutinized the message center activity and made efforts to reformulate it in ways they presumed would restore its initial educational goals. Teachers, for instance, had heated discussions about children's expressions, behaviors, and attitudes in the message center and consulted with one another about pedagogical methods for modifying outcomes perceived as failures. The message center issue of the Rainbow Room, in particular, was shared by the Somang preschool teachers through a weekly conference in which the director, teachers, and sometimes outside experts discussed classroom activities, outcomes, and pedagogies. It became a "problem" to be corrected.

Interestingly, whereas teachers' first and explicit reaction focused primarily on the lack of creativity and diversity of expressions, the main focus of discussions shifted to the issues of communality and relationships as reformulation efforts developed. The following narrative by Ms. Choo nicely illustrates this point: "I think kids don't know how to play together yet. They are together, but don't know what living together really means. They're all too individualistic. In girls' play, Nuri draws very pretty. So other girls look at her drawing, ask her to draw one for them, and then copy what Nuri drew. Nuri won't be excited either. It's not like 'Wow, Nuri, yours are so great.' Kids just ask her to give one to them and that's it. They don't know how to make things together."

Expressing the difficulty of attaining educational goals in the message center, Ms. Choo in this comment problematizes children's tendency to copy one particular child's product. At the same time, however, the overall focus of this comment lies in children's inabilities to play or live together. In particular, Ms. Choo views children's practice of requesting, drawing, and giving pictures as an indication that children "do not know how to make things together" and even interprets it as individualistic. For Ms. Choo, children's exchange of drawings is individualistic or egoistical in that the purpose of exchange lies primarily in possessing or reproducing drawings rather than in constructing reciprocal and mutual relationships as reflected in her statement, "Nuri won't be excited either. It's not like, 'Wow, Nuri, yours are so great.' Kids just ask her to give one to them and that's it."

Teachers also interpret children's longings for competition and hierarchy found in the message center as reflections of egocentricity. In the following interview, for instance, Ms. Park interprets children's status seeking and competition as showing off and criticizes children's expressions for being too egoistic: "They're all into comparing one another's drawings and arguing [that] one's drawing is better than others. They draw just to show off. They never appreciate others' work, [they are] only interested in winning . . . They're only interested in themselves, too egotistic."

Teachers' narratives clearly show that their main concerns lie more on communality and relationality rather than diversity or creativity of expressions. While teachers agonize over the difficulty of attaining the educational goal of diverse and creative expressions, what catches their eyes first when they are confronted with the so-called message center problem is children's lack of cooperation, communality, or thoughtfulness. That is, teachers view children's interactions in the message center through lenses of embodied and implicit cultural beliefs and practices that are rarely articulated in dominant South Korean socialization discourses. Although teachers discarded and erased the sociocentric aspects of the original message center in their adoption of it, what bothered them first and most in children's activities at the message center was insufficient collectivity, modesty, and considerateness.

This view and interpretation, then, led to reforms of the message center. Based on their scrutiny and deliberate discussions about the message center activity, Somang teachers reformed the activity in several ways, all of which are highly geared toward promoting communality and relationships. First, teachers contrived a new space called the decorating center in which children could concentrate on making "pretty" things such as princesses, closets, and so forth. By providing a separate place where children could fulfill their egotistic needs, teachers attempted to restore what they now consider the initial functions and aims of the message center—that is, communication and relationalities. This new space intends to prevent children from competitively producing uniform outcomes in the message center as the following remark by Ms. Park explains:

148 BETWEEN SELF AND COMMUNITY

I couldn't see any delivery going on in the message center today. Everyone is just taking their own. No one is giving his or her drawings to others. It's used totally differently from what we initially planned. We thought the message center was a place to express one's own feelings and communicate one's minds to others. But as I saw today, no one is giving drawings to others. They just draw their own pretty things. Kids just say, "It's pretty, so give it to me" and then take it. If it's like that, I guess we just need a place to make something really pretty for oneself. Why do we need a message center? I'm thinking about rather making a separate place where children can just make pretty things.

Similar to Ms. Choo's statement before, Ms. Park here criticizes children's behaviors in the message center as egocentric and not being relational enough. Problematizing children's tendency to draw pretty pictures simply for themselves and not exchange them, she brings up the idea of making a separate place in which children make "pretty" things without any constraints. A week after this interview, Rainbow teachers made a separate decorating place and urged children to go to the decorating center, not message center, if they would like to make pretty things like princesses, houses, clothes, and so forth (figure 5.2). Interestingly, contrary to her previous interview in which she defined the message center as a place for promoting children's diverse expressions, Ms. Park here explicitly states the initial goal of the message center activity as communication among minds as well as expression of one's own feelings. In the process of teachers' readjustment to children's transformations, the message center now becomes a place for communication and establishing relationships.

If teachers created the decorating center to discourage children's pursuit of uniformity and competition in the message center, they, at the same time, made concerted efforts to promote communicative and relational aspects of the message center through various means. Teachers, for instance, on the table of the message center, provided pictures of all classroom members and papers printed with two blank squares, as shown in figure 5.3. If they simply furnished pencils, crayons, and blank paper to have children freely and individually express their authentic thoughts and feelings before, now they induced children to write letters and produce pictures and artworks for others by providing these new materials. The new materials forced children to indicate to whom they would send a picture or letter by having them fill out the blank squares with names or pictures of classroom members. As shown in figure 5.4, children started to produce pictures or letters for others and their products consisted of signs reflecting peer social relationships. In the first product by Dongju, a four-year-old boy of the Rainbow Room, he puts his name and his classmate's name, Jungeun, in the blank boxes of the paper, draws a picture of a boy and a girl holding hands, and writes, "I love you." Similarly, the second product by Ayeon, a four-year-old girl of the Rainbow Room, is composed of pictures of classroom members—that is, two teachers, herself,

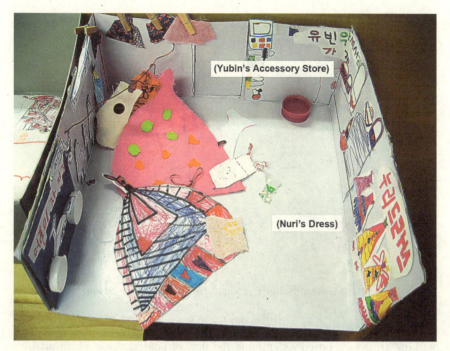

FIGURE 5.2 Decorating center.

FIGURE 5.3 New materials in the message center.

FIGURE 5.4 Children's products from the message center.

and the other girl. Here, Ayeon, by adding hearts and crowns in the pictures and marking arrows supposedly signifying the flow of hearts, produces an artwork about social relations and ties.

To assist children's writing, teachers even provided a list of phrases children are supposed to write on letters as well as the ones children frequently write in the messages. The paper hung in the message center listed the following phrases: love you, teacher, like you, cute, fun, pretty, thank [you], Rainbow Room, twinkle, mom and dad, grandma, cat, meow, butterfly, and, storybook, athletics, summer wave, rainbow, misena princess, yaeri princess, ballerina, heart, dress, Ms. Ahn, Ms. Min, Ms. Lee. This list, made by teachers in consultation with children, is composed mainly of three categories: persons (mom and dad, Ms. Min, Ms. Lee, teacher, etc.), themes frequently appearing in children's artwork (princess, dress, heart, twinkle, etc.), and adjectives and verbs (love you, like you, thank, pretty, etc.). Although the ostensible function of this list lies in helping illiterate children write letters, the list encourages children to make artwork about or for classroom members. The category of adjectives and verbs, in particular, coerces children to express affection, thankfulness, and compliments toward peers. Children are supposed to love, like, or thank others but are not given choices to hate or exclude others or even to delve into their own selves as asked by teachers before. Not only the relational quality but the kinds of relationships and personhood teachers expect of their students are reflected in these newly made materials.

In addition to classroom members' pictures, printed papers, and the list of phrases, teachers also placed the mailbox beside the message center and encouraged children to drop letters and drawings into the mailbox. Teachers, then, opened the mailbox once a day and, during group time, showed who wrote letters to whom

FIGURE 5.5 Mailbox in the message center.

and delivered letters to children. If they urged children to make artwork for and about others through newly contrived materials, teachers here attempt to show reciprocal and relational effects artwork can have on social spheres by having artwork delivered to peers through the mailbox. Children originally drew or made things mainly to compete with peers and possess for themselves; by setting up the mailbox, teachers expect children to make relationships by writing letters or making things for others as the following statement by Ms. Choo during the group time illustrates: "Do we need mailbox if we don't have any letters in it? Mailbox is hungry. I'll see who puts the most in the mailbox. It is useless if we just draw pictures and put them into your own mailbox. Please write many letters to our friends."

Teachers also highly praised letters or drawings children made for others. For instance, as Seryin, a four-year-old in the Rainbow Room, brought mini books she made for classmates during the weekend to school one day, Rainbow teachers had her introduce her mini books during the morning meeting, praised her for making so many mini books for friends, and encouraged children to write letters or make mini books to send to friends by participating in the message center activities. At the same time, teachers emphasized an obligation for a return by encouraging children to reply to the letters they received. After the morning meeting, for instance, Ms. Park asked Minsu how many letters he received, and as Minsu answered that he got six letters, she asked, "How many did you write?" As Minsu hesitated to answer, she mentioned his duty to reply by stating, "Can you write back six letters, then?" Children who did not respond to teachers' efforts to redefine the message center as a place for building relationships and communication were constantly and sometimes explicitly asked to write letters and make artwork for others. Ms. Lee, for instance, approached Ara who drew diagrams using rulers in the message center. Ms. Lee asked why she did not write letters and suggested that she write letters to send to friends. As Ara refused by shaking her head, Ms. Lee said, "Friends gave you many letters. Don't you feel good when you get letters?" Ara kept shaking her head no, and Ms. Lee this time coaxed Ara to write back to her after she (Ms. Lee) wrote one to Ara. Even though Ms. Lee's persuasion failed as Ara focused on drawing her own work while shaking her head no, this teacher's efforts demonstrate that the message center is no more a place for cultivating a child's individual self-expressions but a site for developing relationalities, communalities, and reciprocities. Teachers made this newly established goal explicit by articulating it in the group time through statements such as, "You don't draw a princess standing pretty at the message center" and "It's good to have happy feelings in your own mind, but it's also good to share them. Minds never shrink if we share them."

In the process of reforming the message center, teachers also started to explicitly define and educate the ideal form of expressions as the following classroom lesson illustrates.

SCENE 5.3: "GOOD EXPRESSION LESSON"

Participants: Ms. Lee (teacher), Minjun (boy, 5 years), Sion (girl, 5 years), Jiho (boy, 6 years), Doyun (boy, 5 years), Hawon (girl, 6 years)

1. ((Ms. Lee shows Munch's *The Scream*, Dürer's *Praying Hands*, and a princess cartoon to the students))
2. Ms. Lee: Which one do you think is the prettiest?
3. Children: Princess.
4. Ms. Lee: Yes. Princess is pretty. But you know what? This one ((points to Dürer's picture)) is also a good one because the painter who drew this picture thought of his friend when he drew this picture. The painter had a friend who also liked to be a painter. But they were very poor, so could not go to school. So they promised to help each other. Dürer's friend worked and helped Dürer to go to school. Dürer became a famous painter thanks to his friend and looked for his friend to help him. When the painter found his friend, he was praying for the painter. The friend prayed, "I'm too late to be a painter. But please make my friend Dürer a good painter." Dürer was very impressed and drew his friend's praying hands. ((points to the picture)) This is those praying hands. Isn't it impressive? This picture is a good one because he drew it while thinking of his friend.
5. Ms. Lee: ((points to Munch's *Scream*)) How about this picture? How does this person look like?

"MAYBE WE'RE NOT WRONG"

6. Minjun: He looks funny. ((smiles)
7. Sion: He doesn't have hair. ((giggles))
8. ((Children giggle))
9. Jiho: My younger sister doesn't have hair either. ((giggles))
10. Ms. Lee: Let's go back to pictures again. Which one do you think is better one? ((points to Dürer's picture)) This one? Or princess?
11. Doyun: ((points to Dürer's picture)) That one.
12. Ms. Lee: Yes. If you guys just draw princesses, you can't draw the picture like this. Is this a great prince picture?
13. ((Children shake their heads))
14. Ms. Lee: No. This is not a prince picture, but people are impressed by this picture because in drawing it, the painter thought of his friend and tried to reflect his friend's thoughts. The painter put his own thankful mind in this picture, too. He drew it not to show off but to think of his friend. Showing off is not important. So only pretty princess picture is a good one?
15. Hawon: No. You have to have a loving mind for your friends.
16. Ms. Lee: Right. And it is also a good attitude to appreciate other friends' pictures. This afternoon, I think it will be good to draw something that shows you are thinking of others.

In this scene, Ms. Lee defines "good expression" as reflecting loving minds toward others and consistently compares it with other forms of expressions such as boasting or appearance-focused expressions. Comparing three different types of pictures, the teacher explicitly downgrades the princess drawing, the children's favorite one, as egotistically oriented and valorizes Dürer's painting for reflecting friendship between Dürer and his friend. By framing the princess cartoon as a less desirable form of expression, the teacher implies that the princess pictures the children competitively drew in the message center are inferior. Moreover, she explicitly criticizes bragging and the pursuit of prettiness involved in the children's princess drawings and states that prettiness is not the only standard of good expression. By contrast, Dürer's painting is framed as exemplary of the good expression that children need to follow. The teacher introduces the story behind Dürer's painting, highly praises it for showing a caring attitude toward friends, and encourages children to produce a picture like Dürer's when they are in the message center.

The interesting point here lies in that although the teacher consistently compares Dürer's paintings and the princess cartoon, she never places Munch's *Scream* into the comparative framework, nor does she develop it in discussions on "good expression." Rather, she briefly asks children what they think of the person in the picture and then shifts to compare the other two pictures. Moreover, even though children make fun of Munch's picture and express negative attitudes toward it, the teacher does not make any comments on it. Given that Munch's painting could be a good example with which to discuss creativity or diversity of expressions, the teacher's attitude toward Munch's painting reveals that creativity and diversity, which were initial goals of the message center when Somang preschool first adopted the Reggio's message center, are no longer their primary concerns. Even though teachers mentioned that their reform aimed to restore the initial functions of expressing unique selves through message center activities, in the process of reacting and responding to children's transformations, the initial goal of promoting children's creative and diverse expressions faded and the message center was transformed into a place for cultivating caring expressions for others and making relationships through expressions.

The way teachers reformed the message center activity illustrated so far shows how globally dominant socialization values collide with taken-for-granted local ones in the South Korean classroom. Affection, relationships, and communality are implicit, unmarked, and tacit local socialization values teachers initially rarely articulated and sometimes downplayed in order to emphasize the ideological importance of new socialization values. Yet teachers eventually try to instill these very values through the reform of the message center reintroducing the sociocentric elements stripped off in the initial adoption of this classroom focus. As features of new values collide with local ones, as is the case in which self-expression inevitably involves egotistical pursuit, arrogance, and competition, teachers evaluated and reformed activities in terms of taken-for-granted habitus (Bourdieu 1977) rather than new ideologies.

The interesting point here is that the sociocentric values teachers made concerted efforts to cultivate through the reform were already found and even apparent in children's use of the message center as seen in chapter 4 and examples above. Children fondly drew pictures about their peer relations, actively reflected tastes of peers in their artwork, and exchanged their creations with peers in the message center. Teachers, however, were oblivious to these relational and communicative aspects of children's early participation as they tended to view and evaluate children's creations through the lens of the new socialization ideologies: individuality, creativity, or diversity. They could not simultaneously see the relational, communicative, and collaborative elements manifested in the children's processes. Even when teachers looked closely at children's participation, they were likely to problematize the pursuit of status and exclusivity entailed in children's negotiations of social distances and hierarchies through their artwork. Given that every value has both "good" and "bad" sides, the desirable aspect of sociocentric values cannot be detached from undesirable ones such as exclusivity and hierarchy. That is, when children used artwork as a means of self-expression and building social relations, this involved undesirable qualities such as exclusion, hierarchy, or uniformity as well as desirable ones of affection, alliance, or collaboration. This dual nature is shown in the next microhistory of the message center—that is, children's retransformation.

Children's Retransformation

Teachers' reform of the message center activity did not remain constant but was actively and strategically reinterpreted and retransformed by children, reflecting the mutual, negotiated, and dynamic character of socialization. At a glance, children seemed to conform to newly set educational goals of the message center. Children's final products consisted mainly of letters, pictures, and artwork about peer relationships as shown in figure 5.4 and children increasingly displayed interests in the exchange of their final products. Children's fondness for princess drawings and copying of peers' artwork diminished. In these respects, teachers' reform efforts seemed to work successfully.

Close observation of children's interactions at the message center, however, shows other developments. Although children produced artwork about their peer social relations and used these to construct reciprocal, affectionate, and egalitarian relationships as desired by teachers, at the same time, they actively utilized the newly reformed activity as ways to police behaviors of peers and negotiate social distances among them, the characteristics of peer interactions that teachers typically viewed as undesirable. In conflicts with peers, for instance, children frequently used letters as means to control behaviors of others as the following scenes illustrate.

SCENE 5.4: "BLOCK AREA"

Participants: Junwoo (boy, 4 years), Dongju (boy, 4 years)

1. Junwoo: ((shows the triangular block to Dongju)) Look, look.
2. Dongju: Let me do it. Let me do it.
3. Junwoo: No.
4. Dongju: Then I'm gonna write a letter to you that I hate you. I'm gonna write a letter to you.

SCENE 5.5: "DECORATING AREA"

Participants: Ara (girl, 4 years), Bora (girl, 4 years), Ayeon (girl, 4 years)

1. ((Ara, Bora, and Ayeon make a house using boxes and decorating materials))
2. Bora: ((moves the bed)) You have to put the bed here.
3. Ara: ((raises her voice)) Hey. Hey.
4. Bora: To here.
5. Ara: Hey. Hey.
6. Bora: ((points to the place Ara put the bed)) No, this is a living room. You can't put the bed in the living room.
7. Ara: Don't talk to me.
8. Bora: I mean if the bed is outside the living room . . . ((takes off the bed and moves it to the other side))
9. Ara: Don't take it off.

10. Bora: I'm not taking it off.
11. Ara: Why are you doing everything as you want?
12. Bora: No, I'm not.
13. Ara: Hey, I'm not gonna write a letter to you, then.
14. Ayeon: ((to Ara)) Would you like me to write one for you?
15. Ara: Okay.

In scene 5.4, Dongju, in his conflict with Junwoo over the toy, strategically uses the idea of writing a letter to express his unpleasant feelings toward Junwoo and curb Junwoo's behaviors. Unlike the desired norm of writing an amicable and cordial letter to peers, Dongju states to Junwoo that he will write a letter that he hates Junwoo (line 4), thereby trying to have Junwoo share his blocks with him. Similarly, in scene 5.5, Bora and Ara argue over the spot to place the bed in their making of the house and Ara displays uneasiness toward Bora's attitude by stating, "Why are you doing everything as you want?" (line 11). As Bora continues to disagree with Ara's location of the bed, Ara then withdraws her alliance with Bora by stating, "Hey, I'm not gonna write a letter to you, then" in line 13 and tries, in this way, to influence Bora's behaviors and attitudes. Although writing a letter meant establishing an affectionate relationship with peers in teachers' reform of the message center, children here strategically use it as means to police and control behaviors of peers with whom they are in conflict.

Children also used the reformed activity in the negotiation of social distances among themselves as the following cases illustrate.

SCENE 5.6: "MESSAGE CENTER"
Participants: Soojung (girl, 5 years), Suji (girl, 5 years)

1. ((Soojung puts classmates' pictures on the paper and writes numbers on the top of each picture))
2. ((Suji comes into the Rainbow classroom))
3. ((Soojung runs into Suji holding her artwork))
4. Soojung: ((shows her artwork)) Look at this. Look. You're here.
5. Suji: Here?
6. Soojung: ((points to Suji's picture in the artwork)) Yes, you're the first.

SCENE 5.7: "MESSAGE CENTER"
Participants: Nuri (girl, 4 years), Jiwon (girl, 4 years), Haejin (girl, 5 years), Soojung (girl, 5 years)

1. ((Nuri writes the phrase "persons who can be a princess" in the middle of the paper, draws lines along the top and the bottom of the phrase, and writes "yes" and "no." She then writes the names of the Rainbow Room children))
2. Nuri: ((to Jiwon)) Look, you're here. You can be a princess.
3. ((Jiwon smiles and puts her arm around Nuri's shoulder))

4. ((Haejin looks at Nuri's picture))
5. Haejin: ((to Nuri with threatening voice)) Next time.
6. Nuri: Okay.
7. ((Nuri writes Haejin's name in the "yes" part))
8. Nuri: Who else wants to be a princess?
9. ((Children in the message center raise their hands))
10. ((As Soojung does not pay attention to Nuri's question, Nuri puts Soojung's name in the "no" part))
11. Nuri: Soojung sister can't be a princess, right?
12. ((Jiwon nods))

In scene 5.6, Soojung makes artwork about her relationships with peers as expected by the newly set goal of the activity but strategically appropriates it in order to manipulate social distances with peers. Soojung puts classmates' pictures on the paper and writes names and numbers on each picture. She then shows her artwork to Suji and elucidates it by stating, "Look at this. Look. You're here" and "Yes, you're the first" in lines 4 and 6. As these statements indicate, pictures and numbers of Soojung's artwork signify her preferences for some classmates, therefore having the effect of manipulating peer relationships in the real social sphere. By lining up Suji in the first place of her artwork, Soojung expresses affection toward Suji and endeavors to make alliances with her.

In similar contexts, Nuri in scene 5.7 maneuvers social status and distances in her friendship group by strategically utilizing the message center activity. As her product from the message center in figure 5.6 shows, Nuri's artwork titled "Persons who can be a princess" consists of "yes" and "no" parts. By selectively choosing classmates to be included in these two parts, Nuri skillfully manipulates her status and alignment structure in the peer world. She puts Jiwon's name in the second position (with herself as the first) of the "yes" part and shows it to Jiwon to forge alliances (line 2) and actively recruits members to be included in the "yes" part to both gain authority and build affiliations (lines 8–9). The way she puts Soojung, who does not pay attention to her recruitment, in the "no" part clearly shows that her artwork is a powerful medium through which she attempts to influence her peer relationships.

The way children retransform the reformed message center activity demonstrates the very nature of socialization—that is, the multidirectionality of learning. Whereas teachers, through the reform, expected children to use the message center as a place to construct an idealized social structure in which everyone is affectionate, collaborative, and considerate to one another, children retransformed the reformed activity to address themes of their peer world—that is, building differentiated and hierarchical social relationships. Children were already utilizing the message center as a place to negotiate peer social relations even before the reform when teachers stressed the individuated, expressive, and creative features of the message center activity. Children's appropriation, however, became more explicit and blatant as teachers reinforced sociocentric aspects of the message

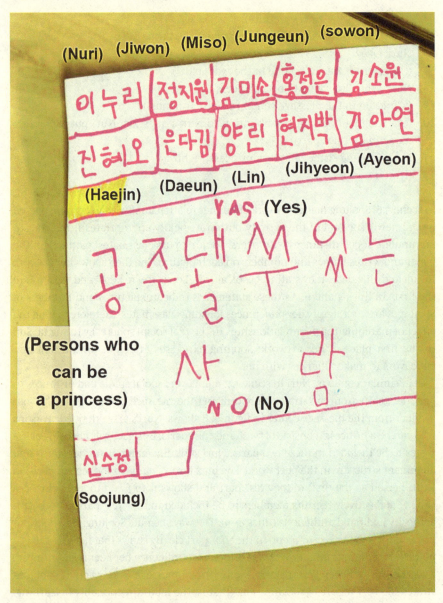

FIGURE 5.6 Artwork from the message center (product from scene 5.7).

center. That is, if children's transformations before focused more on producing the same themes or styles of artwork to belong to the group, reflecting peers' tastes in the production to forge alliances, and comparing products of one another to build hierarchical relationships, as sociocentric elements are stressed and easily accessible through the reform, the retransformation centered more on the open, deliberate, and straightforward utilization of the products in negotiating and manipulating social relations. The focus of children's strategic transformations shifted largely from the pursuit of uniformity, competition, and hierarchy to the manipulation of social distances. At the same time, children's exchange of the products at the message center became more superficial and perfunctory as relationalities came to be the norm and the strategic use of the exchange became rampant in children's interactions. Children often handed over letters to peers without much enthusiasm and the ones who received letters also crassly returned thanks. If the purpose of the reform was to restore the communicative and relational aspects of the message center, it achieved its goal as relationalities became the major themes of children's productions and the exchange of artwork and letters prevailed at the message center. However, if its aim was to have children build affectionate, inclusive, and considerate relationships with peers, teachers' reform efforts were only partially successful. For children, the message center was still a place for constructing hierarchical, differentiated, and exclusive social relationships as well as for building alliances and collaboration.

Nature Expedition: Scout Activity and Reinforcement of Communality and Relationality

Discourses of Children's Undesirable Peer Interactions

As shown in the case of the message center, Somang teachers were highly critical of children's performances, behaviors, and play displayed in a variety of everyday classroom activities. Discourses on children's unsatisfactory performances, in particular, centered on the prevalence of uniformity, hierarchy, competition, and exclusivity in peer interactions. Talking about children's relationships, for instance, the Rainbow Room teacher Ms. Park once stated to other teachers that their room is like *"Our Twisted Hero, the episode littles." Our Twisted Hero* is a bestselling South Korean novel that portrays distorted and corrupted power relations of students in an elementary classroom in a small rural village. First published in 1983, the novel consists of a story about the authoritarian and tyrannical main character student and his rule of other classmates and is typically read as an allegory of South Korea under its corrupt dictatorial regimes. By adding "the episode littles" to the original title and drawing the analogy between peer interactions of their students and those depicted in the novel, she regards her students' social relationships not only as hierarchical but even authoritarian and dictatorial. In a similar vein, looking at children's disputes over the role and the story of pretend play, Ms. Choo, the Rainbow Room teacher, states to the other teacher that their classroom is the "animal kingdom." These two analogies allude to teachers' highly negative and critical gazes toward children's pursuit of power, authority, and hierarchy in peer interactions.

The main reason teachers problematize children's hierarchical social relationship lies in their view of power asymmetry as hindering creativity and diversity of children's activities as the following interviews with teachers illustrate:

We're surprised by powers among children these days. (me: powers?) Yes, I heard yesterday in the conference that Rainbow Room is more serious. I heard that the power among children was the issue in their room. We have similar worries. Children in our room already have something like mainstreams and minorities. Those kinds of things are already happening. . . . And we see only mainstream kids involved in group play.

(Looking at Jiwon playing) Did you see Jiwon this morning? While others were dancing, she was crouching down. As Jungyoon told Jiwon to do *Maum* (play the hamster) while dancing, Jiwon suddenly crouched as her form of Maum. I thought they're getting better (sighs).

In the first interview, Ms. Chung from the Arum Room anxiously views the emerging divide between mainstreams and minorities among her students and problematizes power relations for prohibiting children's diverse expressions in play. As reflected in the statement that "we can see only mainstream kids involved in group play," she perceives power relationships as working in children's enactment of play and as constraining opportunities for minority members to express their own ideas and thoughts. Similarly, Ms. Choo from the Rainbow Room criticizes the play Jungyoon and Jiwon participated in as the director (Jungyoon) and Maum (Jiwon), the hamster raised in the Rainbow Room, for being hierarchical. She, in particular, negatively views Jungyoon's assigning the role of Maum to Jiwon and Jiwon's bodily demeanors of crouching which indexes her lower status. Although the interactions of Jungyoon and Jiwon could be viewed simply as an instance of pretend play and their faithful performance of assigned roles, the teacher problematizes them because she views peers' hierarchical social relationships as hindering individual children's creativity and uniqueness. She regards these two children's pretend play not as a collaborative creation but as a production of Jungyoon's and Jungyoon imposing her ideas on Jiwon.

Along with the pursuit of power and authority, teachers also problematized the prevalence of competition and social exclusion in their children's activities and play. As for competitive behaviors, teachers regarded competition as facilitating and reinforcing uniformity of children's productions and creations. That is, as children were keen to compete with other children, they copied and compared others' products rather than producing their own unique ones, which resulted in the uniformity of final products as evidenced in the case of the message center noted before. At the same time, teachers were highly critical of exclusive behaviors and attitudes prevalent in peer interactions. Looking at children refusing to have others entering into their play on the grounds of the color of their outfits, Ms. Chung, for instance, told me, "See? They don't let them in with this excuse and that excuse. It's more difficult than entering into the country club."

As in the cases of children's aspirations for power and authority, the major reason teachers regard competition and exclusivity as undesirable is that these values contradict with the new, explicit socialization goals and are interpreted as constraining cultivation of those goals. Ironically, as in the case of the message center, teachers, in the process of rectifying undesirable outcomes, focused not so much on facilitating so-called new ideologically laden values of individuality, self-expression, or creativity as on instilling implicit values such as relationality, communality, and cooperation. The logic behind this reform was that "play gets better when children's relationships get better," the phrase frequently mentioned by teachers in their reform of the curriculum and pedagogical practices.

"Play Gets Better When Children's Relationships Get Better"

The phrase "Play gets better when children's relationships get better" reflects transformation of teachers' perspectives on children's play and activities. Dissatisfied with outcomes, teachers scrutinized their curriculum and pedagogical practices, tried to reformulate them in ways that would allow them to attain their initial educational goals, and came up with their own answers. Ms. Park in the following interview, for instance, proposes improvements in children's social relationships as a solution to children's unsatisfactory play: "As you know, it was very difficult at first. . . . But now we've decided to think differently. I think play gets better when there's a change in children's relationships. . . . We had a very distressful time. But children's relationships are getting better. Don't you see some changes? Well, they don't know what getting together really means yet, but they're getting better."

Even though teachers were vastly dissatisfied with outcomes of children's activities and play, their responses tended to be passive or at least reactive at first. One of the main factors causing teachers' passivity in intervention is related to the way Reggio's play- and child-centeredness are indigenized in Somang preschool, more broadly in South Korean early childhood education. That is, as the Reggio approach was adopted as an alternative to previous uniform and didactic education, its play- and child-oriented aspects were typically understood as free play and nonintervention. Teachers were hesitant to intervene in peer interactions fearing that their intervention could hinder children's free and creative expressions. The dichotomy of new and old education led teachers to interpret any type of intervention as promoting uniform and obedient personhood. At the same time, even though the original Reggio approach views play as a place to form social relations and learn through interactions with peers, Somang teachers, similar to their indigenization of the Reggio approach in general, approached play as an educational site for cultivating self-expressions, creativity, or diversity. Adopting currently dominant Western educational discourses of play as "necessary" and "an essential component of developmentally appropriate practice" (Bredekamp and Copple 1997), teachers viewed a play-based approach as natural, child-centered, and responsive to context and directly opposed to formal, decontextualized, and adult-centered instruction. Moreover, they often drew on the romantic discourses of play which conceptualize play as natural, intrinsic, and free (Ailwood 2003); therefore, they tended to expect children's play to be genuine, intrinsically motivated, and free from external standards. The nonintervention ideology combined with the developmental and romantic discourses of play ironically made teachers reluctant to step in and rectify children's play even while that very play reinforced their dissatisfaction with and critiques of children's play.

As illustrated in Ms. Park's statement above that "now we've decided to think differently," Somang teachers' initial view of children's play and activities shifted. In the process of the reform, they started to pay attention to the social and relational components of play and actively intervened in children's interactions. Teachers' own solution that "play gets better when children's relationships get better" emerges from their penetration, even though unconscious, of the unreality of their early indigenized version of play- and child-centeredness. Similar to criticisms made by much of poststructural research on children's play (Ailwood 2003; Bishop and Curtis 2001; Strandell 2000), teachers came to understand that the romantic view of play as solely natural, free, enjoyable, or fun could not be realized in actual contexts and play could never be cut off from social and contextual factors. Based on the perspective that children's play is intrinsically social and interactional, teachers, then, started to view improvements in social relationships as a prerequisite to "good" and "desirable" play. This shift led to drastic transformations of the focus of the explicit curriculum from cultivation of children's individuality, creativity, or diversity to promotion of "good" and "better" social relationships. As discussed in the following, the "good" and "better" social relationships here often meant social relations based on collectivity, cooperation, and communality.

Explicit Teaching of Collectivity, Communality, and Cooperation

Based on the rationale that "play gets better when social relationships get better," Somang teachers actively reformed their explicit curriculum in ways that could promote the desired sociality. The embodied socialities teachers had implicitly used only backstage to evaluate children's dynamic social relations now came to constitute an integral part of the explicit curriculum. The Scout activity called nature expedition mentioned in the beginning of this chapter was one of the representative reform efforts enacted in Somang preschool. Unlike a play-and child-centered curriculum in which children were expected to autonomously express their authenticity and creativity in play and activities and teachers found meanings in the outcomes, the reformed curriculum was enacted in more didactic and teacher-centered ways and had explicit socialization goals of instilling communality and collaboration. In the first day of the nature expedition week, the Rainbow teachers divided the whole class into two teams and designed a variety of team-based activities in which children were expected to produce outcomes as a team. Asking children to come up with the name of their own teams, for instance, Ms. Choo states, "You should pick a name such that nobody gets hurt. You're not supposed to pick what you want." Children here are explicitly expected to suppress individual wishes and wants for the sake of the group and collaboratively produce communal outcomes. Moreover, teachers actively utilized socialization practices they had consciously distanced themselves from in the previous play- and child-centered curriculum to promote uniformity, obedience, or collectivity. To Nuri who drew pictures before the announcement of playtime, for instance, Ms. Park said in a stern voice, "Nuri, did I say to take out crayons? Why are the Gold Treasure team not listening to me?" Ms. Park here attributes the misbehavior of the individual child to the whole group she belongs to, thereby stressing the importance of collectivity. Similar statements such as, "Your wrong-doings are not your own; they become wrongdoings of your team" or to children misbehaving, "Which team are you on?" are frequently heard in the new everyday educational contexts. During group time, teachers also asked children to display and embody collectivity and oneness, for instance, by stating, "Let's clap with one voice. We have to make one voice. . . . Rainbow Room, we're the one. We're the one." Moreover, in Ms. Park's statement to Nuri, she even asks Nuri to show obedience and compliance toward her. Given that Somang teachers were highly critical of hierarchical teacher-children relations for prohibiting the development of children's true selves, teachers' explicit and direct request now for obedience and compliance clearly shows the drastic transformation of pedagogical goals and styles.

In stressing collectivity and communality, teachers also promoted competition among children, the practice explicitly degraded in the previous formal educational contexts and only implicitly enacted in noneducational and more mundane situations. Asking children to name their team on the first day of the nature expedition activity, Ms. Park, for instance, says to one team, "Look, they [the other team] are already done. They are making slogans and dances." The performance as a team was constantly compared to that of other teams, and competitions among teams were strongly encouraged. During the week of the nature expedition, teachers constantly asked children to remember their team through questions such as, "Which team are you on?" and explicitly compared outcomes and performance of two teams. Children were asked to imagine themselves as a member of the group and collaboratively work with group members to compete with other groups. Here, group as a unity works as the basic division of competition. This type of collectivity has also been mentioned as characteristic of Korean social organization by many anthropological studies of Korean social relationships and structures (Janelli and Yim 1993; Kim 1992).

In addition, the reformed curriculum often entailed shifts in pedagogical styles from child- and play-centered activities to more teacher- and content-centered didactic instruction. Teachers, for instance, made a list of the kinds of sociality they expect for children and asked children to recite the list items with one voice every day during the week of the nature expedition. The list constituted an oath containing the following phrases: Love and help friends, Care for and protect nature, Give the winning team a big hand, Don't laugh at the losing team. Teachers also had a session about friends and friendship wherein they stressed the importance of having and being harmonious with friends. As Nuri said that she could play with her mom even if she didn't have friends, Ms. Park even scolded her in an angry voice stating, "That's not a good idea. Do you think you can play with your mom even when you grow up? You have to make good relationships with your friends." Teachers also spoke highly of the previously downgraded values of collectivity and oneness to children in official educational contexts. Ms. Choo in morning group time mentioned the television program she watched during the previous weekend in which the old ladies and gentlemen sang in chorus. Ms. Choo said that she was impressed by them because "they sang as if they're one person." In all these instances, a sense of cooperation, harmony, collectivity, and unity are explicitly mentioned as a major socialization goal and the importance of these values are delivered to children through didactic and content-centered instructions. Previous child- and play-centered approaches faded away, even if they were not completely expunged.

This reformed pedagogical style made teachers more active in intervening in children's social relationships and correcting their undesirable behaviors and attitude. As Haejin says, "Wow, we won" after finishing discussions of the team name, Ms. Park admonishes her by stating, "We don't brag about winning." Teachers, heretofore, tended to problematize children's arrogance and bragging only implicitly or simply felt dissatisfied with those attitudes as we have seen in Rainbow teachers' responses toward Nuri's arrogance and excellence in chapter 3 without trying to change them directly. Ms. Park, however, here, directly and explicitly problematized Haejin's behavior for being overbearing and tries to rectify her demeanor and attitude.

Whereas Ms. Park's admonition intended to inscribe Haejin's character as more modest, caring, and harmonious in relations with classmates, her discipline seems to involve a certain irony and even contradiction. That is, as shown before, teachers promoted competition between two teams in their naming of the team. Therefore, Haejin's statement, "Wow, we won" is responsive to the competitive structure teachers constituted. Children were encouraged to compete with other teams as a group, and when they did and expressed the joy of winning in the competition, they were reprimanded for being boastful and pretentious. The contradictions and conflicts in the reformed curriculum were also apparent on other occasions. For instance, on the last day of the nature expedition activity, Rainbow Room had discussions on how to spend the money they earned through the charity bazaar. Children individually expressed their plans and some children showed disagreement over others' opinions by saying, "I don't want to" or "I don't like his idea." To these statements, Ms. Choo asked the whole class, "Whose money is this?" and as children says "Ours," she states in a stern voice, "Why are you doing as you want while saying it's ours?" Here, children were first asked to express their individual wants and needs and, when they did, were scolded for not agreeing with others' ideas. If teachers provided opposing and contradictory values depending on the contexts of socialization before—that is, new and ideologically dominating ones in formal educational contexts and more implicit ones in less formal and noneducational situations—the conflicting and contradictory values and

Weekend Stories: From Expression to Listening

The weekend story time is another activity that illustrates characteristics and processes of the transformation of Somang curriculum and pedagogical practices. As discussed in the previous chapters, the weekend story time was one of the representative activities of Somang preschool designed to promote children's self-expressions, individuality, and creativity. During group time on Monday mornings, teachers picked students to present their weekend stories and the students came up and narrated how they spent their weekend. By having children verbally articulate their weekend experiences, the activity aims to have children learn how to express their authentic and individual ideas, thoughts, and feelings. Somang teachers proudly spoke of presentation and verbal skills their students displayed during the weekend story times to parents and outsiders such as incoming parents or researchers visiting the preschool. Ms. Shim praised her students' performances during the weekend story time to me when I was still a stranger and a newcomer to the Rainbow Room.

Behind the ostensible complimentary remarks, however, there were also teachers' discontent and uneasy feelings toward children's performance during the weekend story time. As discussed in chapter 3, Somang teachers frequently mentioned the problem of excessive and self-immersed expressions displayed during the story time. Teachers could not have all the students present their stories due to time constraints; therefore, they had to select a limited number of students from among the ones who raised their hands. Children, then, often expressed their disappointment in teachers' selection of presenters. Teachers problematized these responses from children for being too egocentric, self-immersed, and competitive. Criticizing children's complaints, Ms. Choo once told me, "They just can't help expressing their desires. They can't suppress themselves. They think of only themselves. . . . They're only interested in winning in this competition." She considers children's discontent as emerging from egotistical needs to win a competition of expression.

Similar to their responses to other cases discussed before, teachers at first did not actively confront or correct children's unsatisfactory expressions and only tried to solve the problem indirectly. The solution they first came up with was using the ladder game in which the presenters were selected not by teachers but by chance. Every Monday morning, teachers listed children who raised their hands to present their weekend stories, did the ladder game, and announced ones selected as presenters. The selected students, then, were given a chance to present their stories in group time at the end of the day. In declaring the selected students, teachers often made the statement, "This is not decided by teachers but by how the game goes on," which indicates their intention of nonintervention, a tendency similarly found in the cases of other activities. That is, teachers feared that their selection of presenters would create hierarchies between teachers and children and inequalities among children, therefore hindering development of children's true selves. The ladder game was contrived as a way to evade the supposed responsibilities ensuing from teachers' intervention while at the same time resolving the problems of children's excessive desires to express themselves and compete.

If teachers' initial reform of the weekend story time was somewhat passive and indirect as shown in the use of the ladder game, the reform became more extensive and far-reaching as children did not comply with teachers' reform efforts. Children still expressed their dissatisfaction toward teachers' choices despite teachers' indication that the choice was made by the game. The next reform was enacted in ways that could meet the demands of every individual child and solve the problem of time limits. In this reform, teachers asked children to make their weekend stories into artwork such as by drawing, writing, or bringing pictures about their weekend experiences and hanging them on the storyboard on the wall. Teachers then picked up the stories to be presented during the weekend story time. Explaining the changes of the weekend story time, Ms. Park said, "We can't hear how you all spent your weekend, right? So you guys individually draw how you spent the weekend so that the teachers can see and know 'Oh, this person did this and others did that.' And the teachers will select the ones that friends are most likely to [want to] hear about. Okay?" This reform seemed to respond to children's insatiable and excessive desires to express themselves by having every individual child display their experiences on the board. At the same time, the reform also entailed more teacher-centered pedagogical intervention even though teachers had tried to dissociate themselves from intervening when they employed the idea of using the ladder game before. Unlike the ideology of the initial Somang curriculum that expressions need to reflect authenticity, creativity, and diversity of every individual child, teachers here explicitly evaluated children's expressions and position themselves as authoritarian figures who do not only observe but also rank children's performances. As Ms. Park mentions above that she will select the expressions that classmates are likely to favor most, this statement clearly demonstrates that expressions are assessed and ranked by teachers.

If reforms such as the ladder game and the storyboard so far retained some major aspects of the weekend story activity—that is, promoting verbal expression and skills—at the explicit level although implicitly attempting to moderate their children's expressive desires, later reforms even transformed the main purpose of the activity. That is, teachers started to stress the importance of paying attention to others' stories rather than focusing on expressing one's own. As children frowned and sighed at the announcement of presenters, Ms. Choo, for instance, said, "If you guys all just want to tell your own stories, then who would listen to them? . . . You sometimes get to say your stories and sometimes get to listen to others; it's like back-and-forth. You say once and you listen back once. Do only teachers listen to your stories, then?" In this statement, Ms. Choo criticizes children's selfish desires to express themselves and emphasizes the importance of listening to others' stories. Teachers not only articulated the significance of an other-oriented perspective and reciprocity but also implemented pedagogical methods to instill these values. In the initial format of the weekend story time, after each presenter told his or her story, audiences had a chance to ask questions or comment on the presenter's story. This part, however, was replaced by one in which teachers asked questions about the contents of a presenter's story to the audience in order to check whether the children were listening. After Suji told the story of making sushi with her mom, Ms. Park, for instance, asked the audience what kinds of sushi Suji made and praised the students who got the answers such as eel sushi or egg sushi. She also picked some students who were inattentive and distracted during Suji's presentation, asked them details of the story, and reprimanded them for not paying attention. The importance of listening to others' stories—that is, the values of other-orientedness and mutuality—were added and became one of the major purposes of the activity. Moreover, in inculcating these values, teachers actively employed pedagogical styles they were highly critical of before—that is, the content- and teacher-focused instructions such as rote memorization.

"We're Not Doing Tongkuk Anymore": Shunning Perceived Problems

Although Somang teachers made concerted efforts to rectify perceived problems of children's performances, behaviors, and interactions displayed in a variety of school activities and play through reforms of curriculum and pedagogical styles as shown in the cases discussed so far, they, at the same time, frequently displayed elusive attitudes toward children's unsatisfactory behaviors and interactions. Such indecisive responses were attributable largely to frustrations teachers experienced in the process of reformulating curriculum and therefore tended to appear increasingly toward the end of the school year. That is, as children did not produce desirable outcomes in response to teachers' reforms and often even retransformed the reformed curriculum as seen in the case of the message center, teachers felt despair, which then led them to evade or shun perceived problems and sometimes give up reform efforts.

The tongkuk (children's drama) of the Arum classroom was one of those activities that teachers finally responded to by sidestepping. The tongkuk is an activity in which Arum Room children perform a play based on stories they created. The activity emerged from Arum Room teachers' observation of children making stories in the message center using a variety of expressive means such as drawings or letters. This observation, especially children's use of diverse expressive means, reminded teachers of the phrase "a hundred languages" originally used in Reggio's definition of the message center and reinterpreted by Somang teachers as signifying self-expressions and creativity as seen before. Arum Room teachers, therefore, started to closely observe and document the stories children expressed in the message center and then introduced them to the whole class during group time believing that this would cultivate children's verbal expressions and creativity. To this initial format, teachers later added a part in which children collectively performed a play based on one of the stories they made up. Teachers collected children's stories mainly from the message center at first, but their collection expanded into other places such as children's free play or artwork. For instance, Ms. Sung one day approached Jeemin who was drawing a picture in the artwork center about going on a picnic, asked her for details of the picture, and documented her story. She introduced Jeemin's story to the whole class at group time, and as some children commented on and asked questions about the story after Ms. Sung's presentation, she asked Jeemin whether other children could add some stories to hers. Jeemin, however, refused to have others add on her story, and Ms. Sung then had Jeemin choose members to play the roles in her story. Later that day, Arum classroom put a play on the stage based on Jeemin's story and her assignment of play roles.

The tongkuk became one of the main activities of Arum Room curriculum and was even presented to other classrooms. However, the activity suddenly dropped out of Arum curriculum after a few weeks of enactment. When I asked Ms. Chung one day whether they planned to do the tongkuk activity in the afternoon, she answered, "No, we're not doing it anymore. I'll let you know if we resume, but I guess we'll not. We're just introducing stories these days. When we started the tongkuk with children at first, our aim was not like that. But they're just interested in assigning roles. You saw Hajun today, right? He assigns roles and then says that's it. We hoped to have children make relationships, collectively participate and make things together. But they just want to put their own stories into a play. . . . So we're not doing it anymore." To my question of whether those were their initial goals, Ms. Chung described the microhistory of this activity as follows: "No, we were hoping to see children's verbal expressions in the message center. . . . Then we started putting on a play based on children's play in the free-play area and noticed that some marginalized children got to participate. But children got to be interested in assigning roles and directing other children rather than making stories together. So we're thinking about other ways to support children's making things together."

As reflected Ms. Chung's narrative on the microhistory of tongkuk activity as well as its two-part composition—that is, an individual child's creation of the story and the whole class's performance of the play—the activity was initially designed to promote individuality and creativity and then later transformed to add emphasis on sociocentric values such as collaboration, communality, and cooperation. This shift in the focus reflects the overall transformation of Somang curriculum, the phenomenon discussed in this chapter. However, as shown in Ms. Chung's narratives and the response of Jeemin above, children paid keen attention to competitively putting their own stories into a play, which grants an authority to assign roles and direct others. For teachers who conceived of this activity as a place to instill senses of collaboration, cooperation, and communality as manifested in Ms. Chung's statement, "We hoped to have children make relationships, collectively participate and make things together," children's aspirations for authority, power, and hierarchy are seen as a failure of their reform efforts. Confronted with this failure, teachers shunned further reform efforts, unlike the cases of the message center, nature expedition, and weekend story time in which they actively tried to rectify the perceived problems. As alluded to in Ms. Chung's statement "I'll let you know if we resume, but I guess we'll not," tongkuk activity, even the part involving teachers documenting and introducing children's stories, faded away from Arum classroom curriculum.

This strategy of evasion emerged mostly from feelings of helplessness and fatigue teachers experienced from a series of failures of reform efforts despite their active intervention to rectify children's unsatisfactory behaviors, interactions, and attitudes. At the end of the school year, for instance, Ms. Park from the Rainbow Room expressed difficulty mediating and supporting children's social relationships to me by saying, "I won't focus on children's relationship again." Similarly, Ms. Chung in the following narrative reveals the adversity of cultivating children's social relationships and socialities: "I think preschool teachers have really hard work. If you're a middle school teacher, you just need to teach Korean, English, or math. The contents are already set up and your aim is just to teach those contents well. But preschool teachers, it's mostly about children's personality and their peer relations. So most of the time, we're bewildered how to do it. It's really a difficult job."

While teachers contrived their own solution to perceived problems as reflected in the statement "Play gets better when social relations get better" and further reformed the curriculum reflecting this penetrating solution, they, at the same time, realized the difficulty of modifying and improving children's social relationships. From experiences of enacting the reformed curriculum of actively intervening in peer interactions and explicitly instilling the values of communality, cooperation, and collaboration, teachers came to a conclusion that they "won't focus on children's relationship again" and "it's really a difficult job." Similar to the final development of the tongkuk activity, teachers increasingly reformulated the curriculum in ways that consisted mainly of academic subjects such as literacy or math, the ones that do not particularly involve peer relations or conflicts of children's ideas, wishes, or desires. As academic subjects became the focus of the curriculum, the overall curriculum became more content focused than before. However, teachers still tried to teach academic subjects employing child- and play-centered pedagogical styles. Rather than teaching by rote, teachers tried to provide ample room for children to express their own thoughts and ideas about academic subjects and learn by trial and error even when children provide obviously incorrect answers. Teachers endeavored to enact their own indigenized and idealized version of the Reggio curriculum at the beginning of the school year and then reformed the curriculum in response to children's creative transformations as we have seen in the cases of the message center, nature expedition, and weekend story time in this chapter. However, as their reform efforts faltered, teachers

170   BETWEEN SELF AND COMMUNITY

employed the strategy of evasion as shown in the cases of tongkuk and reformulated the curriculum again in ways that allowed them to avoid dealing with and confronting issues of social relationships or socialities, tasks they found difficult, frustrating, and overwhelming.

Conclusion: Communal Creativity and Its Infeasibility

The microhistory of activities described in this chapter shows that children's transformation of global imports significantly influences teachers' indigenizing processes. The characteristically Korean socialization values such as communality and relationality, rarely articulated and sometimes even undermined for prohibiting cultivation of children's genuine selves in the initial adoption of the Western curriculum, come to constitute a major part of Somang curriculum in teachers' reactions to children's transformations. If the excessive ideological importance placed on new socialization values made teachers distance themselves from taken-for-granted local socialization values and only implicitly or unconsciously instill them in more mundane and noneducational contexts, children's transformations incited teachers to articulate, openly emphasize, and incorporate them in their enactments and reform of the curriculum. Children here are, in collaboration with teachers, found to be implicitly resisting the hegemonic force of Western early childhood ideologies. The findings highlight the role children play in indigenization of globally circulating socialization ideologies and multidirectionality of learning in the globalized and globalizing socialization landscape.

In the process of reforming the curriculum, teachers created their own indigenized model of creativity which could be characterized as "communal creativity." As reflected in the frequently mentioned phrase "Play gets better when social relationships get better," teachers came to realize that what they expected from their students was not an individualized creativity but children's communal and collaborative production of creativity. When the teacher asked children to create "the name such that nobody gets hurt" for the nature expedition activity, for instance, she anticipated children to cooperatively and harmoniously produce a creative team name. Although the dichotomous and hierarchical framework and the heuristic use of values made teachers consider global imports as consisting solely of "good" components and local ones as having only "bad" sides, teachers came to unconsciously and vaguely understand that each value has both undesirable and desirable aspects and they produced an indigenized model of creativity by taking the desirable sides of both newly imported and traditional socialization values.[1]

This indigenized model teachers have in mind, however, was rarely articulated nor further elaborated and practiced in actual socialization contexts. Rather, teachers chose certain parts of the model and applied them in inconsistent and contradictory ways. For instance, in enacting the value of "communality," teachers highly emphasized the importance of being cooperative, considerate, and harmonious but at the same time instilled the ideas of uniformity, exclusivity, or competition as shown in the case of the nature expedition activity in which children were asked to cooperatively work as a team but also to compete with and exclude others and display oneness and uniformity as a team. Teachers also provided highly contradictory ideas toward certain values as shown in the case when Ms. Choo harshly reprimanded Haejin for expressing the joy of winning in competition the teacher herself had created. Moreover, even though the indigenized model aimed at producing creativity that is communal in nature, the creative aspects of the model mostly faded away in the actual enactment of the reformed curriculum. In rectifying children's self-immersed and egocentric expressions displayed during the weekend story time and emphasizing the significance of mutuality and other-oriented perspective taking, the expressive and creative parts of the story time—that is, asking questions and commenting on the presenter's story—were largely erased and replaced by content- and teacher-focused instruction. Similarly, as shown in the way the teacher, in the discussion of good expression, did not pay attention to children's comments on Munch's painting which could have been a good place to discuss creativity and diversity, the reformed message center rarely had any emphasis on children's creativity or diversity.

This infeasibility of the indigenized model of "communal creativity" seems to stem from several related factors. First, children's transformations, in combination with teachers' taken-for-granted habitus, provided an impetus for teachers to create their own indigenized model of personhood by selectively taking desirable elements of both imported and local socialization ideologies and values. However, teachers lacked specific strategies, guidelines, and practices to realize this idealized indigenized model. Teachers themselves barely experienced the model of "communal creativity" in their upbringing, nor were they exposed to it in their early childhood education program. The rapidly changing socialization landscape also made it even more difficult for teachers to articulate or conceptualize what they have in mind, and thus they were less able to realize their own vision in actual contexts. Instead, they tended to rely on more embodied and taken-for-granted forms of characteristically Korean traditional communality stressing exclusivity, oneness, uniformity, and competition in their efforts to realize harmonious, cooperative, and collaborative relationships that they believed to be a prerequisite for "good" expression, play, and creativity. Without articulating or enunciating the complex model they have in mind to children, teachers expect children to figure out the optimal guidelines for realizing the model on their own by inference from their diverse and often contradictory and inconsistent experiences.

Second, the indigenized model was also limited by a lack of ideological support resulting mainly from hierarchized socialization ideologies and discourses. Even though teachers attempted to realize their own newly setup model by reforming the curriculum, they were still burdened by the ideological importance placed on new socialization values. Regardless of teachers' emphasis on relationalities and communalities in their own classroom, the outcome of school activities was still evaluated in terms of creativity, diversity, and individuality. In a conference with other classroom teachers, teachers were expected to find something unique and creative from artworks, activities, and play of their children and present them with a verbal gloss such as self, creativity, or potential. Parents also wanted to hear and see their children being equipped with new values required to be successful in a globalized world. Most importantly, public discourses and larger early childhood educational ideologies teachers encountered daily were and still are highly geared toward the importance of global values. As a result, teachers were unable to pursue their own indigenized models fully and thoroughly with enough time span as shown in the cases of evading perceived problems, the issue discussed in the last section of this chapter. The cultivation of communality and relationality inevitably involves hierarchy, exclusion, or uniformity, but teachers were not provided with enough time or opportunity to experiment with their own practices of newly contrived indigenized models. Without ideological support, teachers have no choice but to lament, be frustrated by, and eventually even shun the steps needed to engender a newly desired person.

6

Conclusion

A Journey and Beyond

In chapter 1, I recalled my first impressions of Somang preschool and the puzzling feedback about students I got from teachers afterward. I found teachers' comments puzzling because their interpretation of children's behaviors and performances was completely different from and even the opposite of mine. Whereas I viewed the Somang classroom landscape as faithfully fulfilling the desire to raise self-confident, creative, global children, teachers lamented over what they perceived as the unattainability of their socialization goals and the children's undesirable personhood.

This book has been a journey to understand these perplexing observations and the questions they entail for me. As I immersed myself in and became part of Somang, I came to better understand its members' views and interpretations of, reactions to, and feelings about their ever-changing globalized socialization landscape. By the time I "graduated" from the Somang preschool with the children at the end of the school year, I had completely different views on the scene with which I opened this book. Somang classrooms no longer looked similar to U.S. preschool classrooms I had studied before; instead, they appeared profoundly "Korean." The ostensibly westernized Somang classrooms are filled with heterogeneities, tensions, and conflicts caused by the meeting of the global and the local. This book explores the nature of this meeting by detailing the shifting, contradictory, and conflicting socialization landscapes wherein local children and teachers actively indigenize diverse, floating, global ideologies, aspirations, and imaginings and endeavor to solve their dilemmas in a variety of ways. They have developed their own strategies, constructed new indigenized hybrid models of personhood, implicitly resisted global imports, or sometimes eagerly pursued global ideals.

Locating Somang Preschool in Scholarly Discussions of Globalization and Socialization

Like any ethnographic work, this thick description of a local socialization landscape requires both an active engagement with various intellectual grounds from socialization and globalization studies and a deep understanding of the multifaceted experiences, feelings, views, and interactions of local members and interpretations of them in terms of larger sociopolitical structures. The ethnographic accounts in this book are advanced by and, at the same time, advance various theoretical discussions and intellectual discourses of globalization, socialization, and childhood.

Most of all, the tensions, confusions, and contradictions described in this book attest to a primary tenet of anthropological discourses on globalization: global imports get "creolized" and indigenized to reflect local realities (Appadurai 1996; Hannerrz 1996; Kearney 1995; Lewellen 2002). Local actors extensively transform and reinterpret imported global ideologies and practices to accommodate local contexts and priorities that change over time and vary greatly. As seen in chapter 3, teachers, for instance, rather than straightforwardly adopting imported models of self-expression, create highly complex and contradictory models that not only expect children to have confidence in their own authentic needs, feelings, and ideas but also expect them to be considerate, modest, and reserved in their expression of themselves. Similarly, in chapter 5, teachers, by utilizing the desirable sides of both newly imported and traditional socialization values, produce an indigenized model of creativity that could be characterized as "communal creativity." Children also create their own meanings and practices of self-expression as social relationships to address goals of their culture-laden peer world, as discussed in chapter 4. The rampant indigenization and the very complex and conflicting lived experiences that are under pressure from global forces, as shown in this book, highlight the need to pay attention to the contextualized meanings and practices behind ostensibly similar global repertoires and the cultural contingencies that play on and enter into local realizations of global desires.

The ethnographic description of local actors' responses to global forces, in particular, highlights the everydayness of indigenization. Teachers featured in this book rarely criticize or resist globally dominant socialization ideologies but rather highly valorize and pursue them while consciously dissociating themselves from anything that seems "traditional" or "local." The traditional values that teachers view as backward and obsolete, however, lurk and survive as exogenous influences. Teachers unconsciously enact them in every socialization context, as we have seen in instances of their problematizing children's excessive and self-absorbed expressions or in the complex models of personhood teachers hold in mind in their actual evaluation of a child's character. Teachers' prioritization of traditional values became more blatant when the context moved to less formal and noneducational

CONCLUSION

arenas, as shown in teachers' explicit instruction of so-called traditional values, such as hierarchy, collectivity, comparison, or shame, in their everyday care of children. The inevitable gap between imported models and actual practice and the uneven implementation across cultural contexts, as described in the book, reveal that indigenization rarely occurs at the level of imported policy, ideology, or discourse but more in the pragmatic process of local actors' enactment of them in everyday socialization contexts. The findings urge future studies of globalization and socialization to pay more attention to ethnographically informed approaches in order to fully account for the very nature and processes of indigenization.

Furthermore, the everydayness of indigenization manifested in this book supports theories of socialization and cultural learning that stress the forces of implicit, habitual, and embodied practices in cultural transmission. The socialities of modesty, considerateness, and harmoniousness that teachers implicitly expect from their pupils and the values of collectivity, hierarchy, and comparison that are heavily imbued in noneducational contexts are all parts of what Bourdieu (1977) calls "taken-for-granted habitus," embodied and deeply felt understandings and beliefs formed largely as a result of teachers' own growing-up experiences. This habituated feature of socialization has been conceptualized in various terms such as "implicit cultural practices" (Tobin, Hsueh, and Karasawa 2009), "folk pedagogy" (Bruner 1996), "culturally patterned psychodynamic formation" (Chapin 2010, 2014), and "practical knowledge" (Rogoff and Lave 1984), but they all emphasize the power of unconscious, habitual, and embodied practices in immersing the child into a cultural world. Given that Somang teachers unconsciously but repeatedly and redundantly enact so-called characteristically traditional values, and these embodied practices are primary sources of creating conflicts with teachers' explicitly stated socialization goals, then the significance of paying attention to such habitual, unconscious, and embodied practices becomes salient, especially in the context of the transforming socialization sphere. Moreover, if we accept teachers' evaluation that children's performances are highly geared toward traditional values of uniformity, comparison, or hierarchy, thereby falling short of global personhood, it becomes more evident that implicit messages, rather than explicit injunctions and lessons, significantly shape children's learning experiences. In particular, as teachers are oblivious to their own enactment of traditional values, the unconscious and unmarked nature of habituated practices makes inculcation all the more powerful; socializers find their deeply felt, culturally distinctive practices to be natural and therefore effortlessly enact them without being self-reflective or critical. Through these cumulative but unmarked learning experiences, children then are predisposed to develop and form culturally distinctive and embodied conduct, moralities, and sentiments—what LeDoux (2002, 27–29) called implicit selves.[1]

Along with habitual and embodied features of socialization, this book advocates the view of socialization as a multidirectional process in which children, as active participants, play a significant role in shaping and reshaping their own learning experiences. Previous research on globalization and childhood discusses the complexities and heterogeneities that local actors such as teachers, parents, or administrators bring to the shifting socialization scene; however, the research also tends to marginalize children and their active engagement with global imports. By situating children's perspectives and voices at the center of analysis, this book demonstrates children's agency in the indigenization of globally circulating socialization ideologies and dynamisms they bring to a globalizing socialization terrain. The detailed description of children's phenomenal social worlds in chapter 4 reveals that children, rather than passively adopting global imports as indigenized by teachers, create their own meanings, practices, and models of self-expression, personhood, and conduct, which are not only distinct from but are even more refined and penetrating than those of teachers. For instance, children, exposed to a conflicted semiotic system in which new, explicit socialization ideals and implicit traditional values are inconsistently expected across contexts, construct and pursue complex but highly consistent and coherent ideas of self-expression and personhood—unlike teachers, who tend to display inconsistent and conflicting models, as shown in chapter 3. Moreover, children's active transformation of global imports does not result in separate cultural meanings and practices for their peer world but significantly constrains, facilitates, and encourages teachers' views on and practices of globally dominant socialization ideologies, as shown in the micro-histories of classroom activities in chapter 5. Although teachers provided highly inconsistent models of self-expression and personhood in the initial adoption of the curriculum—and criticized children for not fulfilling their desire to raise self-sufficient global children—they, in the process of responding to children's strategic transformations, came to emphasize taken-for-granted local values and beliefs and created a revised model of ideal personhood that intuitively combines local values with global imports. These empirical findings attest to the mutual involvement and interplay of children and teachers in indigenizing processes. The findings also highlight the importance of theorizing globalization and socialization as sites of contestation and negotiation, where both children and teachers, as active local participants, mutually attune, collaborate, and shape each other's learning experiences.

Practical Implications and Possibilities for South Korean Early Childhood Education

As much as the ethnographically grounded findings and arguments of this book expand various strands of scholarship on globalization, socialization, and childhood, I hope they also provide practical suggestions for the current, rapidly transforming South Korean socialization terrain. More specifically, the findings in this book may inform local education participants who, like Somang's teachers and children, are bewildered by the dilemmas and contradictions caused by the intrusion of the global into their everyday socialization spheres. To discuss some possibilities for change, I start by introducing a conversation I had with Rainbow Room teachers at the end of the school year.

It was a cold, sunny winter day, almost at the end of the school year. I was about to finish my fieldwork, just as the five-year-old children of the Rainbow Room were graduating Somang preschool, and the three- and four-year-olds were moving into new classrooms. I went to the playground with the Rainbow Room, and Ms. Choo approached and started talking to me about the conference she attended over the previous weekend. Ms. Choo said:

> It was a conference about emergent pedagogy. After the conference, I thought, "This job is not a good one." You know what? Being a preschool teacher is a lousy job. A lot of professors came up and presented. . . . The first professor talked about documentation, about how important it is for teachers to incessantly document classroom activities, and for fellow teachers to document these teachers' documentation processes. It's documentation and collaboration in name only. It's actually an evaluation. Think about other teachers documenting what you're doing. . . . And the second presenter was our director. She presented what we have done so far—how we share our classroom activities and outcomes through weekly teacher conferences, how difficult it was, and some limitations of our collaborations. She then also said that if teachers made more of an effort and saw the big picture, there would be more possibilities.

At that moment, Ms. Park approached and joined us by saying:

> Well, if that's what the director had in mind, if that's really what she meant, how come she thinks in that way? . . . I mean, if she really wanted us to teach in that way, she should have given us at least three months in the year to just run a teacher-directed curriculum. I mean, just applying what we memorized . . . or at least given us time to persuade moms to wait until we make some progress. How come she expects us to do so many things and still accomplish that? . . . The director always tells us that today and tomorrow should be continuous, and we should see the big picture to find children's self. But how could our everyday be that way? I myself barely survive day to day, hoping today goes smoothly and nothing bad happens tomorrow. If the teacher feels this way, how come today and tomorrow should be continuous? At the conference, I met a teacher who said that she suffered from insomnia because of documentation requirements. She was worried whether she might have missed something, whether she did it right or could she finish it tomorrow.

Ms. Choo added, "Everyone there, I mean even teachers, looked like directors and professors, until one attendant asked, 'How democratic are we?'" Ms. Park then left us to settle a conflict on the playground, and Ms. Choo told me, "These days, I envy teachers who have just spent many years with children, not teachers who make fancy posters and document children's play. I dream of being an old teacher who has just spent many, many years with children."

Teachers had frequently expressed the anxieties, frustrations, and agonies they experienced in pursuing the "new" global socialization ideals, but this conversation at the end of the school year was somewhat different from those I encountered before. Although teachers agonized over the unattainability of socialization goals and later came to be more lenient toward so-called traditional values—as shown, for instance, in their explicit but unwitting inculcation of uniformity, competition, and comparison in the reform of the curriculum—they never abandoned faith in the superiority of globally dominant socialization ideologies and practices. Cultivation of global personhood, values of self-expression, creativity, and diversity, a child-centered curriculum, and entailed pedagogical practices such as documentation, student participation, and active and hands-on learning were all maxims to be followed instead of targets for criticism. This unwavering faith spurred teachers to painstakingly revise and reform their curriculum by scrutinizing and reflecting on their own pedagogical practices and to willingly take any advice from outside authorities—whether through attending the Reggio conference they could hardly understand or by participating in weekly teacher conferences wherein they shared their classroom activities and documentations with the director, other classroom teachers, and outside members like early childhood education professors.

Ms. Choo and Ms. Park, however, in the conversation above, throw doubt on and are even skeptical of their pedagogical practices. Ms. Choo confronts the professor's emphasis on documentation, for implying an evaluation of teachers' pedagogical practices; she even downgrades it, as reflected in her remark, "not teachers who make fancy posters and document children's play." Similarly, Ms. Park shows her disapproval of documentation when she mentions the teacher who experienced insomnia due to the burden of documentation. These teachers' reactions might stem in part from the exhaustion of pursuing unattainable goals and may come more directly from their own director's open criticism of them at the conference. Teachers seemed to be frustrated when they found out that the director was not satisfied with and even thought negatively of their performance.

The last remark by Ms. Choo, that she would like to be an old teacher who just spent time with children, however, alludes to more fundamental stories in teachers' source of frustrations. Even though Ms. Choo did not articulate it, nor was she aware of it, her statement that she would like to "just" spend "many" years with children reveals her desire to stop striving for unachievable and implausible socialization goals and to "just" naturally enact embodied practices. Here, she intuitively perceives the mismatch between global ideals and local, ordinary, implicit values and practices. She articulates this disjuncture by differentiating two kinds of teachers. The first kind survives day to day, "making fancy posters and documenting children's play" to make meaningless, unachievable daily connections under the big picture of addressing the global ideal of finding children's selves, as impelled by the director. The second type of teacher naturally enacts their own, already embodied, taken-for-granted habitus and therefore could have a long career as a preschool teacher, as reflected in her expression "many, many years." Ms. Choo now aspires to be the latter, which contrasts sharply with her current state of being in a "lousy job." If teachers before tended to pit the dichotomous, hierarchical framework—wherein globally dominating socialization ideologies and practices are valorized against the old, backward, characteristically traditional one—, Ms. Choo now rejects that framework. Instead, she employs a different and somewhat opposite one that undermines global ideals and endorses implicit local practices.

Earlier in the school year, Ms. Choo told me that even though her father sees her job as changing children's soiled diapers, she loves her job and the Reggio curriculum, especially its documentation practice, which fulfilled her, so she could grow and find herself while observing and documenting children's play. What made this passionate and well-intended teacher become so frustrated and pessimistic toward her job? How can we help her fulfill the dream of being an old teacher who will have been in the field for a long time?

As Ms. Choo already alluded to in her last remark, the first step to realizing her dream might be to acknowledge the huge gap between global ideals and local implicit values and practices, as well as the heterogeneities and fragmentations this gap brings to the socialization sphere—one of the main findings of this book. If practitioners of early childhood education, including teachers, directors, and administrators, and authorities like professors and policymakers paid due attention to how discordant globally dominant socialization ideals are within the long-standing South Korean socialization sphere and how these discrepancies create inevitable conflicts and contradictions in practice, they would not force teachers to recklessly pursue global ideals and then blame them for failing to achieve the goals. Moreover, if we take into consideration that the global ideals these practitioners and many other sectors of South Korean society eagerly seek are, in fact, imagined ones that do not even exist in the West, it becomes more evident that none of the local participants, including teachers and children, are responsible for failing to realize these illusive and imaginative global ideals.

This first step in recognizing the disruption would potentially be to create space for rethinking and reevaluating the place of global imports in the South Korean early childhood socialization landscape. If global imports cause conflict and confusion on a local level, this suggests a need to be wary of and vigilant against the precarious assumption of global ideals as necessary for "good" and "quality" education, as is argued by much of anthropological and cross-cultural literature on globalization, childhood, and education (Ailwood 2003; Anderson-Levitt 2003; Ouyang 2003; Pence and Marfo 2008; Viruru 2005). This shift in viewpoint would equip teachers with critical awareness of global imports, thereby enabling them to confidently experiment with various practices and develop indigenized models that are not simple copies of imposed global imports but are, instead, responsive to the conditions and concerns of local communities. As shown in the book, teachers have, in fact, already constructed various indigenized models that reflect local concerns and contexts. Without ideological support, however, these models exist only fragmentarily and in rupture, as shown, for instance, in teachers' inconsistent emphasis on so-called global and traditional socialization values across educational and noneducational contexts. As long as the larger South Korean early childhood education community is caught up in the ideological baggage of perceiving globally dominant socialization values and practices as "necessity," teachers will be deprived of an opportunity to fully test, examine, and refine their own indigenized models. Instead, teacher performance will continue to be evaluated by a supposedly more advanced and superior global pedagogical standard that lacks local resonance in many regards.

If we create an environment that fully supports and acknowledges teachers' experience, expertise, and intuition and more broadly recognizes the significance of taken-for-granted local values and habitus, teachers might develop more refined, durable indigenized models and accompanying strategies for enacting them—unlike the current improvised and expedient ones that disappear rapidly, despite great potential and penetrating insights. As shown in chapter 5, teachers' keen findings, intuitions, and constructs, such as "play gets better when children's relationships get better" or "communal creativity," were not further refined and elaborated as models and rather soon faded away, sometimes becoming objects of evasion.

Teachers are exposed to and are expected to actively participate in various ostensibly collaborative settings, such as weekly teacher conferences or outside conferences. However, these are often the places where global socialization ideologies are passed down from on high and imposed on teachers; they are not constructed as places to keenly examine or question imported curricula, frankly express difficulties and articulate requests, or openly discuss not-yet-fully developed ideas and pedagogies that embrace local values and practices. Teachers in these settings were asked to reflect on and be critical of their own enactments of the imported curriculum, not the philosophies, aims, and pedagogies of the curriculum themselves. As well reflected in Ms. Choo's narrative, that one attendant asked, "How democratic are we?" the environment wherein teachers can frankly disclose their reservations about the imported curriculum, openly discuss emergent ideas and implicit expectations they have in mind, and freely develop their own indigenized models and practices in collaboration with experts, parents, and local community with enough time is what Somang teachers unconsciously desire and what is most needed if teachers are to successfully enact consistent and continuous everyday practices under the big picture, as expected and constantly stressed by the director. Allowing for the inclusion of taken-for-granted local values and habitus, as valuable and legitimate sources for creating "good" and "quality" educational practices, would enable teachers to construct feasible, durable models and practices. In turn, teachers would be more content to remain in the profession for a long time, without losing their initial enthusiasm, sincerity, and goodwill.

Such a supportive, collaborative atmosphere is essential not only for realizing the wishes, goals, and dreams of teachers like Ms. Choo but more fundamentally for constructing "good" and "better" learning environments for the children growing up in a rapidly globalizing and transforming South Korea. The current South Korean socialization terrain is built up in a way that tends to hamper adequate communication between teachers and children. Miscommunication limits children's opportunities to fully practice and refine their richly developing senses of good personhood and socialities. When teachers are constrained by the ideology of global imports as inherently superior and their performance is evaluated on how well they implement inflexible global ideals, then children's profound sense of creativity and their sophisticated practices of communality are not properly noticed and acknowledged by teachers. As this book's detailed descriptions of children's culture-laden coconstructed social worlds illustrate, these worlds are saturated with unique and creative rituals, practices, expressions, and products. However, children's creativity and uniqueness go unnoticed by teachers since they often appear in the context of constructing competitive and hierarchical social relationships, one of the main characteristics of children's peer worlds. Teachers, in this context, applying the dichotomous and hierarchical framework onto children's performance, pay exclusive attention to problems of hierarchy, competition, and comparison—the lingering residue of backward traditional socialization practices—and are oblivious to children's creative, unique, and self-confident expressions, constructs, and interactions. It is not that children lack self-confidence, creativity, or individuality; the dichotomous and hierarchical framework blinds teachers to the possibility that those global values could go hand in hand with characteristically traditional values of comparison, competition, and hierarchy. As a result, children are deprived of opportunities to further craft their developing creativity, uniqueness, and self-expression.

More importantly, children's highly sophisticated senses of communality and relationality are not properly acknowledged as virtues to be cultivated in order to realize the ideal personhood and social relationships teachers envision. The Somang children's own contrived and highly creative rituals, such as the eating ritual (ttala meki) and the play ritual (ttala haki) for instance, are collaborative, interactional routines that reflect children's deep awareness of communality and the practical means to realize it. In these rituals, children, along with the pursuit of differentiation and hierarchy, display and construct elaborate and intricate practices of collaboration and cooperation. The rituals, however, go unnoticed by teachers, whose tendency to distinguish between educational and mundane contexts prevents them from recognizing the great potential of informal contexts as resources for constituting the hybrid form of personhood that teachers hold in mind but struggle in vain to realize.

Similarly, children's reformulation and reinterpretation of self-expression as social relationships have great potential to be developed into the model of "communal creativity" that teachers contrived in their curriculum reform efforts. For instance, children's artwork that reflects the tastes and preferences of peers and their ongoing fluctuating social relationships could be instances of "communal creativity" in that children mutually pay close attention to the needs and likes of peers and constantly attune their individual efforts to collaboratively and cooperatively produce artwork. The great pressure to find global values of unique self-expression, creativity, and diversity in the children, however, made teachers focus exclusively on outcomes and therefore engage critically with children's artwork that was typically uniform in output. The communal and relational aspects embedded in the process of production, then, go unnoticed.

If children were exposed to a learning environment wherein diverse values, practices, and conduct were equally respected and appreciated, their deep and elaborate sense and awareness of communality, human relationships, and creativity displayed in peer play, interaction, and production would be fully appreciated and therefore could be further developed and refined. Although the South Korean early childhood socialization sphere valorizes diversity, the actual socialization environment, ironically, is not diverse enough in that global imports are more recognized and rewarded and treated as more legitimate than local forms of ideas, values, and practices. The children and teachers in this book already possess immense potential and ample resources to construct advanced models of good personhood that have a competitive edge in the global world.

The journey into the everyday lives of Somang teachers and children tells us that in the pursuit of good personhood and socialities, it might be worth delving into the practices, ideas, sentiments, and moralities of local actors rather than exclusively attending to ideals imposed from the outside. The need for this respect and appreciation is especially acute in this historical time, when South Korea is fraught with demands to construct a new type of personhood for individuals who will excel in a competitive, neoliberal world system but will still be sufficiently responsive to deeply rooted local virtues, orientations, and sentiments.

ACKNOWLEDGMENTS

Although my name alone appears on the cover, this book is a product of the "communal," the virtue that my informants implicitly and tenaciously pursue. Among many people involved in the production of this work, my greatest debt is to the Somang teachers and children who opened not only their classroom doors but also their hearts and minds to this strange fieldworker. Teachers accepted my abrupt intrusion into their lives, gladly shared their everyday feelings and thoughts with me, and taught me how to be sincere in one's job. Children willingly included me in their peer world as an atypical adult, and I was privileged to be part of their play and sometimes even conflicts, wherein I acquired insights I present in this book. The director unconditionally supported my research from the first time we met at her office. Although I have to use pseudonyms to ensure anonymity, they all deserve recognition. I hope this book will somehow repay the kindness, generosity, support, and faith they showed me.

This book grew out of intellectual inspiration and support I received along my journey to become an anthropologist. I was introduced to this fascinating field of childhood and socialization through my graduate training in anthropology at the University of Michigan, where I met my advisors Larry Hirschfeld and Barbra Meek. They taught me through their own brilliant research and guidance that "children are not trivial," a theoretical perspective that forms the basis of this book and has been critical in shaping my thinking of children and childhood. I am very fortunate to have had Hansok Wang as my advisor during my master's program at Seoul National University. He has been my example of an anthropologist, a scholar, and a mentor. He told me how important it is for a scholar to carry out a probing second research project after getting a PhD, and his advice spurred me to plan and conduct the long-term research on which this book is based.

Many people have sharpened the analysis and arguments that I make in this book through comments on various portions and versions of the manuscript. Their responses often drove me into territory I might otherwise have neglected. Any list is necessarily incomplete, but I would like to especially thank Naomi Quinn, Claudia Strauss, Hyangjin Jung, Boomi Lee, Yoonhee Kang, and Jinsook Choi for sharing their insights, intelligence, and skills. As I have developed this book over a decade, I have presented parts of it at various conferences and workshops, including at meetings of the American Anthropological Association, the Society for East

Asian Anthropology, the Society for Cross Cultural Research, the Korean Society for Cultural Anthropology, and the Korean Society for Sociolinguistics. I would like to thank fellow panelists, discussants, and audiences for insightful comments and questions. I am especially indebted to two anonymous reviewers who offered detailed and extensive commentary on the manuscript and the proposal, which resulted in stronger and clearer arguments in this book. Kimberly Guinta and Carah Naseem, my editors at Rutgers University Press, generously guided me through every step of the publication process with their expertise and speedy feedback.

When I first read Janet Keller's books and articles in my culture and cognition class as a graduate student, I never imagined myself receiving proofreading assistance from her. As any anthropologist might infer, her proofreading was certainly more than correcting my inaccurate English grammar and expressions as a nonnative speaker. She closely read various versions of the whole manuscript and provided extremely detailed and incisive comments from which this book has greatly benefited. Jennifer Delliskave's proofreading at the final stage of this book was also crucial in improving clarity and concision of my arguments. If the book is readable and makes sense to audiences, it is due to their efforts to make this a better work.

The Department of Urban Sociology at the University of Seoul is a special place where everyone is pleasant, generous, and supportive. I was fortunate to start and continue my career in this special environment, where I could take time to conduct this long-term fieldwork even during semesters. I thank my former and current colleagues for their warmth, support, and humor. I am also thankful to my students at the University of Seoul for always inspiring me with their curiosity, sincerity, and energy. Special thanks to Narae Yun for reworking images and gladly assisting with other administrative procedures for the book. The financial support from the University of Seoul has been crucial in moving this project to completion. This work was supported by the Basic Study and Interdisciplinary R&D Foundation Fund of the University of Seoul (2020).

I am blessed to have a very special family whose genuine interest in my academic work makes the process of a project like this one fulfilling, reassuring, and joyful when it could otherwise be quite lonely. Having spent his entire academic career in an applied field, my father enjoys talking with me about the possible practical value of work like mine. If this book makes any practical contribution to the field, it is largely due to the discussions I had with him about this project at the dinner table and while strolling together. My mother has always been the first audience of my books, and I'm sure she would have read the draft of this book if it were written in Korean. If I make any progress through this book, it is because she taught me how to proceed (move forward) by setting herself as an example. My sister Shinhui encouraged my everyday writing by humorously asking me whether I finished chapter 4 and how many paragraphs I wrote. Her witty cheering magically comforts me and helps me pass each milestone smoothly. To my family, thank you for everything.

NOTES

CHAPTER 1 INTRODUCTION

1. Show-and-tell is a classroom activity in which a child brings an item from home and talks to the class about it. In a typical show-and-tell time, a child verbally presents information about the item and receives questions and comments from the audience. It is a common classroom practice for young children in the United States, United Kingdom, New Zealand, and Australia.

2. For the interpretive turn in anthropology, see Clifford and Marcus (1986) and Marcus and Fischer (1986).

3. The dichotomy is described by different labels such as "egocentric" and "sociocentric" (Shweder and Bourne 1984), "independent" and "interdependent" (Markus and Kitayama 1991), or "individual-centered" and "situation-centered" (Hsu 1953), but they all focus on describing cultures and individuals in terms of oversimplified categories.

4. This implicit, unmarked, and embodied nature of socialization has been articulated in theories of socialization and cultural learning through concepts such as folk pedagogy (Bruner 1996), culturally patterned psychodynamic formation (Chapin 2010, 2014), or practical knowledge (Rogoff and Lave 1984).

CHAPTER 2 NEW PERSONHOOD AND TRANSFORMATION OF SOUTH KOREAN EARLY CHILDHOOD SOCIALIZATION

1. Early childhood education and care in South Korea includes a wide range of programs funded and delivered by both the public and private sectors. Preschool and kindergarten are the two most typical early childhood institutions, and they differ by age and supervisory agency. Preschool provides care and education for children from zero to five years of age and is under the supervision of the Ministry of Health and Welfare. Kindergarten is an educational institution for children from three to five years old and supervised by the Ministry of Education. Both preschools and kindergartens are classified again by whether they are delivered by the public or private sector. (Since tuition for preschool and kindergarten are supported by the nation regardless of parents' income or the type of institution, the costs for sending children to these institutions are basically the same. However, the extracurricular activities and program focuses make a difference in the overall cost and kind of education they offer.) Although each institution has its own characteristics, the private ones tend to deliver more customized and focused programs such as play-focused, English-only, or study-focused programs, whereas public preschools and kindergartens tend to follow stated-mandated requirements and curricula. When Ms. Shim mentions "kids from private schools," she refers to study-focused and academically oriented programs delivered in affluent, upper-middle-class areas where many five-year-old children enrolled in the Somang preschool had gone before

185

they came to Somang. The "kindergartens attached to elementary schools" are public institutions that tend to follow more strict curriculum criteria and use teacher-centered pedagogical styles, so they are thereby considered more "traditional" by her. As will be detailed in this chapter, Somang preschool is a private institution that runs a child-centered program, adopting the Reggio curriculum.

2. Parents, for instance, evaluate the Montessori program as relatively static and rule-focused and compare it with other recently imported curriculums such as Reggio or Waldorf, which they perceive as more child- and play-centered and therefore better fit for cultivating children's creativity and self-expression.

CHAPTER 3 "WHY DON'T WE FIND A UNIQUE SELF CONCEPT DEVELOPING IN OUR CHILDREN?"

1. *Hyenga* is another form of *hyeng*, a nonhonorific kinship term used to address and refer to the superior.

2. Lo and Fung (2012) list *son tulko seisski* as a typical example of an embodied practice of shaming in Korean schools. This practice asks the child being shamed to hold her arms straight up in the air in a location visible to others such as in the front or back of the classroom or hallways. The authors mention that feeling the gazes of others is an integral part of this shaming practice.

CHAPTER 4 "I WANT TO COPY MY BEST FRIEND'S ARTWORK"

1. Corsaro (1997) and Goodwin (1990) make similar points in their study of children's social organization. They note that the fluidity and complexity of children's social organization increase when competition itself is valued more than actually winning.

2. The names in children's drawings and artifacts in the pictures are all changed to pseudonyms for the purpose of anonymity.

3. The message center is an activity and a place in which children write or draw messages using various materials. Most Reggio Emilia preschools have message centers in their classrooms. Implementing the Reggio approach, Somang preschool also adopted the message center as a core part of their curriculum. In adopting the message center, however, Somang preschool downplayed the original goals of this activity such as cultivation of social relationships and communication skills and transformed it as a place in which children cultivate their individuated self-expressions, creativity, or diversity. This indigenizing process will be more closely discussed in chapter 5.

CHAPTER 5 "MAYBE WE'RE NOT WRONG"

1. In addition to the forces children's agency and teachers' implicit embodied local beliefs exert on the reform of curriculum, Reggio's original characteristics also seem to provide space for teachers to create their own indigenized model of creativity that incorporates communality and cooperation. That is, while teachers did not attend to Reggio's original sociocentric trends when they initially adopted this foreign Western curriculum, its original characteristics, such as an emphasis on learning through relationships with peers, teachers, and community, or project-based pedagogy, seem to accommodate teachers' emphasis on a newly constructed model of creativity with communal focus. As with the influence of teachers' embodied local habitus on the reform of curriculum, the operation of the original characteristics of Reggio's curriculum is never conscious or intentional.

NOTES

187

CHAPTER 6   CONCLUSION

1. LeDoux (2002), in his discussion of neural foundations of the self, distinguishes conscious and nonconscious aspects of the self and term them as explicit and implicit selves. He states that in spite of the long tradition of emphasis on the self as a conscious entity in philosophy and psychology, nonconscious aspects of the self are central to neural processes that endow each person with a self.

REFERENCES

Abelmann, Nancy, Jung-Ah Choi, and So Jin Park. 2013a. Introduction to *No Alternative? Experiments in South Korean Education*, edited by Nancy Abelmann, Jung-Ah Choi, and So Jin Park, 1–10. Berkeley: University of California Press.

Abelmann, Nancy, Jung-Ah Choi, and So Jin Park, eds. 2013b. *No Alternative? Experiments in South Korean Education*. Berkeley: University of California Press.

Abelmann, Nancy, So Jin Park, and Hyunhee Kim. 2009. "College Rank and Neo-liberal Subjectivity in South Korea: The Burden of Self-Development." *Inter-Asia Cultural Studies* 10 (2): 229–247.

Abu-Lughod, Lila, and Catherine A. Lutz. 1990. "Introduction: Emotion, Discourse, and the Politics of Everyday Life." In *Language and the Politics of Emotion*, edited by Catherine A. Lutz and Lila Abu-Lughod Lutz, 1–23. Cambridge: Cambridge University Press.

Adler, Patricia A., and Peter Adler. 1998. *Peer Power: Preadolescent Culture and Identity*. New Brunswick, NJ: Rutgers University Press.

Ahearn, Laura M. 2001. "Language and Agency." *Annual Review of Anthropology* 30:109–137.

Ahn, Junehui. 2011. "'You're My Friend Today, but Not Tomorrow': Learning to Be Friends among Young US Middle-Class Children." *American Ethnologist* 38 (2): 294–306.

Ailwood, Jo. 2003. "Governing Early Childhood Education through Play." *Contemporary Issues in Early Childhood* 4 (3): 286–299.

Alanen, Leena. 1988. "Rethinking Childhood." *Acta Sociologica* 31 (1): 53–67.

Anderson-Fye, Eileen P. 2003. "Never Leave Yourself: Ethnopsychology as Mediator of Psychological Globalization among Belizean Schoolgirls." *Ethos* 31 (1): 59–94.

Anderson-Levitt, Kathryn, ed. 2003. *Local Meanings, Global Schooling: Anthropology and World Culture Theory*. New York: Palgrave.

Anderson-Levitt, Kathryn M., and Boubacar Bayero Diallo. 2003. "Teaching by the Book in Guinea." In *Local Meanings, Global Schooling: Anthropology and World Culture Theory*, edited by Kathryn M. Anderson-Levitt, 75–97. New York: Palgrave.

Appadurai, Arjun. 1996. *Modernity at Large: Cultural Dimensions of Globalization*. Minneapolis: University of Minnesota Press.

Apple, Rima. 2006. *Perfect Motherhood*. New Brunswick, NJ: Rutgers University Press.

Azuma, Hiroshi. 1994. "Two Modes of Cognitive Socialization in Japan and the United States." In *Cross-Cultural Roots of Minority Child Development*, edited by Patricia M. Greenfield and Rodney R. Cocking, 275–284. New York: Psychology Press.

Bandura, Albert, and Frederick J. McDonald. 1963. "Influence of Social Reinforcement and the Behavior of Models in Shaping Children's Moral Judgment." *Journal of Abnormal and Social Psychology* 67 (3): 274–281.

Barlow, Kathleen. 2004. "Critiquing the 'Good Enough' Mother: A Perspective Based on the Murik of Papua New Guinea." *Ethos* 32 (4): 514–537.

Beach, J. M. 2011. *Children Dying Inside*. Scotts Valley, CA: CreateSpace.

Behar, Ruth. 2012. "What Renato Rosaldo Gave Us." *Aztlán: A Journal of Chicano Studies* 37 (1): 205–211.

Bellah, Robert N., Richard Madsen, William M. Sullivan, Ann Swidler, and Steven M. Tipton. 2007. *Habits of the Heart, with a New Preface: Individualism and Commitment in American Life*. Berkeley: University of California Press.

Benedict, Ruth. 1946. *The Chrysanthemum and the Sword: Patterns of Japanese Culture*. Boston: Houghton Mifflin.

Berentzen, Sigurd. 1984. *Children Constructing Their Social World: An Analysis of Gender Contrast in Children's Interaction in a Nursery School*. New York: Lilian Barber Press.

Best, R. 1983. *We've All Got Scars: What Boys and Girls Learn in Elementary School*. Bloomington: Indiana University Press.

Bishop, Julia, and Mavis Curtis. 2001. *Play Today in the Primary School Playground: Life, Learning, and Creativity*. Maidenhead, UK: Open University Press.

Bluebond-Langner, Myra, and Jill E. Korbin. 2007. "Challenges and Opportunities in the Anthropology of Childhoods: An Introduction to Children, Childhoods, and Childhood Studies." *American Anthropologist* 109 (2): 241–246.

Boggs, Stephen T. 1978. "The Development of Verbal Disputing in Part-Hawaiian Children." *Language in Society* 7 (3): 325–344.

Boli, John, and Francisco O. Ramirez. 1986. "World Culture and the Institutional Development of Mass Education." In *Handbook of Theory and Research for the Sociology of Education*, edited by J. G. Richardson, 65–90. New York: Greenwood.

Bourdieu, Pierre. 1977. *Outline of a Theory of Practice*. Durham, NC: Duke University Press.

Bredekamp, Sue, and Carol Copple. 1997. *Developmentally Appropriate Practice in Early Childhood Programs (Revised Edition)*. Washington, DC: National Association for the Education of Young Children.

Briggs, Jean L. 1998. *Inuit Morality Play: The Emotional Education of a Three-Year-Old*. New Haven, CT: Yale University Press.

Bruner, Jerome. 1986. *Actual Minds, Possible Worlds*. Cambridge, MA: Harvard University Press.

———. 1990. *Acts of Meaning*. Cambridge, MA: Harvard University Press.

———. 1996. *The Culture of Education*. Cambridge, MA: Harvard University Press.

Burman, Erica. 1994. "Innocents Abroad: Western Fantasies of Childhood and the Iconography of Emergencies." *Disasters* 18 (3): 238–253.

Cadwell, Louise Boyd. 1997. *Bringing Reggio Emilia Home: An Innovative Approach to Early Childhood Education*. New York: Teachers College Press.

———. 2002. *Bringing Learning to Life: The Reggio Approach to Early Childhood Education*. New York: Teachers College Press.

Cannella, Gaile Sloan, and Radhika Viruru. 2004. *Childhood and Postcolonization: Power, Education, and Contemporary Practice*. New York: Routledge.

Caputo, Virginia. 1995. "Anthropology's Silent 'Others': A Consideration of Some Conceptual and Methodological Issues for the Study of Youth and Children's Cultures." In *Youth Cultures: A Cross-Cultural Perspective*, edited by Vered Amit-Talai and Helena Wulff, 19–42. New York: Routledge.

Casey, Conerly, and Robert B. Edgerton. 2005. Introduction to *A Companion to Psychological Anthropology: Modernity and Psychocultural Change*, edited by Conerly Casey and Robert B. Edgerton, 1–14. Malden, MA: Blackwell.

Castañeda, Claudia. 2002. *Figurations: Child, Bodies, Worlds*. Durham, NC: Duke University Press.

Chabbott, Colette, and Francisco O. Ramirez. 2000. "Development and Education." In *Handbook of the Sociology of Education*, edited by Maureen T. Hallinan, 163–187. New York: Springer.

REFERENCES

Chapin, Bambi L. 2010. "'We Have to Give': Sinhala Mothers' Responses to Children's Expression of Desire." *Ethos* 38 (4): 354–368.

———. 2014. *Childhood in a Sri Lankan Village: Shaping Hierarchy and Desire*. New Brunswick, NJ: Rutgers University Press.

Christensen, Pia, and Alan James, eds. 2008. *Research with Children: Perspectives and Practices*. London: Routledge.

Christou, Miranda, and Spyros Spyrou. 2012. "Border Encounters: How Children Navigate Space and Otherness in an Ethnically Divided Society." *Childhood* 19 (3): 302–316.

Clancy, Patricia M. 1986. "The Acquisition of Communicative Style in Japanese." In *Language Socialization across Cultures*, edited by Bambi B. Schieffelin and Elinor Ochs, 213–250. Cambridge: Cambridge University Press.

Clark, Alison, and Peter Moss. 2011. *Listening to Young Children: The Mosaic Approach* (2nd ed.). London: National Children's Bureau.

Clark, Cindy Dell. 2003. *In Sickness and in Play: Children Coping with Chronic Illness*. New Brunswick, NJ: Rutgers University Press.

Clifford, James, and George E. Marcus. 1986. *Writing Culture: The Poetics and Politics of Ethnography: A School of American Research Advanced Seminar*. Berkeley: University of California Press.

Connolly, Paul. 2004. *Boys and Schooling in the Early Years*. London: Routledge.

Corsaro, William A. 1985. *Friendship and Peer Culture in the Early Years*. Norwood, NJ: Ablex.

———. 1997. *The Sociology of Childhood*. Thousand Oaks, CA: Pine Forge.

———. 2017. *The Sociology of Childhood*. 2nd ed. Newbury Park, CA: Sage.

Corsaro, William A., and Peggy Miller. 1992. *Interpretive Approaches to Children's Socialization*. San Francisco: Jossey-Bass.

Cross, Toni G. 1979. "Mothers' Speech Adjustments and Child Language Learning: Some Methodological Considerations." *Language Sciences* 1 (1): 3–25.

Crystal, David S., W. Gerrod Parrott, Yukiko Okazaki, and Hirozumi Watanabe. 2001. "Examining Relations between Shame and Personality among University Students in the United States and Japan: A Developmental Perspective." *International Journal of Behavioral Development* 25 (2): 113–123.

Dahlberg, Gunilla, Peter Moss, and Alan R. Pence. 1999. *Beyond Quality in Early Childhood Education and Care: Postmodern Perspectives*. London: Falmer.

Dahrendorf, Ralf. 1966. *Homo Sociologicus*. Rome: Armando.

Doi, L. Takeo. 1973. "The Japanese Patterns of Communication and the Concept of Amae." *Quarterly Journal of Speech* 59 (2): 180–185.

Douglas, Mary. 1970. *Natural Symbols: Explorations in Cosmology*. New York: Vantage.

Dumont, Louis. 1982. "A Modified View of Our Origins: The Christian Beginnings of Modern Individualism." *Religion* 12 (1): 1–27.

Dunn, Judy. 2013. *The Beginnings of Social Understanding*. Cambridge, MA: Harvard University Press.

Dyson, Anne Haas. 2016. *Child Cultures, Schooling, and Literacy: Global Perspectives on Composing Unique Lives*. New York: Routledge.

Edwards, Carolyn P., Lella Gandini, and George Forman. 1998. *The Hundred Languages of Children: The Reggio Emilia Approach—Advanced Reflections*. Westport, CT: Greenwood.

Erickson, Frederick, and Gerald Mohatt. 1982. "Cultural Organization of Participation Structures in Two Classrooms of Indian Students." In *Doing the Ethnography of Schooling*, edited by G. Spindler, 131–174. New York: Holt, Rinehart, & Winston.

Evaldsson, Ann-Carita. 2005. "Staging Insults and Mobilizing Categorizations in a Multiethnic Peer Group." *Discourse & Society* 16 (6): 763–786.

Ewing, Katherine P. 1990. "The Illusion of Wholeness: Culture, Self, and the Experience of Inconsistency." *Ethos* 18 (3): 251–278.

REFERENCES

Falgout, Suzanne. 1992. "Hierarchy vs. Democracy: Two Strategies for the Management of Knowledge in Pohnpei." *Anthropology & Education Quarterly* 23 (1): 30–43.

Fiala, Robert, and Audri Gordon Lanford. 1987. "Educational Ideology and the World Educational Revolution, 1950–1970." *Comparative Education Review* 31 (3): 315–332.

Fivush, Robyn, and Catherine Haden. 2003. *Autobiographical Memory and the Construction of a Narrative Self: Developmental and Cultural Perspectives.* Mahwah, NJ: Lawrence Erlbaum.

Flinn, Juliana. 1992. "Transmitting Traditional Values in New Schools: Elementary Education of Pulap Atoll." *Anthropology & Education Quarterly* 23 (1): 44–58.

Fong, Vanessa L. 2007. "Parent-Child Communication Problems and the Perceived Inadequacies of Chinese Only Children." *Ethos* 35 (1): 85–127.

Fraser, Susan, and Carol A. Wien. 2001. "Authentic Childhood: Experiencing Reggio Emilia in the Classroom." *Canadian Journal of Infancy and Early Childhood* 8 (4): 75–78.

Fuller, Bruce. 1991. *Growing-Up Modern: The Western State Builds Third-World Schools.* London: Routledge.

Fung, Heidi. 1999. "Becoming a Moral Child: The Socialization of Shame among Young Chinese Children." *Ethos* 27 (2): 180–209.

Fung, Heidi, and Eva Chian-Hui Chen. 2001. "Across Time and beyond Skin: Self and Transgression in the Everyday Socialization of Shame among Taiwanese Preschool Children." *Social Development* 10 (3): 419–437.

Gandini, Lella. 1993. "Fundamentals of the Reggio Emilia Approach to Early Childhood Education." *Young Children* 49 (1): 4–8.

———. 2005. "From the Beginning of the Atelier to Materials as Languages: Conversations from Reggio Emilia." In *In the Spirit of the Studio: Learning from the Atelier of Reggio Emilia*, edited by L. Gandini, L. Caldwell, and C. Schwall, 6–15. New York: Teachers College Press.

Geertz, Clifford. 1984. "From the Native's Point of View." In *Culture Theory: Essays on Mind, Self, and Emotion*, edited by Richard A. Shweder and Robert A. Levine, 123–136. Cambridge: Cambridge University Press.

Goodwin, Marjorie Harness. 1980. "He-Said-She-Said: Formal Cultural Procedures for the Construction of a Gossip Dispute Activity." *American Ethnologist* 7 (4): 674–695.

———. 1990. *He-Said-She-Said: Talk as Social Organization among Black Children.* Bloomington: Indiana University Press.

———. 2006. *The Hidden Life of Girls: Games of Stance, Status, and Exclusion.* Oxford: Blackwell.

Goodwin, Marjorie Harness, and Amy Kyratzis. 2007. "Children Socializing Children: Practices for Negotiating the Social Order among Peers." *Research on Language and Social Interaction* 40 (4): 279–289.

Griswold, Olga. 2007. "Achieving Authority: Discursive Practices in Russian Girls' Pretend Play." *Research on Language and Social Interaction* 40 (4): 291–319.

Hallowell, A. Irving. 1955. *The Self and Its Behavioral Environment in Culture and Experience.* Philadelphia: University of Pennsylvania Press.

Han, Namhee. 2004. "Language Socialization of Korean-American Preschoolers: Becoming a Member of a Community beyond the Family." Doctoral diss., UCLA.

Hanks, William F. 1996. *Language and Communicative Practices.* Boulder, CO: Westview.

Hannerrz, Ulf. 1996. *Transnational Connections.* New York: Routledge.

Hardman, Charlotte. 2001. "Can There Be an Anthropology of Children?" *Childhood* 8 (4): 501–517.

Harter, Susan. 1999. *The Construction of the Self: A Developmental Perspective.* New York: Guilford.

Hinton, Alexander Laban. 2005. "Genocide and Modernity." In *A Companion to Psychological Anthropology*, edited by Conerly Casey and Robert B. Edgerton, 419–436. Malden, MA: Blackwell.

REFERENCES

Hirschfeld, Lawrence. 2002. "Why Don't Anthropologists Like Children?" *American Anthropologist* 104 (2): 611–627.

Hofstede, Geert. 1980. "Culture and Organizations." *International Studies of Management & Organization* 10 (4): 15–41.

Holland, Dorothy, and Andrew Kipnis. 1994. "Metaphors for Embarrassment and Stories of Exposure: The Not-So-Egocentric Self in American Culture." *Ethos* 22 (3): 316–342.

Hollos, Marida, and Philip Leis. 2001. "Remodeling Concepts of the Self: An Ijo Example." *Ethos* 29 (3): 371–387.

Holloway, Susan D. 2000. *Contested Childhood: Diversity and Change in Japanese Preschools.* New York: Routledge.

Howard, Kathryn. 2007. "Kinterm Usage and Hierarchy in Thai Children's Peer Groups." *Journal of Linguistic Anthropology* 17 (2): 204–230.

———. 2012. "Socializing Hierarchy." In *Handbook of Language Socialization*, edited by Alessandro Duranti, Elinor Ochs, and Bambi B. Schieffelin, 341–364. Malden, MA: Wiley-Blackwell.

Hsu, Francis L. K. 1953. *Americans and Chinese: Two Ways of Life.* New York: Henry Schuman.

Hu, Hsien Chin. 1944. "The Chinese Concept of 'Face.'" *American Anthropologist* 46:45–64.

Hutchby, Ian, and Jo Moran-Ellis. 1998. "Situating Children's Social Competence." In *Children and Social Competence: Arenas of Action*, edited by Ian Hutchby and Jo Moran-Ellis, 7–26. London: Falmer.

Jacoby, Sally, and Patrick Gonzales. 1991. "The Constitution of Expert-Novice in Scientific Discourse." *Issues in Applied Linguistics* 2 (2): 149–181.

James, Allison. 2007. "Giving Voice to Children's Voices: Practices and Problems, Pitfalls and Potentials." *American Anthropologist* 109 (2): 261–272.

James, Allison, Chris Jenks, and Alan Prout. 1998. *Theorizing Childhood.* New York: Polity Press.

James, Allison, and Alan Prout. 1997. *Constructing and Reconstructing Childhood: Contemporary Issues in the Sociological Study of Childhood.* New York: Routledge.

Janelli, Roger L., and Dawnhee Yim. 1993. *Making Capitalism: The Social and Cultural Construction of a South Korean Conglomerate.* Stanford, CA: Stanford University Press.

Katriel, Tamar. 1987. "'Bexíbudim!': Ritualized Sharing among Israeli Children." *Language in Society* 16 (3): 305–320.

Kaye, Kenneth. 1982. *The Mental and Social Life of Babies: How Parents Create Persons.* Chicago: University of Chicago Press.

Kearney, Michael. 1995. "The Local and the Global: The Anthropology of Globalization and Transnationalism." *Annual Review of Anthropology* 24:547–565.

Keeler, Ward. 1983. "Shame and Stage Fright in Java." *Ethos* 11 (3): 152–165.

Killen, Melanie, and Cecilia Wainryb. 2000. "Independence and Interdependence in Diverse Cultural Contexts." *New Directions for Child and Adolescent Development* 2000 (87): 5–21.

Kim, Choong Soon. 1992. *The Culture of Korean Industry: An Ethnography of Poongsan Corporation.* Tucson: University of Arizona Press.

Kirkpatrick, John, and Geoffrey M. White. 1985. "Exploring Ethnopsychologies." In *Person, Self, and Experience: Exploring Pacific Ethnopsychologies*, edited by Geoffrey M. White and John Kirkpatrick, 3–32. Berkeley: University of California Press.

Kitayama, Shinobu, Hazel Rose Markus, and Hisaya Matsumoto. 1995. "Culture, Self, and Emotion: A Cultural Perspective on 'Self-Conscious' Emotions." In *Self-Conscious Emotions: The Psychology of Shame, Guilt, Embarrassment, and Pride*, edited by J. P. Tangney and K. W. Fischer, 439–464. New York: Guilford.

Kondo, Dorinne K. 1990. *Crafting Selves: Power, Gender, and Discourses of Identity in a Japanese Workplace.* Chicago: University of Chicago Press.

Kusserow, Adrie. 2004. *American Individualisms: Child Rearing and Social Class in Three Neighborhoods.* New York: Palgrave Macmillan.

REFERENCES

Kwon, Young-Ihm. 2004. "Early Childhood Education in Korea: Discrepancy between National Kindergarten Curriculum and Practices." *Educational Review* 56 (3): 297–312.

Kyratzis, Amy. 2004. "Talk and Interaction among Children and the Co-construction of Peer Groups and Peer Culture." *Annual Review of Anthropology* 33:625–649.

Kyratzis, Amy, and Jiansheng Guo. 2001. "Preschool Girls' and Boys' Verbal Conflict Strategies in the United States and China." *Research on Language and Social Interaction* 34 (1): 45–74.

Lancy, David F. 2008. *The Anthropology of Childhood: Cherubs, Chattel, Changelings*. Cambridge: Cambridge University Press.

Lebra, Takie Sugiyama. 1983. "Shame and Guilt: A Psychocultural View of the Japanese Self." *Ethos* 11 (3): 192–209.

———. 1994. "Mother and Child in Japanese Socialization: A Japan-US Comparison." In *Cross-Cultural Roots of Minority Child Development*, edited by P. M. Greenfield and R. R. Cocking, 259–274. Mahwah, NJ: Lawrence Erlbaum.

LeDoux, Joseph. 2002. *Synaptic Self: How Our Brains Become Who We Are*. New York: Viking.

Lee, Ju-Ho. 2004. "The School Equalization Policy of Korea: Past Failures and Proposed Measure for Reform." *Korea Journal* 44 (1): 221–234.

Lee, S. 1987. *Modern History of Kindergarten Education in Korea*. Seoul: Ewha Womans University Press.

Lett, Denise Potrzeba. 1998. *In Pursuit of Status: The Making of South Korea's "New" Urban Middle Class*. Cambridge, MA: Harvard University Asia Center.

Levin, Paula. 1992. "The Impact of Preschool on Teaching and Learning in Hawaiian Families." *Anthropology & Education Quarterly* 23 (1): 59–72.

Levine, Robert A. 2007. "Ethnographic Studies of Childhood: A Historical Overview." *American Anthropologist* 109 (2): 247–260.

Levy, Robert Isaac. 1984. "Emotion, Knowing and Culture." In *Culture Theory: Essays on Mind, Self, and Emotion*, edited by Richard A. Shweder and Robert A. Levine, 214–237. Cambridge: Cambridge University Press.

Lewellen, Ted C. 2002. *The Anthropology of Globalization: Cultural Anthropology Enters the 21st Century*. Westport, CT: Bergin & Garvey.

Li, Jin, Lianqin Wang, and Kurt Fischer. 2004. "The Organization of Chinese Shame Concepts." *Cognition and Emotion* 18 (6): 767–797.

Lim, Jae Hoon. 2013. "South Korea's 'School Collapse' Debates." In *No Alternative? Experiments in South Korean Education*, edited by Nancy Abelmann, Jung-ah Choi, and So Jin Park, 28–43. Berkeley: University of California Press.

Lindholm, Charles. 1997. "Does the Sociocentric Self Exist? Reflections on Markus and Kitayama's 'Culture and the Self.'" *Journal of Anthropological Research* 53 (4): 405–422.

Linger, D. 2005. "Identity." In *A Companion to Psychological Anthropology: Modernity and Psychocultural Change*, edited by B. Casey and R. Edgerton, 186–200. Malden, MA: Blackwell.

Lo, Adrienne, and Heidi Fung. 2012. "Language Socialization and Shaming." In *The Handbook of Language Socialization*, edited by Alessandro Duranti, Elinor Ochs, and Bambi B. Schieffelin, 169–189. Malden, MA: Blackwell.

Lutz, Catherine. 1985. "Ethnopsychology Compared to What? Explaining Behavior and Consciousness among the Ifaluk." In *Person, Self, and Experience: Exploring Pacific Ethnopsychologies*, edited by G. White and J. Kirkpatrick, 35–79. Berkeley: University of California Press.

Malaguzzi, L. 1993. "History, Ideas and Basic Philosophy." In *The Hundred Languages of Children: The Reggio Emilia Approach to Early Childhood Education*, edited by C. Edwards, L. Gandini, and G. Forman, 41–89. New York: Ablex.

Marcus, George E., and Michael Fischer. 1986. *Anthropology as Cultural Critique: An Experimental Moment in the Human Sciences*. Chicago: University of Chicago Press.

Markus, Hazel R., and Shinobu Kitayama. 1991. "Culture and the Self: Implications for Cognition, Emotion, and Motivation." *Psychological Review* 98 (2): 224–253.

Mauss, Marcel. 1985. "A Category of the Human Mind: The Notion of Person; the Notion of Self." In *The Category of the Person: Anthropology, Philosophy, History*, edited by M. Carrithers, S. Collins, and S. Lukes, 1–25. Cambridge: Cambridge University Press.

Maynard, Douglas W. 1985. "On the Functions of Social Conflict among Children." *American Sociological Review* 50 (2): 207–223.

McHugh, Ernestine. 2004. "Moral Choices and Global Desires: Feminine Identity in a Transnational Realm." *Ethos* 32 (4): 575–597.

Menon, Usha, and Richard A. Shweder. 1994. "Kali's Tongue: Cultural Psychology and the Power of Shame in Orissa, India." In *Emotion and Culture: Empirical Studies of Mutual Influence*, edited by Shinobu Kitayama and Hazel Rose Markus, 241–282. Washington, DC: American Psychological Association.

Meyer, John W., and Francisco O. Ramirez. 2000. "The World Institutionalization of Education." In *Discourse Formation in Comparative Education*, edited by Jürgen Schriewer, 111–132. New York: Peter Lang.

Miller, Neal E., and John Dollard. 1941. *Social Learning and Imitation*. New Haven, CT: Yale University Press.

Miller, Peggy J., Heidi Fung, Shumin Lin, Eva Chian-Hui Chen, and Benjamin R. Boldt. 2012. "How Socialization Happens on the Ground: Narrative Practices as Alternate Socializing Pathways in Taiwanese and European-American Families." *Monographs of the Society for Research in Child Development* 77 (1): 1–140.

Miller, Peggy J., Heidi Fung, and Judith Mintz. 1996. "Self-Construction through Narrative Practices: A Chinese and American Comparison of Early Socialization." *Ethos* 24 (2): 237–280.

Miller, Peggy J., Judith Mintz, Lisa Hoogstra, Heidi Fung, and Randolph Potts. 1992. "The Narrated Self: Young Children's Construction of Self in Relation to Others in Conversational Stories of Personal Experience." *Merrill-Palmer Quarterly* 38 (1): 45–67.

Miller, Peggy J., Su-hua Wang, Todd Sandel, and Grace E. Cho. 2002. "Self-Esteem as Folk Theory: A Comparison of European American and Taiwanese Mothers' Beliefs." *Parenting: Science and Practice* 2 (3): 209–239.

Mishler, Elliot G. 1979. "'Wou'you Trade Cookies with the Popcorn?': The Talk of Trades among Six Year Olds." In *Language, Children and Society: The Effect of Social Factors on Children Learning to Communicate*, edited by Olga K. Garnica and Martha L. King, 221–236. New York: Elsevier.

Mok, Ka-ho, Kiok Yoon, and Anthony Welch. 2003. "Globalization's Challenges to Higher Education Governance in South Korea." In *Globalization and Educational Restructuring in the Asia Pacific Region*, edited by Ka-ho Mok and Anthony Welch, 58–78. New York: Springer.

Montgomery, Heather. 2008. *An Introduction to Childhood: Anthropological Perspectives on Children's Lives*. Malden, MA: Wiley.

Morgan, Jane, Christopher O'Neill, and Rom Harré. 1979. *Nicknames: Their Origins and Social Consequences*. New York: Routledge.

Murray, David W. 1993. "What Is the Western Concept of the Self? On Forgetting David Hume." *Ethos* 21 (1): 3–23.

Myers, Fred R. 1979. "Emotions and the Self: A Theory of Personhood and Political Order among Pintupi Aborigines." *Ethos* 7 (4): 343–370.

Napier, Diane Brook. 2003. "Transformations in South Africa." In *Local Meanings, Global Schooling: Anthropology and World Culture Theory*, edited by Kathryn Anderson-Levitt, 51–74. New York: Palgrave.

Nelson, Katherine, ed. 1989. *Narratives from the Crib*. Cambridge, MA: Harvard University Press.

New, Rebecca S. 1993. "Reggio Emilia: Some Lessons for US Educators." Eric Digest.

———. 2007. "Reggio Emilia as Cultural Activity Theory in Practice." *Theory into Practice* 46 (1): 5–13.

Ochs, Elinor, and Lisa Capps. 2001. *Living Narrative: Creating Lives in Everyday Storytelling*. Cambridge, MA: Harvard University Press.

Ochs, Elinor, and Tamar Kremer-Sadlik. 2007. "Introduction: Morality as Family Practice." *Discourse and Society* 18 (1): 5–10.

Ochs, Elinor, and Bambi B. Schieffelin. 1984. "Language Acquisition and Socialization." In *Culture Theory: Essays on Mind, Self, and Emotion*, edited by Richard Shweder and Robert Levine, 276–320. Cambridge: Cambridge University Press.

———. 2012. "The Theory of Language Socialization." In *The Handbook of Language Socialization*, edited by A. Duranti, E. Ochs, and B. Schieffelin, 1–11. Malden, MA: Wiley-Blackwell.

Organisation for Economic Co-operation and Development (OECD). 1998. *Reviews of National Policies for Education: Korea*. Paris: OECD.

Ouyang, Huhua. 2003. "Resistance to the Communicative Method of Language Instruction within a Progressive Chinese University." In *Local Meanings, Global Schooling*, edited by K. M. Anderson-Levitt, 121–140. New York: Palgrave.

Paley, Vivian Gussin. 1993. *You Can't Say You Can't Play*. Cambridge, MA: Harvard University Press.

Park, Eunhye, Jeehyun Lee, and Hong-Ju Jun. 2013. "Making Use of Old and New: Korean Early Childhood Education in the Global Context." *Global Studies of Childhood* 3 (1): 40–52.

Park, So Jin. 2007. "Educational Manager Mothers: South Korea's Neoliberal Transformation." *Korea Journal* 47 (3): 186–213.

Parsons, Talcott. 1951. *The Social System*. Glencoe, IL: Free Press of Glencoe.

Pence, A. R., and K. Marfo. 2008. "Early Childhood Development in Africa: Interrogating Constraints of Prevailing Knowledge Bases." *International Journal of Psychology* 43 (2): 78–87.

Philips, Susan U. 1992. "Colonial and Postcolonial Circumstances in the Education of Pacific Peoples." *Anthropology & Education Quarterly* 23 (1): 73–78.

Pontecorvo, Clotilde, Alessandra Fasulo, and Laura Sterponi. 2001. "Mutual Apprentices: The Making of Parenthood and Childhood in Family Dinner Conversations." *Human Development* 44 (6): 340–361.

Prout, Alan, and Allison James. 2015. "A New Paradigm for the Sociology of Childhood? Provenance, Promise and Problems." In *Constructing and Reconstructing Childhood*, edited by Allison James and Alan Prout, 6–28. New York: Routledge.

Quinn, Naomi. 2005a. *Finding Culture in Talk: A Collection of Methods*. New York: Palgrave Macmillan.

———. 2005b. "Universals of Child Rearing." *Anthropological Theory* 5 (4): 477–516.

Raeff, Catherine. 2006. "Individuals in Relation to Others: Independence and Interdependence in a Kindergarten Classroom." *Ethos* 34 (4): 521–557.

Rao, Nirmala. 2010. "Preschool Quality and the Development of Children from Economically Disadvantaged Families in India." *Early Education & Development* 21 (2): 167–185.

Resnick, Lauren B., Roger Säljö, Clotilde Pontecorvo, and Barbara Burge, eds. 1997. *Discourse, Tools, and Reasoning: Essays on Situated Cognition*. New York: Springer.

Rogoff, Barbara. 1990. *Apprenticeship in Thinking: Cognitive Development in Social Context*. Oxford: Oxford University Press.

———. 2003. *The Cultural Nature of Human Development*. Oxford: Oxford University Press.

Rogoff, Barbara, and Jean Ed Lave. 1984. *Everyday Cognition: Its Development in Social Context*. Cambridge, MA: Harvard University Press.

Rosaldo, Renato. 1993. *Culture & Truth: The Remaking of Social Analysis*. Boston: Beacon.

REFERENCES

Rosaldo, Michelle. 1984. "Toward an Anthropology of Self and Feeling." In *Culture Theory: Essays on Mind, Self, and Emotion*, edited by Richard A. Shweder and Robert A. Levine, 137–157, Cambridge: Cambridge University Press.

Rosen, David M. 2007. "Child Soldiers, International Humanitarian Law, and the Globalization of Childhood." *American Anthropologist* 109 (2): 296–306.

Rosen, Lisa. 2003. "The Politics of Identity and the Marketization of US Schools." In *Local Meanings, Global Schooling: Anthropology and World Culture Theory*, edited by Kathryn Anderson-Levitt, 161–182. New York: Palgrave.

Sacks, Harvey, Emanuel A. Schegloff, and Gail Jefferson. 1974. "A Simplest Systematics for the Organization of Turn-Taking for Conversation." *Language* 50 (4): 696–735.

Schriewer, Jürgen, and Carlos Martinez. 2004. "Constructions of Internationality in Education." In *The Global Politics of Educational Borrowing and Lending*, edited by Gita Steiner-Khamsi, 29–53. New York: Teachers College Press.

Schwartzman, Helen. 2001. "Children and Anthropology: A Century of Studies." In *Children and Anthropology: Perspectives for the 21st Century*, edited by Helen Schwartzman, 15–38. Westport, CT: Bergen & Garvey.

Seth, Michael J. 2002. *Education Fever: Society, Politics, and the Pursuit of Schooling in South Korea*. Honolulu: University of Hawaii Press.

———. 2013. "South Korea's Educational Exceptionalism." In *No Alternative? Experiments in South Korean Education*, edited by Nancy Abelmann, Jung-ah Choi, and So Jin Park, 17–27. Berkeley: University of California Press.

Seymour, Susan. 2004. "Multiple Caretaking of Infants and Young Children: An Area in Critical Need of a Feminist Psychological Anthropology." *Ethos* 32 (4): 538–556.

Shaver, Phillip R., Shelley Wu, and Judith C. Schwartz. 1992. "Cross-Cultural Similarities and Differences in Emotion and Its Representation." In *Emotion*, edited by M. S. Clark, 175–212. Thousand Oaks, CA: Sage.

Sheldon, Amy. 1996. "You Can Be the Baby Brother, but You Aren't Born Yet: Preschool Girls' Negotiation for Power and Access in Pretend Play." *Research on Language and Social Interaction* 29:57–80.

Shim, Sook-Young, and Joan E. Herwig. 1997. "Korean Teachers' Beliefs and Teaching Practices in Korean Early Childhood Education." *Early Child Development and Care* 132 (1): 45–55.

Shin, Kwang-Yeong. 2000. "The Discourse of Crisis and the Crisis of Discourse." *Inter-Asia Cultural Studies* 1 (3): 427–442.

Shweder, Richard A. 1990. "Cultural Psychology: What Is It?" In *Cultural Psychology: Essays on Comparative Human Development*, edited by James W. Stigler, Richard A. Shweder, and Gilbert Ed Herdt, 1–44. Cambridge: Cambridge University Press.

Shweder, Richard A., and Edmund J. Bourne. 1984. "Does the Concept of the Person Vary Cross-Culturally?" In *Culture Theory: Essays on Mind, Self and Emotion*, edited by Richard A. Shweder and Robert A. Levine, 158–199. Cambridge: Cambridge University Press.

Silova, Iveta. 2004. "Adopting the Language of the New Allies." In *The Global Politics of Educational Borrowing and Lending*, edited by Gita Steiner-Khamsi, 75–87. New York: Teachers College Press.

Sirota, Karen Gainer. 2010. "Fun Morality Reconsidered: Mothering and the Relational Contours of Maternal-Child Play in US Working Family Life." *Ethos* 38 (4): 388–405.

Skinner, Burrhus Frederic. 1957. *Verbal Behavior*. New York: Appleton-Century-Crofts.

Snow, Catherine E. 1990. "10 Building Memories: The Ontogeny of Autobiography." In *The Self in Transition: Infancy to Childhood*, edited by Dante Cicchetti and Marjorie Beeghly, 213–243. Chicago: University of Chicago Press.

Sobo, Elisa. 2015. "Anthropological Contributions and Challenges to the Study of Children and Childhoods." *Reviews in Anthropology* 44 (1): 43–68.

Song, Jesook. 2003. "Shifting Technologies: Neoliberalization of the Welfare State in South Korea, 1997–2001." PhD diss., University of Illinois at Urbana-Champaign.

Sorensen, Clark W. 1994. "Success and Education in South Korea." *Comparative Education Review* 38 (1): 10–35.

Spiro, Melford E. 1993. "Is the Western Conception of the Self 'Peculiar' within the Context of the World Cultures?" *Ethos* 21 (2): 107–153.

Steiner-Khamsi, Gita. 2004. *The Global Politics of Educational Borrowing and Lending*. New York: Teachers College Press.

Strandell, Harriet Anita. 2000. "What Is the Use of Children's Play: Preparation or Participation?" In *Early Childhood Services: Theory, Policy and Practice*, edited by H. Penn, 147–157. Maidenhead, UK: Open University Press.

Strauss, Claudia. 1990. "Who Gets Ahead? Cognitive Responses to Heteroglossia in American Political Culture." *American Ethnologist* 17 (2): 312–328.

———. 1997. "Partly Fragmented, Partly Integrated: An Anthropological Examination of 'Postmodern Fragmented Subjects.'" *Cultural Anthropology* 12 (3): 362–404.

Takanishi, Ruby. 1994. "Continuities and Discontinuities in the Cognitive Socialization of Asian-Originated Children: The Case of Japanese Americans." In *Cross-Cultural Roots of Minority Child Development*, edited by Patricia M. Greenfield and Rodney R. Cocking, 351–362. New York: Psychology Press.

Thorne, Barrie. 1993. *Gender Play: Girls and Boys in School*. New Brunswick, NJ: Rutgers University Press.

Tobin, Joseph. 2005. "Quality in Early Childhood Education: An Anthropologist's Perspective." *Early Education and Development* 16 (4): 421–434.

Tobin, Joseph, Yeh Hsueh, and Mayumi Karasawa. 2009. *Preschool in Three Cultures Revisited: China, Japan, and the United States*. Chicago: University of Chicago Press.

Van Ausdale, Debra, and Joe R. Feagin. 2001. *The First R: How Children Learn Race and Racism*. Oxford: Rowman & Littlefield.

Viruru, Radhika. 2005. "The Impact of Postcolonial Theory on Early Childhood Education." *Journal of Education* 35 (1): 7–30.

Waksler, Frances Chaput. 1986. "Studying Children: Phenomenological Insights." *Human Studies* 9 (1): 71–82.

Walkerdine, V. 1984. "Developmental Psychology and the Child-Centered Pedagogy: The Insertion of Piaget into Early Childhood Education." In *Changing the Subject: Psychology, Social Regulation and Subjectivity*, edited by Julian Henriques, Wendy Hollway, Cathy Urwin, Couze Venn, and Valerie Walkerdine, 153–202. London: Methuen.

Wang, Xiao-Lei. 1992. "Resilience and Fragility in Language Acquisition: A Comparative Study of the Gestural Communication Systems of Chinese and American Deaf Children." PhD diss., University of Chicago.

Watson-Gegeo, Karen Ann, and David Welchman Gegeo. 1992. "Schooling, Knowledge, and Power: Social Transformation in the Solomon Islands." *Anthropology & Education Quarterly* 23 (1): 10–29.

Weisner, Thomas S., and Edward D. Lowe. 2005. "Globalization, Childhood, and Psychological Anthropology." In *A Companion to Psychological Anthropology: Modernity and Psychocultural Change*, edited by Conerly Casey and Robert B. Edgerton, 315–336. Malden, MA: Wiley.

Wellenkamp, Jane C. 1988. "Notions of Grief and Catharsis among the Toraja." *American Ethnologist* 15 (3): 486–500.

White, Geoffrey M. 1992. "Ethnopsychology." In *New Directions in Psychological Anthropology*, edited by Theodore Schwartz, Geoffrey M. White, and Catherine A. Lutz, 21–46. Cambridge: Cambridge University Press.

REFERENCES

White, Geoffrey M., and John Kirkpatrick, eds. 1985. *Person, Self, and Experience: Exploring Pacific Ethnopsychologies.* Berkeley: University of California Press.

Willis, Paul. 1977. *Learning to Labour: How Working Class Kids Get Working Class Jobs.* New York: Routledge.

Wolfenstein, Martha. 1951. "The Emergence of Fun Morality." *Journal of Social Issues* 7 (4): 15–25.

Woronov, T. E. 2008. "Raising Quality, Fostering 'Creativity': Ideologies and Practices of Education Reform in Beijing." *Anthropology & Education Quarterly* 39 (4): 401–422.

Wyness, Michael G. 1999. "Childhood, Agency and Education Reform." *Childhood* 6 (3): 353–368.

Xu, Jing. 2014. "Becoming a Moral Child amidst China's Moral Crisis: Preschool Discourse and Practices of Sharing in Shanghai." *Ethos* 42 (2): 222–242.

———. 2017. *The Good Child: Moral Development in a Chinese Preschool.* Stanford, CA: Stanford University Press.

INDEX

abandonment, 68
affection, 81, 82, 124, 150, 154–157, 159
age-based norms, 63, 129, 131, 143
agency of children, 6–8, 24, 137, 176, 186n1
aka, ayki (baby), 62
alliance formation and exclusions, 80–83, 86–88
Anderson-Fye, Eileen P, 10
apprenticeship model, 136
arrogance, 49, 154, 164
artwork activity, 46–47
artwork area, 96, 97–98, 99–100, 103–105
authenticity, 41, 97, 107–108, 162, 166
authority, 17–18, 79, 100–108
autonomy, 7, 15, 31, 32, 34

Behar, Ruth, 22
belonging, 75, 83–86
Benedict, Ruth, 64
bipolar model of selfhood, 11–12
Bruner, Jerome, 23, 71
bullying, 125

ca-a, as term, 34, 38, 48. *See also* selfhood
Cadwell, Louise Boyd, 138
child-initiated curriculum, 26, 33, 42–43, 161–162. *See also* curriculum
children's agency, 6–8, 24, 137, 176, 186n1
China, 5, 7, 15, 34, 64
Chun Doo Hwan, 30
citizenship, 5, 22, 26–31, 43, 138. *See also* selfhood
cleanup time, 62–63
collaborative learning, 48, 83–86, 96–100, 135
collectivity, 63–68, 162–165
communality, 108–114, 159–165, 170–172, 181
communication skills, 138–139, 147–148, 181, 186n3
comparison, 55–63, 74
competence, 46, 48, 75, 123, 130–131, 136
competence paradigm, 7
competition, 55–58, 100–108, 147
competitive talk, 74–75, 77–79. *See also* social hierarchy
conformity, 26–27
Confucian cultural heritage, 29
considerateness: expectations of, 49, 69, 157, 159, 170, 174, 175; expressions of, 53; lack of, 51, 52, 70, 147. *See also* inconsiderateness

content-focused curriculum, 32, 40, 46. *See also* curriculum
cooperation, 135, 162–165
copying, 2, 24; of artwork, 104, 155; *vs.* belonging, 83–86; expressions and behaviors of, 108–122; in message center, 137–138, 146; in wire play activity, 102. *See also* uniformity
Corsaro, William A., 20, 79
creative reading activity, 44–45, 84–85, 107–108
creativity: in building project, 41; as core value, 1–3; indigenized models of, 186n1
culturally patterned psychodynamic formation, 175, 185n4
curriculum: child-initiated, 26, 33, 42–43, 161–162; content-focused, 32, 40, 46; play-oriented, 26, 32, 161–162; self-oriented, 40, 42–43, 51; teacher-centered, 16, 26, 32, 40, 162, 166, 186. See also *names of specific activities*

decorating center, 148, 149, 155–156
Developmentally Appropriate Practice (DAP), 4, 32, 161
discourse-centered approach, 10–11, 42, 161
diversification, 4, 16, 31
diversity: expectations of, 50; in explicit curriculum, 55, 100, 136; as explicit socialization goal, 8, 37–39, 55, 75–76, 88, 136, 162
documentation, 40–41, 177–179
Douglas, Mary, 59
Dürer, Albrecht, 152–153

early childhood education, overview, 32, 176–182, 185n1
eating rituals, 108–114. *See also* lunchtime activities
educational reform, 29–31
education fever *(kyoyukyeol)*, 15, 29, 31
egocentricity, 75, 147, 148, 165, 171, 185n3
egoistic, 147, 153, 154, 165
embodied practices, 6, 13, 23, 28, 58, 61, 70
empathy, 21, 49
English class activity, 106–107
enni (elder sister), 60
ethnographic fieldwork, 14–22
ethnopsychology, 10
evaluation, 96–100

202 INDEX

excellence, 16, 26, 31, 49–50, 70, 126, 164
exchange, 131, 138–139, 147, 148
exclusivity, 154, 159, 160–161, 171
expert-novice relation, 136
explicit curriculum, 23, 38, 39–50, 54–55, 70–71, 135, 162
explicit rankings of expressions, 105–108
expressions: of copying *vs.* belonging, 83–86; reflecting relationships in, 88–89; social hierarchy and, 100–108. *See also* personhood; self-expression; selfhood

fieldwork, 14–22
folk pedagogy, 19, 23, 71, 175, 185n4
Fong, Vanessa L., 5, 7, 10, 35, 71
Fraser, Susan, 138
free choice time, 121
Fung, Heidi, 64, 66

Gandini, Lella, 138
global desires, 24, 174
global ideals, 178
global imports, 3–8, 23–25, 34, 134, 170, 173–176, 179
globalization of socialization landscapes, 6–8, 118–122, 135–137, 174–176. *See also* socialization ideologies
group time activity, 60, 62, 66, 119–121
guided participation, 136
guilt, 63–64
gymnastics, 54–55

Han, Namhee, 64
harmony, 53–54, 69, 135, 163–164, 170
heteroglossia, 9, 10, 133, 134
hierarchical view: implicit practices, 5–6, 23, 38, 54–55, 71. *See also* social hierarchy
high school equalization policy, 30
homogeneity, 30, 31, 32, 71
horizontal containment, 133–134
Hsueh, Yeh, 5, 23, 71
hula-hoops, 54–55
hyeng, 59, 60
hyenga (elder brother), 60, 186n1
hyengnim (elder brother + honorific suffix), 59–60, 123–125

"imagined West," 12, 22, 27, 33–35, 42–43
implicit cultural practices, 5–6, 23, 38, 54–55, 71–72, 175
inconsiderateness, 51, 52, 70, 147. *See also* considerateness
independence, 12, 15, 38–39, 42–43, 72, 185n3
indigenized models, 4–6, 24–25, 170–176, 180, 186n1
individuality: as core value, 1–3; Reggio Emilia approach to, 42; teacher's agony over lack of, 36, 52–54, 69–73
integration, 9–10, 133–134
interdependence, 185n3
International Monetary Fund (IMF) crisis, 31
intervention, 5, 161, 166, 169

Japan, 5, 15, 64

Kangnam area, Seoul, 15
Karasawa, Mayum, 5, 23, 71
khunhyeng (eldest brother), 60
kinship term, 59–60
Korean Association for the Reggio Emilia Approach, 37
kyoyukyeol, 15, 29, 31

language socialization, 7, 11
leadership, 48–49, 112
Lebra, Takie Sugiyama, 64
LeDoux, Joseph, 175, 187n1
Lee Hae Chan, 31
Lo, Adrienne, 64, 66
lunchtime activities: alliance formation and exclusions in, 80–81; communicative activities and, 114–17; *hyengnim* and, 61–62, 123–125; power and authority in, 77–78; role-appropriate behaviors during, 129–131; seeking commonality in, 111–112; traditional values and, 56–57, 66–67. *See also* eating rituals

Malaguzzi, Loris, 39
Mauss, Marcel, 9
McHugh, Ernestine, 9
message center activities, 84, 89–96, 97, 137–159, 186n3
modesty, 49, 52, 54, 69, 147, 164, 174
Montessori, 32, 186n2
moralities, 7–8, 64, 68, 75, 102, 123–125, 175, 182
multidirectional learning, 135–137, 157
Munch, Edvard, 152–153
mutual dependence, 72, 129–131
mutuality, 167, 171

National Association of Early Childhood Education (NAEYC), 32
National Kindergarten Curriculum, 32
nature expeditions, 135, 137, 159–165
neoliberalism, 2, 7, 27, 30–31, 182
Nepal, 9–10
North Korea, 26
Nuri, 2, 48–50, 69

obedience, 28, 34, 38, 123, 131, 163
one-child policy (China), 5
Organisation for Economic Co-operation and Development (OECD), 29
ostracism, 68. *See also* shaming
other-orientedness, 167
Our Twisted Hero (Yi), 159
outside play, 81–82

Park Chung Hee, 30
participant observation, 11, 18. *See also* research methods
peer culture, 8, 13, 23, 76–83
penetration, 24, 76, 118–122, 133, 162, 176, 180
personhood: core values of, 1–3; shifting socialization practices and, 31–33; transformation of, 9–11
Play-Based Learning, 32

INDEX

play-oriented curriculum, 26, 32, 161–162. *See also* curriculum
play table activity, 113–114
playtime, 60–61, 67–68, 117, 125–127, 132
poem writing, 44, 45–46, 86–88, 105–108
Pontecorvo, Clotilde, 136
postmodern fragmented subjects, 132–134
power, 100–108, 159–165
practical knowledge, 175, 185n4
praise, 118–119
Praying Hands (Dürer), 152–153
preschool quality, 4
pretend frame, 89–92, 94–95, 123, 128–132
pretentious, 49, 53, 70, 164
private after-school education policy, 30
Project Approach, 32
psychological globalization, 9–11

Quinn, Naomi, 13

ranking practice. *See* social hierarchy
reading time, 44–45, 51–52
reciprocity, 123, 131, 147, 151, 152, 155, 167
Reggio Emilia approach: about, 15–16, 33; message center in, 137–140, 154, 167, 169, 186n3; pedagogy of, 39–43, 161–162; use in Korea of, 32, 137–138
relationality, 43, 133, 145, 147, 159–165, 170, 172, 181
relation-based learning, 48
research methods, 14–22
retransformation, 155–159
ritualistic expressions, 102, 104, 114–116
ritualistic routine, 104
Rogoff, Barbara, 136
role and status, 125–127. *See also* social hierarchy
role-based behaviors, 128–132
Rosaldo, Michelle, 21
rote memorization, 30, 167
rubber band play, 98–99

sameness, 24, 27, 50, 84, 86, 114. *See also* uniformity
Scout activity, 135, 159–165
Scream, The (Munch), 152–153, 171
self, as term, 34, 38, 48. *See also* selfhood
self-centered. *See* egocentricity
self-confidence, 3, 39, 41, 42, 45–46
self-expression, 1–3, 48–55. *See also* expressions
selfhood: in actual educational context, 48–55; bipolar model of, 11–12; in explicit curriculum, 39–43; individuated senses of, 43–48; LeDoux on, 187n1; postmodern fragmentation of, 132–134; socialization and cultural values on, 11–13, 27–29. *See also* citizenship; expressions; personhood; self-expression
self-oriented curriculum, 40, 42–43, 51. *See also* curriculum
Seth, Michael J., 29–30
shaming, 63–68, 71, 124, 130, 186n2. *See also* ostracism
Sheldon, Amy, 132

shifting time, 64–65
show-and-tell activity, 1, 129, 185n1
social hierarchy: children's eagerness and, 79; cultural models of, 122–132; eating rituals and, 108–114; expressions and, 100–108. *See also* competitive talk; hierarchical view
socialization ideologies: about, 1–3; emerging personhood and, 31–33; globalizing practices in, 6–8, 118–122, 135–137; landscape of, 3–8; on selfhood, 11–13, 27–29; transformation of landscapes of, 9–11, 29–31, 140–146; Western *vs.* traditional, 33–35
sociocentric values, 12, 34, 42–43, 138–140, 147, 154, 157–158, 168, 185n3
Somang preschool, overview, 1, 15–16, 185n1
son tulko seisski, 186n2
standardization, 27, 31, 40, 43, 97
storybook reading time, 51–52
Strauss, Claudia, 9, 10, 133–134
student-centered curriculum, 31. *See also* curriculum

taken-for-granted habitus, as term, 175
teacher-centered curriculum, 16, 26, 32, 40, 162, 166, 186. *See also* curriculum
Thorne, Barrie, 19
thoughtfulness, 49, 51, 53, 147
Tobin, Joseph, 5, 23, 71
tongkuk (children's drama), 137, 167–170
tongsayng (younger brother or sister), 62
"traditional" Korean socialization, 33–35
transformation of socialization landscape, 9–11, 29–31, 140–146. *See also* socialization ideologies
trash pickup activity, 57–58
trust, 16–19
ttala haki (copying other's behaviors), 108–114, 181
ttala meki (copying other's eating), 108–114, 181

uniformity, 55–63. *See also* copying; sameness
United States: author's work in, 1, 14, 48; childhood education in, 28, 185n1 (intro.); personhood in, 9; preschool culture in, 5, 64; Reggio Emilia approach in, 15, 43
U.S. National Association for the Education of Young Children (NAEYC), 32

verbal gloss, 10, 172
vertical containment, 133–134
video-watching activity, 128–129

Waldorf, 32
weekend story time, 1, 51, 70, 100, 137, 165–167, 169
Western socialization, 33–35
Wien, Carol A., 138
Willis, Paul, 122
wire play area, 101–103, 121–122
world culture theory, 4
Woronov, T. E., 5
Wyness, Michael G., 6–7

Xu, Jing, 7, 10, 34

ABOUT THE AUTHOR

JUNEHUI AHN is a professor of urban sociology at the University of Seoul. She received her PhD in anthropology from the University of Michigan, Ann Arbor. Her main research area is the anthropology of childhood and socialization, with particular focus on the development of self, emotion, and sociality in cultural context. Based on long-term ethnographic fieldwork in preschools of the United States and South Korea, her research delves into the critical importance of children's agency to sociocultural and political matters, the interactions of culture and human psychology, and the cultural groundings of human sociality. Her work has appeared in *American Ethnologist, Ethos, Anthropology and Education Quarterly, Childhood, Children and Society,* and *Linguistics and Education.*

Available titles in the Rutgers Series in Childhood Studies:

Amanda E. Lewis, *Race in the Schoolyard: Negotiating the Color Line in Classrooms and Communities*

Donna M. Lanclos, *At Play in Belfast: Children's Folklore and Identities in Northern Ireland*

Cindy Dell Clark, *In Sickness and in Play: Children Coping with Chronic Illness*

Peter B. Pufall and Richard P. Unsworth, eds., *Rethinking Childhood*

David M. Rosen, *Armies of the Young: Child Soldiers in War and Terrorism*

Lydia Murdoch, *Imagined Orphans: Poor Families, Child Welfare, and Contested Citizenship in London*

Rachel Burr, *Vietnam's Children in a Changing World*

Laurie Schaffner, *Girls in Trouble with the Law*

Susan A. Miller, *Growing Girls: The Natural Origins of Girls' Organizations in America*

Marta Gutman and Ning de Coninck-Smith, eds., *Designing Modern Childhoods: History, Space, and the Material Culture of Children*

Jessica Fields, *Risky Lessons: Sex Education and Social Inequality*

Sarah E. Chinn, *Inventing Modern Adolescence: The Children of Immigrants in Turn-of-the-Century America*

Debra Curtis, *Pleasures and Perils: Girls' Sexuality in a Caribbean Consumer Culture*

Don S. Browning and Binnie J. Miller-McLemore, eds., *Children and Childhood in American Religions*

Marjorie Faulstich Orellana, *Translating Childhoods: Immigrant Youth, Language, and Culture*

Don S. Browning and Marcia J. Bunge, eds., *Children and Childhood in World Religions*

Hava Rachel Gordon, *We Fight to Win: Inequality and the Politics of Youth Activism*

Nikki Jones, *Between Good and Ghetto: African American Girls and Inner-City Violence*

Kate Douglas, *Contesting Childhood: Autobiography, Trauma, and Memory*

Jennifer Helgren and Colleen A. Vasconcellos, eds., *Girlhood: A Global History*

Karen Lury, *The Child in Film: Tears, Fears, and Fairy Tales*

Michelle Ann Abate, *Raising Your Kids Right: Children's Literature and American Political Conservatism*

Michael Bourdillon, Deborah Levison, William Myers, and Ben White, *Rights and Wrongs of Children's Work*

Jane A. Siegel, *Disrupted Childhoods: Children of Women in Prison*

Valerie Leiter, *Their Time Has Come: Youth with Disabilities on the Cusp of Adulthood*

Edward W. Morris, *Learning the Hard Way: Masculinity, Place, and the Gender Gap in Education*

Erin N. Winkler, *Learning Race, Learning Place: Shaping Racial Identities and Ideas in African American Childhoods*

Jenny Huberman, *Ambivalent Encounters: Childhood, Tourism, and Social Change in Banaras, India*

Walter Hamilton, *Children of the Occupation: Japan's Untold Story*

Jon M. Wolseth, *Life on the Malecón: Children and Youth on the Streets of Santo Domingo*

Lisa M. Nunn, *Defining Student Success: The Role of School and Culture*

Vikki S. Katz, *Kids in the Middle: How Children of Immigrants Negotiate Community Interactions for Their Families*

Bambi L. Chapin, *Childhood in a Sri Lankan Village: Shaping Hierarchy and Desire*

David M. Rosen, *Child Soldiers in the Western Imagination: From Patriots to Victims*

Marianne Modica, *Race among Friends: Exploring Race at a Suburban School*

Elzbieta M. Gozdziak, *Trafficked Children and Youth in the United States: Reimagining Survivors*

Pamela Robertson Wojcik, *Fantasies of Neglect: Imagining the Urban Child in American Film and Fiction*

Maria Kromidas, *City Kids: Transforming Racial Baggage*

Ingred A. Nelson, *Why Afterschool Matters*

Jean Marie Hunleth, *Children as Caregivers: The Global Fight against Tuberculosis and HIV in Zambia*

Abby Hardgrove, *Life after Guns: Reciprocity and Respect among Young Men in Liberia*

Michelle J. Bellino, *Youth in Postwar Guatemala: Education and Civic Identity in Transition*

Vera Lopez, *Complicated Lives: Girls, Parents, Drugs, and Juvenile Justice*

Rachel E. Dunifon, *You've Always Been There for Me: Understanding the Lives of Grandchildren Raised by Grandparents*

Cindy Dell Clark, *All Together Now: American Holiday Symbolism among Children and Adults*

Laura Moran, *Belonging and Becoming in a Multicultural World: Refugee Youth and the Pursuit of Identity*

Hannah Dyer, *The Queer Aesthetics of Childhood: Asymmetries of Innocence and the Cultural Politics of Child Development*

Julie Spray, *The Children in Child Health: Negotiating Young Lives and Health in New Zealand*

Franziska Fay, *Disputing Discipline: Child Protection, Punishment, and Piety in Zanzibar Schools*

Kathie Carpenter, *Life in a Cambodian Orphanage: A Childhood Journey for New Opportunities*

Norbert Ross, *A World of Many: Ontology and Child Development among the Maya of Southern Mexico*

Camilla Morelli, *Children of the Rainforest: Shaping the Future in Amazonia*

Junehui Ahn, *Between Self and Community: Children's Personhood in a Globalized South Korea*